NOW IS THE TIME

A Van Life Road Trip

By Andrew Singer

The events, places, and conversations in this memoir have been recreated from the author's recollection, journal entries, news articles, and interviews with those familiar with the events described. Many of the names and identifying characteristics of individuals have been changed to protect the privacy of those depicted. A majority of the dialogue has been recreated from memory and should not be taken verbatim. Certain location names have been intentionally omitted. Additionally, this book is not a how-to guide; do not consider the van build chapter as a set of instructions.

First paperback edition 2025
Cover design by Gülsah Keles
Map by Sarah May © 2025 by Authors on Wheels

ISBN 979-8-9926996-0-9 (paperback)
ISBN 979-8-9926996-1-6 (ebook)

To Sarah, for more reasons than I have words.

Table of Contents

Prologue
Home, Part 1

THERE'S A WORD in van life that should never be uttered. It's the very word my partner spoke one cold, damp morning in the dense forests of the Pacific Northwest.

"I think we should get a *hotel*," said Sarah.

Gasp. The h-word. Hotel, that place with more plush pillows than you need, temperature-controlled rooms, soft towels, and hot showers—yes, endless, steamy showers. Nothing says vacation like a nice hotel.

There was just one problem: we weren't on a vacation. We were six weeks into a new lifestyle that involved turning a van into a home, the road into our driveway, and America's glorious public lands into our backyard. Besides, van-lifers don't get hotels—at least not the ones who are in it for more than just the 'Gram. No, we rough it, we explore, we go back to basics.

With a year of dating under our belt, Sarah knew me well enough to understand that you can't just drop the h-word because you want a hot shower. Hell, I refuse to pay for campgrounds.

"I know you don't want to spend the money," she continued, "but look at yourself, you're miserable, bubs."

I threw off the blanket and looked down at my legs. Bug bites dotted each one and burned with such ferocity that it felt like my shins had chlamydia. We began counting all the little red mounds: seventy-five on my legs, several on my forearm and waistband; all in, I had nearly one hundred. She took to the internet to diagnose the problem—fleas.

1

I attempted to look over at Sarah, but a searing pain shot across my upper spine, locking my head in an awkward position. *Van life, we have another problem.* My neck had gone out a couple of nights back, a consequence of switching to a considerably smaller bed. I was putting the elder in elder millennial. To sleep for longer than thirty minutes at a time, I had made a makeshift neck brace with an orange towel. So, there I sat, in my underwear, covered in flea bites, with a neon orange towel wrapped tightly around my neck. At any moment an aspiring influencer might burst in, video us in our misery, then post it to the internet with the clickbait title, "Van Life Actually SUCKS!"

"I don't want to get a *hotel*," I grumbled. The h-word sounded evil coming out of my mouth, like it shouldn't be said too loudly or Voldemort might appear with a bell cart and a continental breakfast voucher.

"C'mon, you're a mess."

Sarah was right. I was an itchy, throbbing, ridiculous-looking mess. Turning my head was impossible. Scratching my legs made it worse. Beat and vulnerable, I said it—the *other* H word.

"Ugh. I wish I was *HOME!*"

Ah, *Home.* That oasis of a place with a worn-in mattress that has never seen a flea. Netflix, Hulu, Disney+. A freezer filled with ice cream. An actual sofa. All of it at the ready. All of it familiar. All of it comfortable.

And this comfort—found at my grandfather's house back in San Diego, California—was the closest thing I had to a home. I'd spent the last seven years there, even met Sarah and fell in love there. But was it really home? Though it still said so on my driver's license, I wasn't so sure anymore.

Nor was home where I had been born and raised: Texas. Twenty-five years of my life had been spent there, shaped by a complicated childhood, only to crash and burn from a descent into alcoholism. Helped by strangers, angels, and fellow addicts, Texas was also where I got sober and started life anew. With this transformation, I began to question if home might actually be within, so I moved away and found a new addiction—travel.

And if I were to ask myself: where have I felt the most "at home"? The answer would undeniably be on the road, namely an old SUV that I'd spent portions of my late twenties living out of, lying on a makeshift bed in the backseat, ending my days staring at a road atlas from the light of a headlamp. Sure, not the most spacious place, but it was where I'd felt the most at peace, the most myself.

It's why I thought I could make the road my home again, this time in a more enduring and intentional way. And that home, the one now infested with fleas, turned out to be different from all the rest. Not merely because of its limited size, mobility, and simplicity, but because Sarah and I had built it with our own hands. Nevertheless, I was now ready to throw in the towel, and I'm not talking about the one holding my spine together.

"Do you really want to go back home?" Sarah whispered as she massaged my neck.

"I don't know. Maybe."

"C'mon, you don't mean that. Let's just get a hotel. We can take showers and even try out the bug bomb, maybe get some takeout."

She had me at takeout.

"Okay, okay. *You're right*," I conceded. "Let's get a hotel."

Van life was over. Maybe for a day, maybe forever.

Chapter 1
The Vandemic

MY SOUL HAS a big appetite and requires constant feeding. I hunger for new experiences, am satiated by different sights. The most nourishing setting of all is turning onto a road I have never been down.

If anything rivals my love for the road, it's a woman who also feels happiest when home is on four wheels. I learned this while dating Sarah. To end 2019, we spent our first trip together in my car, camping and motel-crashing, driving across a state we knew little about—Nevada. We had no van yet, but it didn't matter, because the Silver State was filled with so much nothing and I loved every mile of it. Long, quiet roads snaked through mountains, craving attention like a neglected child. Days went by, counting more miles than cars.

Sarah and I had only been dating for three months and filled the hours getting to know one another more intimately. We often discussed the last decade, an era that had seen us both overcome the drama and dysfunction that nearly took our lives. Like me, Sarah had also spent the 2010s evolving—from a codependent escaping an abusive marriage to a free-spirited and confident woman. It never ceases to amaze me how much can change in a year, and how one decade can feel like two lives.

As the sun set on January 1, 2020, I pulled the car into an overlook. This remote section of western Nevada featured rugged, treeless mountains. Wispy lavender clouds shifted shapes as the sun sank. The two of us got lost in the thousand-mile stare. The silence felt longer, more intense, as we both settled in, not needing conversation to fill each moment.

Eventually, Sarah broke the void, whispering, "What are you thinking?"

I sighed, my eyes fixated on the horizon. "My goal for 2019 was to be less judgmental, but I think I got worse. So, I'm rolling it over. This feels like the right year to try again."

Yeah … 2020, what a great year to try and be less judgmental.

I looked over at Sarah as she gazed unflinchingly toward the edge of the Earth. The desert felt as mysterious as ever.

"And what's on your mind?" I asked.

Her contemplation stretched time. If I were not in love, I would have been more intrigued by the nothing than by an answer.

She kept her eyes fixed ahead, her words drifting into the wind, "I just want to keep doing this. Not go back. Not have to work. Just keep driving wherever we want, and leave whenever we want."

"Yeah, that's the dream," I said.

That night the wind blew hard. Maybe it was God's laughter, maybe it was the unseen turbulence of a wish taking flight.

A historical interruption came in the following months. By the end of March 2020, I was temporarily laid off from my job teaching business to international students. By May, permanently. Come June, Sarah joined me and the millions of unemployed whose jobs clashed with a global pandemic. Everyone's plans and ambitions vanished overnight. In this shared unraveling of control, complaining lost its power, for complaints are like picking out a formal dress—you don't want anyone else to have the same one.

In all honesty, 2019 had been a turbulent year for me. Diagnosed with an anxiety condition called panic disorder, I'd spent a good portion of the year in and out of debilitating panic attacks. Little did I know, with the disruption of 2020 around the corner, that 2019 had been an ideal year to get into therapy.

As the world shut its doors, many of us questioned what we had been doing and why we had been doing it. The restlessness, the isolation, they made me rethink it all. Could I shut off the news and the internet? Could I slow down and simplify my life? Could I make this big world smaller? Maybe immerse myself in nature and reawaken the explorer within? Deep down, I knew myself well enough to accept this: if I changed nothing, nothing would change.

If you want to challenge a society's structure, give it a pandemic. If you want to test a culture's intelligence, give it the internet. If you want to examine a person's mental fortitude, make them stay at home. And if you want to inspire wanderlust, give the restless time and money.

At this time, I was living with my ninety-two-year-old grandfather, Papa Herb. Sarah joined us for much of the lockdown, bringing a newness to our conversations. After all, tell a woman you live with your parents and you're a loser; tell them you live with your grandfather and you're a saint. This is especially true if your grandfather's name is Herbert, who has a plump belly and a cute shuffle for a walk. He had a handkerchief, a landline telephone, and ended conversations with, "Be of good cheer!" If you're still not convinced of his appeal, then ask one of his girlfriends. When I first moved in with him, he was dating five different women.

No surprise, Sarah fell for Papa Herb immediately. And he for her. Sarah's well-thought-out questions prompted stories from my grandfather that I had never heard. When she asked about his late wife, his voice would crack, and his eyes would water. My grandmother passed away from cancer in 2011, but Papa Herb's emotions never reached room temperature. I think this enduring tenderness made watching Sarah and me fall in love all the sweeter for him.

I inherited a passion for travel from Ole Herbie. He had been around the world and was still at it into his nineties (though by then he had slowed down and now only had one girlfriend). At ninety-one, he took our family to Iceland, where he shuffled with his cane to waterfalls, glaciers, and volcanoes. And even in 2020, Papa Herb encouraged Sarah and me to continue seeing the world, even if it meant quieting the part of his heart that wanted us to stay with him until his forever ended.

It was timely, because as the stay-at-home orders dragged on, my wanderlust was a dog's underbelly begging to be scratched. The homelands of the Sierras, Cascades, and Rockies had scratched the itch before—surely, they could again. Sarah's words, the ability to *just keep going*, looped in my mind that rambled back roads in the vehicle of our dreams.

Only a fool thinks that his best ideas belong to him alone, and I was a fool to not consider the thousands of other Americans out there: bored, financially stimulated, eager to hit the road, and as hell-bent as we were to travel in the comforts of the growing #vanlife trend.

Sarah and I began to search in earnest for something we could afford. The only built-out van in our budget was so old that the bottom had rusted straight through to the flooring. At this point we made a big shift in our thinking. And though I had never built anything, some tank-top-wearing Gen Z'er on YouTube made van conversion look so easy that I thought even I could do it. What can I say? I had been influenced.

An arduous month went by as Sarah and I searched, dealing with Craigslist swindlers, banks offering bad loans, shady used-car dealers, and even an unsuccessful online auction where I bid our savings on a van we'd never even seen in person. So much for my theory, that with nearly 15 percent unemployment, dealers would be sitting on excess inventory and willing to sell for less. Trickle-up economics was in full force. As a business teacher, I should have known better—that if you distribute a bunch of money to the masses, you'd better expect Americans to immediately spend it all on an assortment of toys.

As prices for everything, from houses and RVs to electronics and groceries, began to skyrocket, I concluded that we couldn't keep chasing a fantasy that was running away faster than we could keep up.

But before I fully abandoned the idea, one ad remained on my laptop. It was for our ideal van: a RAM ProMaster with an empty interior. A 2016 model with 42,000 miles, only a forty-five-minute drive away. The owner was responsive and oddly polite.

"Sarah," I said, as I slammed the laptop shut, "this is the last van I'm willing to look at."

It was June 4, 2020 when Sarah and I arrived at a house in Chula Vista, California. A wooden cross adorned the lawn. Along the curb was a large white van, which towered over the owner. At 5'4", he stood just barely taller than Sarah, and significantly shorter than me.

"Hi, Rodolfo. I'm Andrew, this is Sarah."

"Call me Rudy," he smiled and extended his hand.

There used to be a time you could tell a lot about a man from his handshake, and Rudy's handshake told me he knew of that time. Integrity was not just in the grip of his palm, it was written on the side of his van in big blue letters: INTEGRITY PLUMBING AND LANDSCAPE.

I slid the side door open and stepped in. Stainless-steel streaks scarred the interior, telling the story of hard labor and Rudy's well-earned retirement. The 159-inch wheelbase made for ample cargo space, and the high-roof edition provided four extra inches of clearance from the top of my head to the tin. I pictured a floor and ceiling, imagining myself standing up tall with enough space to brush out knots of unwashed hair.

Rudy's voice was gentle and spiced with a Mexican accent, "It's a diesel, so it's a little bit different. Have you ever driven a diesel?"

"No," I replied. In fact, I had never driven a cargo van—or any type of vehicle of this size—before.

"Here's the key," he said. I reached out and grabbed the fob. The key swung out switchblade style.

"Don't turn the ignition until all the electronics are on and the beeping stops. You can drive it like a manual using the gearshift, or you can keep it in automatic. If you do, it'll feel different because it's used to me driving it, and I drive like an old man."

Sarah entered the passenger side, while I got behind the wheel. I cranked the key all the way; the engine didn't turn. Rudy smiled and leaned in to start the motor. The four cylinders rumbled to life. The van handled the hills of Chula Vista at a different torque than I was used to, jerking us with each gear change until the engine warmed up. Pipe fittings, loose screws, and soil slid around the cargo space. I looked over at Sarah. Her seafoam eyes were bulging with delight. My heart marinated in them. We didn't need to speak because we both had the same question on our minds: *Could this be the one?*

After the test drive, I gave the key back to Rudy. He sounded more like an inspector than a salesman. "The van's in great shape. Here's the paperwork from all the oil changes and work I had done. Here's the CarFax. You can see where the loan was paid off here." He handed me a manila folder filled with paper-clipped documents. "I just had new tires put on it back in April. You have to take it on the freeway regularly—it drives best when you get it up to speed for a while. Oh, and make sure you let it idle for a few minutes before you shut it off."

Rudy took a step forward and eyed the van from grill to taillight. Then he took a hard look at Sarah, then at me. "This van has done a lot for me. Jobs from San Bernardino and back. I took it down to Mexico many times too, for mission work." His moist eyes drifted elsewhere. A soft smile seized his demeanor. "We built a family a house down there. The family and their kids slept in this van while their home was being built. I love this van."

Sarah and I returned the next day with a cake wrapped in a ribbon, a bouquet of purple flowers, and a cashier's check for $22,000. Rudy met us in the street, his wife gushing from the stoop of their one-story home.

"Will you take a picture with us?" Sarah asked, ever the millennial. The three of us squeezed in for a selfie.

"I love this van," Rudy's voice fractured, "I got many offers, but I would rather take less money from the right people than more money from the wrong ones. May God bless you both, your home, and your trip."

Rudy handed me the key. Nerves reddened my cheeks. I had so much to say, but my lips stayed sealed, in that state of emotion that disconnects the vocal cords—overwhelmed with gratitude.

For some, it was simply a key to a plumber's dirty van. For others, it was a young couple making a big mistake, betting their savings and relationship on a home the size of a walk-in closet. But for Sarah and me, it was the actualization of a dream. Our dream didn't come with an escrow, inspection, picket fence, or a yard. It didn't even have insulation or flooring. What it did have was love, potential, and the blessing from a dying breed of human.

I started the engine, the van still smelling of fertilizer. We rolled away from the curb. In the passenger seat, Sarah appeared happier than ever. This soil-scented tin box was to be our first home together. So much possibility resided on its four tires: open roads, perspective-changing landscapes, unquenchable freedom.

Excitement, that's what Sarah's shining emerald eyes said.

I looked into the side-view mirror at the man who made it all possible. Rudy got smaller and smaller, waving his hand, smiling as we drove away.

"I think we should name the van Rudy," I said.

Sarah squeezed my hand, "I think that's perfect."

I turned us onto the freeway. A loose screw slid across the empty cargo space, rattling over each rib of the steel flooring. I started thinking about all the work we had in front of us, all the tiny details required to successfully convert an empty cargo van into a tiny home-on-wheels. The worries in my head became like that loose screw, clanking away in unorganized chaos.

Now Is the Time

With dream morphing into reality, one great fact now over-shadowed all the fantasies: We didn't know what the fuck we were doing.

Chapter 2
The Build

EVERY PERSON HAS a setting that makes them horrifically insecure, where their confidence whimpers like a forgotten kitten and their inner critic barks like a rabid dog. For some people this is public speaking or a job interview; for others it's a first date or hitting the gym. For me, it's undeniably The Home Depot.

That's because I come from a long line of accountants. Papa Herb, my grandfather, was an accountant. My dad, an accountant. Mom, she was a CPA too. And my brother? You guessed it, he's also a bean counter. This is the kind of family whose tools collect more dust than the top of a ceiling fan. In fact, prior to buying the van, I was one of those flannel-wearing millennials who had never even sawed a piece of wood. I don't know how far back I have to go in my family tree to find someone in our Jewish gene pool who built their own home, but it's far. Like, Joseph-may-have-been-the-carpenter far.

Sure, no epic tale starts with, "I am Hercules, son of Zeus, head of accounting!" But hey, heroes need spreadsheets too. Matter of fact, the only thing of value I was bringing to the van build was a color-coded spreadsheet that tracked every item we purchased, how much it cost, and when to expect its arrival. Not only that, I created an equation that forecasted how many months Sarah and I could travel before our money ran out. Impressive? Perhaps. But let's be real, no one ever put a man with a spreadsheet on a wall calendar.

Like me, Sarah had a construction resume that started and ended with "Ikea furniture assembly." Thankfully, she had earned a master's degree in conflict resolution. While an apprenticeship with a wood-worker would have been more practical, at least her background came with useful tools for argument de-escalation. This was valuable considering that we had only been dating for nine months when we combined our savings to buy the van, with the intention of building it out, moving in together, and starting a new lifestyle that excluded a permanent bathroom. You might be thinking: Nine months *might* be a little too soon to move in together, and nine months is *definitely* too soon to move into a van together. Oh, and these two kooks are going to do all the construction themselves? Yeah, talk about putting the stress in stress test.

Sarah and I envisioned one of those vans you double tap on Instagram, with ingenious storage hacks, adjustable lighting, glossy woodwork, artfully placed macrame, and a few vibrant plants. Beyond aesthetics, we wanted a van designed for off-grid living, powered by the sun, and not dependent on campground amenities. Overflowing with ignorance, we assumed we could do the entire buildout in one month—after all, we weren't working and had nothing else to do. Nevertheless, we were self-aware enough to know that to pull this off we would need some serious help.

Enter YouTube, the wonder platform that can make anyone a teacher and everyone a student. You can learn how to get the perfect booty, start a cryptocurrency, find a like-minded militia, or create a solar-powered electrical system. But before we learned how to—wire electricity; insulate, frame, and mount walls; lay flooring; build a bed, table, bench seats, and cabinets; then install a refrigerator, stove, and swivel chair—we had to figure out what tools we needed and how the heck to use them.

Sarah and I decided to jump right in with a complicated task: installing a ceiling fan through the roof of the van. We entered the garage, Sarah humming, me grinding my teeth. I turned on *The Best of Sade*. I was hoping Sade's angelic voice would deter me from a temper tantrum when things got overwhelming. We grabbed all the necessary tools: jigsaw, steel cutting blades, power drill, drill bits, Flex Seal, stainless-steel paint, paint brushes, paper towels, gloves, and safety glasses (because we can all agree that safety *definitely* needed to come first).

One of these YouTubers passed on the DIY adage his father gave him that you measure twice and cut once. Sarah and I clearly had a lot to compensate for. Therefore, every project had a ritual where I measured twice, then Sarah measured twice, then I reverse-measured, measured again, and finally cut. This ritual felt important on a twenty-dollar sheet of plywood, and it was damn near sacred when making irreversible cuts into the steel of our van.

Rudy's roof flexed and popped as I awkwardly crawled onto the top of the van. I arranged my tools like a surgeon. With the drill bit case open, I analyzed the three different designs. The one with the pointed tip seemed logical, so into the drill it went. I hadn't used a power drill since high school, over fifteen years ago. Turns out, they have more settings than I recalled. I put the drill in forward, easy enough, then examined the two rows of numbers. *Let's go for the medium speed and take it from there.*

"You got this, bubs!" yelled Sarah. Everyone deserves a Sarah.

Go time. I pulled the trigger. The drill bore into the roof, making a tiny silver imprint, but no hole. *More power,* said my monkey brain. I cranked up the settings, fired it back up, and used my body weight to push harder into Rudy's frame. *Whack!* The bit snapped in half, sending me face-first into the roof.

"Everything okay up there?" Sarah asked.

"Yeah, yeah. Just broke a drill bit. Hold on, I need to look something up." The YouTube search box reinforced my insecurities, as I switched from: "How to install a MaxxFan on a RAM ProMaster" to "How to use a power drill." Sade was working away too, and "Your Love is King" was barely preventing me from throwing the drill into the side of the garage.

Sarah fired up the vacuum cleaner, drowning out Sade's voice. Rudy needed a deep cleaning. This sounded simple, but every project would prove to be more challenging than anticipated, even cleaning the damn thing.

Let's try this again. A YouTuber told me that the pointed-tip drill bit is actually used for wood. I switched it out, then pressed the bit designed for metal into the roof and pulled the trigger. It punched through the van. *Rudy, we have a hole.*

I put the drill down and grabbed the jigsaw. The day before, a video taught me the difference between a jigsaw, circle saw, table saw, and hacksaw. Have you ever seen the movie *Saw*? Well, I have not. The title alone terrifies me. Earlier, I had watched a video on how to secure the blade, then tested the jigsaw out on an old fence post. It went well, considering it was the first, *and only*, time I had ever used a jigsaw. In fact, it was the first and only time I had ever used *any* type of saw.

The jigsaw blade slid into the hole. *Game time.* I squeezed the trigger. The van's roof began vibrating violently like my table was now ready at The Cheesecake Factory. I released my finger. The earthquake ended.

"Everything okay up there?" Sarah asked.

"Yeah, babe. Just shakin' a lot."

Your love is king . . .

I pulled the trigger again and tried to keep my eye on the line. One wrong move and our roof would be ruined. Sparks and metal filings sprayed out, landing on my forearms. They burned hot, making me feel sexy. Sade still sang, but her voice couldn't be heard over the grinding metal. The roof's wobbling intensified, which came to an abrupt end when the saw blade bent and snapped in two.

"MOTHERF——!"

My profanities flew further than the broken metal.

Come on, Sade. Work with me, girl.

"Everything okay?" Sarah yelled. (This question would be asked a few times a day for the next several weeks.)

"Just broke a blade. Can you hand me another one? They're on the counter."

A minute later, Sarah climbed the ladder, handed me the blade, and stabbed me with an emotional dagger. "Here you go. This is the last metal cutting blade. We can always go back to Home Depot if we need more."

Our first trip to The Home Depot quickly surfaced some new relationship findings. For instance, whenever I suggested a shade of paint not to Sarah's liking, she would make a verbal gagging sound and pretend to vomit. On the ride home she said, "You're pretty clean for a guy," which I translated to, *But could you get more on my level of OCD organization?* However, there was hope for us, namely that if we could survive building the van, *maybe* we could thrive living in it. Needless to say, there was no way I was going back to The Home Depot, at least not on Sade's watch.

"Okay, thanks babe. Give me a minute."

"How to cut metal with a jigsaw" was typed into the search box. The algorithm team at Google thought they had me figured out because each video started with the same advertisement: some shirtless bro with chiseled abs telling me cardio is a waste of time. A tortuous five seconds elapsed until I skipped the ad and let the engineers at Google know that they were targeting the wrong insecurity.

The jigsaw went back to work, the roof went back to shaking. I finished the first line and returned to my phone, where I learned how to cut corners (no pun intended) from a woman sponsored by some tool company. Everyone on the 'Tube was sponsored, promoting affiliate links and telling you to "like and subscribe." My default reaction to judge arose, but I saw that these influencers and I were similar in more ways than not. Sure, I didn't know how to do anything handy, let alone film and edit a video of it. Nonetheless, these content creators wanted to be on their own—no boss and no breakroom that smelled of burnt popcorn. I could respect that.

With one final section left, I finished the cut and punched the metal square. It landed in the hanging garbage bag and fell to the van's floor. Sarah looked up, through the new hole in our ceiling.

"Ahhh! You did it!" she screamed.

A boyish pride consumed my face. Sade thought I was a "Smooth Operator."

Together, Sarah and I completed the fan's installation. Sure, it took us several hours to do what the influencers did in ten minutes. Regardless, we had something to celebrate. Photos were taken. Hugs were had. Messes were cleaned up. The cocky phrase, *You can do anything!* rattled through my head until I fell asleep, where my subconscious shifted into a nightmare about the next day's project.

Typical build days began when I awoke from a nightmare. These ranged from blowing up the van to electrocuting Sarah. No coffee needed after that. With a cup full of anxiety, it was time to scour the various forums, blogs, and YouTube channels to learn how to do that day's project.

Turns out every decision you make to build a camper van comes with at least three competing options, each heavily debated on the World Wide Web:

For power, should I use a generator, alternator, or solar panels?

You'll need some batteries, and your three options are: lithium, absorbent glass mat, or flooded lead acid.

How about insulation? There's wool, foam board, or Thinsulate.

And you can't forget about a toilet: compost, cassette, or the good ole bucket?

Needless to say, these were not the kind of three-ways I had fantasized navigating in my thirties. Sarah and I discussed every decision, and analysis paralysis usually claimed at least one of us before 9 a.m.

We spent so many hours searching *How to do this* and *How to do that*. One more shirtless bro advertisement and I was going to end up on an ice cream bender. After installing the fan, windows, and insulation it was time to move on to one of the most technical aspects of the build—electricity. I spent an entire week studying: solar panels, charge controllers, batteries, fuse boxes, wire sizing, and lighting. Nothing challenged me more than this vital element. As Rudy sat idle, not making any visible progress, I quite literally plugged away. Each step came with a nervous perfectionism, and I feared that one misstep would electrocute me or my lover.

Judgment Day arrived when I finally hooked everything up to the battery bank. So many connections. So many things that could go wrong. My finger trembled over the light switch. If it worked, glory. If it didn't: defeat, depression, rage. We would have to undo a weeks' worth of work to figure out where we had gone wrong.

I took one final look at the ceiling. Two parallel lines of white LED puck lights lined the pine planks. Would they turn on?

I said a prayer and looked at Sarah. "Are you sure you don't want to press it?"

"No, you do it. You've worked so hard. You got this," she said, her eyes focused on my hand.

"Okay, here we go …"

I flipped the switch.

Nothing. Not a flicker, not a glow. Dark, lightless, nothing. Sarah's head sank.

"Ugh!" A burst of hot fury was working its way to the surface. Then I glanced from the ceiling to the switch. The power bar was at its lowest setting.

"Oh, the dimmer!" I exclaimed.

Duh. I pushed the slider up. Clean, white light brightened the half-built camper van.

Sarah's eyes bulged out of her head. "Oh my gosh! It works! Ahhh!" She skipped across the plywood subfloor and leaped into my arms. The van's chassis bounced up and down as we cheered. Most couples share these marquis moments for marriage proposals or pregnancy announcements ... we had working lights.

I held Sarah's body extra tight and looked up at the ceiling. Tears began to build in my eyes until gravity pulled one drop from the right, then another from the left. The liquid slowed down in the thickness of my beard stubble. I let Sarah go. She looked into my face. The tears on my cheeks glistened under the new lights. Sarah's own eyes started to moisten, not because of the lights, but because she knew the journey I had been on.

When I started therapy, the intake questionnaire asked what I wanted to get out of the treatment. Amidst my overflowing answer were the words: *to finally cry.* Despite my willingness, I had not had a good cry in sixteen years. I always expected the initial breakdown would occur during some intense therapy session or privately while listening to Billie Eilish. Don't ask me why a working light switch cracked that longstanding wall. Perhaps it has to do with all the pressure I put on myself.

When our one-month goal to finish Rudy came and went, the inside of the van was nothing more than exposed wires and insulation. Each item on the to-do list represented a hundred thoughts. As the list grew, so did my sense of overwhelm.

Somehow, Sarah maintained her optimism, transforming into an architect, a plumber, and my motivational coach. Thanks to her, Rudy had custom windshield covers and detachable bug screens for the doors. She made sheets of paper with pictures and dimensions on how to cut each wall panel, including how to navigate the different bumps and curves that make up the van's internal structure. She was a machine—priming, painting, staining, varnishing, measuring, templating, and yelling, "You got this!" as I grew more and more comfortable with a saw.

With electrical out of the way, it was woodworking in overdrive. Our quadruple measuring technique paid off, and within two weeks, Rudy had white walls and a broad kitchen counter that sat atop drawers, a cabinet, and a refrigerator. Sarah also installed our kitchen sink, with running filtered water that pumped out of a stainless-steel faucet. Together we adhered crossbeams over the rear tires, creating the structure that would support our bed.

Sarah's optimism must have been contagious because my dreams started invoking solutions, not worst-case scenarios. I would wake up with the designs for our custom bench seats and cabinets. When it came time to build our retractable table that suspends from the bed frame, I awoke and told Sarah, "Okay, I know how we're gonna do it. We need ten corner brackets, a couple of one by twos, drawer slides, and some bolts."

"You sure this will work?" she asked.

Somehow, by the end of the day, we had a concealed table that pulled out between two bench seats. Design it, build it, fix it—*I can do anything!* Tickle my toes and call me Tim "The Tool Man" Taylor!

It wasn't the first time my ego needed recalibration. My new confidence was taking me into the red warning level, but I didn't know it. I usually don't until it's too late. I especially don't if food is involved.

Pizza. Cookies. Lasagna. Who said living in a van meant a diet of canned soup? So, we purchased a fancy RV range that came with an oven and three-burner stove. That's right ... an oven ... in a van. The range needed a safe propane connection, something an experienced planner would have considered before making a non-refundable purchase.

Of all the projects, this one terrified me the most. Sarah and I discussed what to do at great length. Permanent solutions existed, including mounting a tank outside the van or building a sealed, vented locker indoors. However—like my past bachelor life—I prowled for something easier, cheaper, and less committal. And where do you go when you want something cheap, easy, and undeniably questionable? Well, the internet of course.

On page seven of a Google search, I found an obscure blog that proposed a solution: use a variety of adapters and hoses to connect the oven to a one-pound propane can. I should have known better, but here's an important disclaimer: *I have a reputation for making mistakes.*

I arrived at the local hardware store to track down a mysterious wizard. Eddie, if legend holds, was the man to talk to regarding plumbing. According to my source back at The Home Depot, Eddie knows it all, especially propane.

The aisle walls became an optical illusion as my eyes tried to put into focus the overwhelming collection of brass, PVC, and steel fittings. Elbows, flares, adapters, three-way tee connectors—each sealed in small plastic bags, hanging off hundreds of hooks. Every size imaginable existed, in both standard and metric.

The plumbing wizard Eddie power-walked down the aisle with his shirt half-untucked. He looked nothing like Merlin or Potter. In fact, he was a portly little man who looked more like a hungover hobbit.

I introduced myself and handed him the manual that came with our oven. "I'm trying to run this oven from a one-pound propane can," I told him.

"Boy, I need a beer!" he replied. "You're the last guy I'm helping before I get out of here and crack open some cold ones. I'm not sure this is gonna work, *or if it's a good idea,* but let's see what we can do."

Eddie talked fast and moved faster. He grabbed a package and ripped it open, placing the fitting on the floor. Then another package, and another. The company walkie-talkie started to jabber at him. He unplugged his earpiece and shut it off.

"Next week I'm off, so it's nothing but fishing and drinking for me." He placed a final fitting on the floor. "Here, this oughta do it. Don't think your manual is right, it says 5/8ths but these things are always 3/8ths. I betcha anything."

He lined up the pieces in the proper order. I snapped some photos so I wouldn't forget.

"Okay, I hope this works," I said.

"Here's my phone number. Let me know how it goes. And here's the name of the cabin I'm renting in the Sierras. If you're up there on your trip next week, come swing by. I'll have plenty of beers and whiskey."

I thanked Eddie, shook his hand, and left. It was a kind and generous offer, but for someone like me, it probably posed a greater threat than the propane experiment I was about to conduct.

Back in the garage, Sarah helped me connect everything. Some YouTuber suggested spraying soapy water over each connection to locate any leaks. No music played, and a throbbing silence radiated through the garage as I spritzed the soapy water in the appropriate places. Sarah double-checked to make sure every stove knob was off and that we were not near any pilot lights, chain smokers, or lit fireworks.

While the one-pound canister held significantly less propane than the bigger tanks, I knew the damage it was capable of. In high school, my degenerate friends and I left our Houston suburb for the back-woods of East Texas. There, we got the idea to put one of these small propane cans in the fire pit and shoot it with a .22-gauge rifle. From self-built bunkers, we watched it explode, creating a horrifying burst of fire. No one was hurt, but sixteen years later, the image returned to haunt me.

With a slight tremble in my hands, I screwed in the small, green propane can. A hissing sound followed. My heart thumped harder and harder. Bubbles formed around two of the connections. I sniffed, no propane smell. *Whew*, should be an easy fix with some tightening from the wrench.

I turned off the oven and went to unscrew the propane can. As I twisted, an adapter popped loose from the hose. A vicious hissing sound echoed through the garage as propane shot out. The nightmare was in my hand. Canister. Propane. *Pipe bomb!* One spark and I explode.

My heart hung from my tonsils. Sarah froze in disbelief. I was holding a live grenade with time running out. Before any logic entered my brain, I heaved the can over the driveway and into the neighbor's brush. The smell of rotten eggs blew in the wind.

Sarah broke the silence, "Thank God it didn't hit the driveway and spark. You could have started a wildfire."

"Yeah, I didn't think that through. What should we do?"

"I don't know."

We watched the can empty. My body trembled, my chest hurt. I felt lightheaded, not from the fumes, but from the surge of adrenaline. It was the familiar symptoms of a panic attack.

"I need a moment," I mumbled to Sarah.

Her fingers grazed my back as I walked away.

Inside the house, I closed myself off. My trapezoids coiled into mounds of tension. Cortisol breached the self-help floodgates surrounding my brain.

I just want to get away.

The pressure from the build swirled in my mind. It had passed the point of contemplation, entering the realm of obsession. How badly I didn't want to hurt myself, or worse, Sarah. How badly I wanted Rudy to be perfect. What would happen if I had a panic attack on the road? The physical space I so desperately needed in these moments would no longer be available, leaving nowhere to run, nowhere to hide.

Ten minutes later, a gentle knock on the door. "You okay, bubs?" Sarah said softly before she entered.

"Yeah," I mumbled.

"What do you want to do?"

I sighed, "Let's just buy a portable camping stove."

"What about the oven?"

"I'm burnt out, Sarah. Let's connect it another time, after our trip. We can pay a professional or something. In the meantime, it'll just be an overpriced cabinet and counter."

"Okay," she agreed.

Pizza and perfectionism could wait. After all, first builds are never perfect builds.

I knew the end was finally nearing when the dreaded visits to IKEA came. As summer continued in California, parts of the 2020 COVID lockdown began phasing out. Lines were commonplace at any grocery or retail store, but no line compared to the one at IKEA, which extended around the sidewalk like they were selling Taylor Swift concert tickets.

If The Home Depot is a maze, then IKEA resembles some interdimensional portal that leads to an angry alternate universe. Couple fights break out over the shape of cutting boards. Relationships end over the preferred depths of cereal bowls. Losing your significant other in IKEA is akin to losing your child at Disney World—send out a search party and anticipate at least an hour before you are reunited.

Years of failed relationships meant I neared Jedi mastery on when to bite my tongue and when to make loaded comments:

"Yeah, but did you see the price?"

"It looks cool, but I don't think it's useful."

And the *never* beneficial: "Are we almost finished?"

Apparently, I was still a Padawan in training because we left IKEA with bed slats and a shared commitment that next time we would be better off if I stayed at home.

Neither Sarah nor I had ever built anything. Not a jewelry box. Not a bookshelf. And definitely not our own home. For two months, we put in fifty-plus hours a week. Every night ended in exhaustion, usually more mental than physical. After our near-death experience, I am forever grateful that we didn't end up the poster children for millennials gone wrong.

On our last night in San Diego, I rolled the garbage and recycling cans to the curb. Layers of empty cardboard boxes with various labels filled the bin. That is exactly where labels belong. How good we are at labeling people and putting them in boxes. How many people had I alone categorized and judged? Not to mention how good I was at limiting myself—*I'm not a handy guy. I'm not good at relationships. I'm not a crier.* I had created many boxes for myself and still couldn't decide which ones I fit in: *I'm a tough guy; no, I'm a sensitive dude. I'm a Texan; no, I'm a Californian. I'm Jewish; no, I'm not religious.* Surely the open road would provide many opportunities to question my affiliations and ponder these thoughts.

Most of our friends and family had expected a rustic van-home, with exposed plywood and a mattress on the floor. Instead, Sarah and I had built something we were proud of. Of course, Rudy had some flaws, namely small gaps in the flooring and a few rough edges of woodwork. And while we had a proper sink, our plumbing didn't include a shower, dishwasher, or washing machine. But the van had most modern amenities, which were functionally placed and easy to use. We even had house plants and a color scheme. Even more impressive than the van itself was the fact that Sarah and I got through the entire build with only one moment that came close to a fight (something about a mattress).

Before a proper departure comes a proper goodbye. On August 6, 2020, Sarah and I moved into the van for the rest of the year. By that afternoon, Rudy was fully-loaded and ready for his grand exodus.

My grandfather/roommate walked out of his house and slowly shuffled towards Rudy. I grabbed the step stool and propped it up against the sliding door. With support, Papa Herb stepped into the van—our first guest. His hair was white and thick, making him look a day or two over eighty. However, at ninety-two years old and in the heart of a pandemic, goodbyes took on a deeper meaning.

Rudy smelled of fresh-cut wood and new paint. Papa Herb craned his neck to look up at the ceiling. I flipped the light switch to show off.

"You did that!" he shouted in his Brooklyn accent. "How the fuck did you do that? You're just a Jewish kid from Texas!" Then he smiled; after all, a new deep end had been added to our gene pool.

My grandfather marveled at the finished creation; I marveled at him. I thought about all the meals I had cooked for us. The stories we had shared. The lessons he had passed on. Though my uncle would be caring for him in my absence, I still entertained the frightening thought that this could be our final goodbye.

"What you've done with this is incredible, just incredible." Papa Herb's voice started to break. Emotions clouded his watery eyes. "I just wish you guys have the most amazing trip."

"Thanks, Papa Herb," I said.

We began to do that thing, the one males are really good at. The tears built up. Our eyes lost contact. The ability to say what we truly felt disappeared.

"And thanks for everything you've done for me. It's been great … just great," Papa Herb admitted, the old emotional resistance slowly giving way. "I'll miss you guys."

"Thank you." My throat tightened, the words came out squeaky, "I'm so grateful. It's … it's been a special time. We'll call you from the road."

My tears started to fall. So did Sarah's. So did Papa Herb's.

Sarah and I climbed into Rudy. We closed the doors and opened our minds. We started the engine and began a new chapter. We said goodbye to one life and hello to another. We drove.

Chapter 3
Love on the Run

"WANT TO SCREAM with me?" I asked.

Sarah grinned. "Yeah."

"One ... two ... three ..."

"AHHH!" Our voices echoed down the street as we rolled away from a life rooted in bricks and mortar. When our lungs ran out, our smiles ran on. Quoth the addict: give me more.

Another deep inhale. I screamed again, as loud and as long as I could. Satisfaction, excitement, and joy flew out the opened windows. The gales of momentum blew them right back into my grinning face.

"We're on vacation forever!" I yelled.

Sarah laughed. "I can't believe we did it, I can't believe we built this frickin' thing!"

I inventoried it all as I drove us away in what would surely become a nostalgic memory. Steam rose from the tarmac as the sun heated the manicured road. Tall palms swayed in the sea breeze. The marine layer over the Pacific Ocean reflected off the side-view mirror. The wind whipped through the cab windows. We drove past million-dollar cookie-cutter houses and hundreds more being built.

Our plan, looser than a windless sail, pointed us north to the mountains. First the Eastern Sierras, then the Cascades to Oregon and Washington. Changing leaves and cold winds would be our indicators, telling us when to move southward and eventually into the deserts of the Southwest. Our only firm plans were months away: Thanksgiving in Houston with my family, then back to California for Christmas with Sarah's. Surely different in some capacity, we would return to San Diego for New Year's Eve.

Sarah and I both shared the goal of hitting every national park in our lifetime. Now, with no jobs and no restraints, we intended to use this time to check several parks off the list. Vagabond or nomad fit this new lifestyle by definition, but a posh van-home felt unworthy of the labels adventurer or explorer (after all, our faces lit up anytime Google Maps showed a Trader Joe's on our route).

Life would be different, nonetheless. Cities would transition from home to respite from nature, if we ever desired it. Towns would be there for errands and education (I intended to Wikipedia them all). We viewed crowds as curses, campgrounds too. I'd use the pandemic to make that sound more congenial, that taking space from people was the safer strategy, but the truth is I'm less judgmental when there's no one around to judge.

With shiny tires, Rudy was more eager than any of us to get his waxed frame coated with some boondocking dust. Boondocking (also known as dispersed, primitive, or wild camping) is a style of off-grid camping that is usually accessed down dirt roads on public lands. Typically limited to fourteen days, the accommodation is free but features no amenities or guarantees. Though Sarah was new to the concept, we budgeted and committed to this way of life, having designed Rudy with solar power and water storage configured for this purpose. So, boondock or bust, we bound for the dirt roads of our public lands, seeking millionaire views with everybody prices.

Turning onto the I-15 northbound, Rudy roared and jerked into a higher gear, then another one. I brought the windows into interstate position—closed. I thought for a song—the perfect song to sound-track this moment. Bluetooth and an iPhone gave me access to millions of tracks. The pressure to choose was too much; perhaps shuffle would find the song my brain could not. I rolled the dice. "Follow me" by Aly-Us, came on. A simple beat, gentle strings, that deep bass line, the soulful lyrics, an unforgettable memory. My lover, my home, my soul all riding away into the unknown. Let the road ramble and the music ride.

San Diego had been home for seven memorable years. I thought of the solo hikes I'd taken in the desert; the glorious waves I had surfed; the nights I danced until the moon went to sleep. I replayed the emotional goodbye with my grandfather, tracing fresh tears as they left uninterrupted trails on my cheeks like the do-not-cross lines of a double-lane road. Tony Bennett sang that he left his heart in San Francisco; well, I declared that San Diego gave me mine. In that moment of sweet departure, I promised to return one day and reflect on how I had grown.

As we left the suburbs behind, I thought about the man who had arrived in 2013. I had concluded a solo road trip, which had taken me three months and 11,000 miles, before ending in Southern California. That trip proved to be a pivotal journey because it was there, on the road, where I learned the ever-rewarding lesson on how to be alone. The road is a catalyst for many, especially the heartbroken. I was fresh off a breakup and it had taken several weeks, loneliness squirming under my skin, until I was able to distinguish the pain from the problem. Until I was not only okay with being alone, but preferred it. Everyone should have such an experience, to see and drive, captaining a ship of one. To fall in love with solitude and its everlasting revelations.

I thought of the man I was now, coupled up and departing once again. This road trip was going to be quite different. I had demonstrated that I could go it alone, but had I proven I could sustain a true partnership with another person?

The song changed. I began wondering if the honeymoon phase would vanish as our personal space disappeared. I feared that this new lifestyle could ruin the one relationship I cherished more than anything, a relationship I once thought I was incapable of having.

In the spring of 2019, I found myself in the doctor's office.

"Take a deep breath," I was told. The doctor pressed the cold metal plate of a stethoscope against my chest. My hands crinkled the wax paper that covered the examination table.

The inhale hurt, but I breathed.

"Another one." She moved the plate. The cold surface awoke the skin on my back. "Deep breath ... another one ... one more."

She removed the earpieces and slung the device around the back of her neck. "Well, your lungs sound fine. So, that's good news."

"So, what is it then? Not bronchitis or anything?" I asked.

"Nope. Are you under any stress?"

Planned questions get planned answers. "Umm, just the usual stuff," I mumbled.

"Well, keep an eye on it. If it gets worse, come back in."

The following day, I awoke gasping, sucking, hurting for air. The center of my chest had a tightening, attention-hungry hurt. The pain radiated whether I breathed or not, whether I thought or didn't. But of course, I thought, and thought, and thought some more. It was in that nightmarish, crack-of-dawn moment that my soul knew without a doubt: *this is not a physical problem, it is a mental one.*

Thus, I found myself in one of those little offices with a couple diplomas on the wall, some books on a shelf, opposing chairs, and the ears of a professional. It didn't take long until the diagnosis: panic disorder.

"Really, that's a panic attack?" I asked.

"Yes, it is," said the therapist, Mary.

I was surprised. It didn't resemble the movies. No panting into a paper bag, no frantic crying. Just chest pains, shallow breaths, and spells of lightheadedness. This kind of anxiety couldn't be exercised or meditated away. I know, because I had tried. And how badly I want to say that the trigger came from big wave surfing or mountaineering, or simply a stressful job, but it did not. It came from dating.

"I was reviewing the timeline of life events you submitted—alcoholism, an abusive stepmother, a … um, challenging childhood," said Mary. "There's a lot for us to look at."

Perhaps I had been downplaying things, that we did have plenty to look at. Yet all I could muster on the outside was a simple, robotic nod.

"Have you ever heard of EMDR?" she asked.

"No."

"Oh, well I think you'd be a perfect candidate for it. It stands for eye movement desensitization and reprocessing. It's a form of trauma therapy that allows us to reprocess some of the moments in your life that are impacting you as an adult. Together, we can discover why emotional intimacy and conflict trigger the primitive responses that are overloading your nervous system."

"Will it make the panic attacks stop?"

"I have seen a lot of success with other clients."

"Okay, then I'll try it," I said, unsure what the treatment entailed, simply desperate to return to some semblance of normal.

I used to think that routine made life boring. However, in those bleak and uncertain days when I was undergoing treatment, routine kept me alive. My habitual presence at alcohol recovery meetings preserved my sobriety, as it had since March of 2010. I started going to 6 a.m. yoga classes to help stave off panic attacks before work, although this was often unsuccessful. The biweekly therapy visits felt like dental work for the soul, invasive but necessary.

Mary honed in on specific areas of my life. Whenever she would initiate the EMDR by handing over two vibrating tactiles, I'd grip them tight and close my eyes, knowing we were about to revisit something I'd rather avoid. As we relived and reprocessed, different muscles in my body would knot then unfurl. Some visits I'd leave the office feeling more exhausted and overwhelmed than ever, flooded with more emotions and thoughts than my body could handle. But I trusted her, and she earned every out-of-pocket penny I spent because eventually a light appeared at the end of that punishing tunnel. Sure enough, one day the chest pains went away, my diaphragm softened, and that taken-for-granted smile returned.

"I think it's time you start dating again," said Mary one day.

"*Really?* I don't think so."

"Why not?"

"I don't know. I still feel pretty broken, like it wouldn't be responsible to date until I'm not so messed up."

"Andrew, the only way we can truly gauge your progress is if you're faced with the situations that brought you here in the first place."

"Ugh."

"Is there anyone you're attracted to at the moment?"

I paused. "Yeah, there is."

"Tell me about them."

"Her name is Sarah."

❖

Sarah and I did not meet online. There was no Tinder, Bumble, or Hitch. No Match.com, Christian Mingle, or Farmers Only. In fact, the only thing I was swiping was sweat from my brow.

On March 1, 2019, I walked into the hot yoga studio. The air was dense and smothering. Rubber mats in varying colors unfolded across the floor. Flexible people meditated and stretched. I scanned for a place in the back with my insecure and inflexible companions. Then, my feet stopped. *The instructor.*

She had big, almond eyes the color of emeralds. A single braid of sun-streaked, dirty blonde hair draped over her shoulder. Yoga pants and a tank top accentuated her short frame, striking a balance of strength and curves.

She sat back on her heels. "Good morning everyone, my name is Sarah and I'll be guiding you through today's class. Before we dive in, I want to take a moment and say how grateful I am to be sharing this practice with you. Yoga saved my life during an incredibly dark time. And every time I step on the mat, I'm reminded of my own journey. Whatever you might be going through, may today's practice remind you of your own strength. Let's begin."

Maybe I was drooling, I don't know. I was most certainly sweating. The poses began. I stumbled, repeating my mantra: *Don't fart, don't die.* By the time savasana came around, a pond of perspiration surrounded my mat. It took a while for me to regain enough vigor to stand up. When I did, only one person in class remained. It was Sarah. She had a mop and was waiting for me to leave so she could attempt to disinfect the floor from my pool of sweat. Yeah, probably not the ideal time to present myself. Still, it was a chance, my opener.

"Great class," I said with a smile.

"Aw, thanks," she replied. "What's your name?"

"Andrew."

"I'm Sarah."

"I haven't seen you here before."

"Yeah, I just started teaching. I'll be here every Friday at six."

She moved the mop over Perspiration Pond. The words tripped out of my mouth, "It, uh, was a hot one."

"Yeah," she mumbled, streaking my sweat across the floor. *It was a hot one? You creepy, sweaty oaf.*

We continued chatting, until time ran out. "Maybe I'll see you next week," I said with a grin.

"I hope so," she replied.

Maybe wasn't really authentic because *every* Friday morning, I would wake up at 5 a.m., eager to see my new favorite instructor. Sweating, stumbling, nearly passing out. Yet the hardest pose came after class—the creeper's clam—where I shut in the chemical craziness of deep attraction and strived to be friendly and sensible. After all, I didn't want to be the creepy guy hitting on the yoga teacher—well, at least not the creepy part.

Sarah would mop the floors as I cherished whatever amount of conversation I could sweep in. Our chats grew longer and longer each week. She told me stories about traveling across Europe by herself at the age of sixteen, and how a volunteer trip to a refugee camp in the West Bank changed her life. Her other job was working for a non-profit focused on conflict resolution. Like me, she loved to write. The more I learned, the more my attraction intensified. It was the kind of fascination that keeps you awake at night and asleep to the world during the day.

I was smitten, infatuated. A big, mind-consuming, feel-like-you-are-in-high-school again crush. *And* I knew her last name. So, what would any sensible person do before making a move? Yup, an internet search. And there it was on social media: a boyfriend. *Of course she has a boyfriend. And the son of a bitch has abs. But how come she never talks about him?*

It didn't matter. I was in that horrible crevasse that every nice guy dreads—the friend zone. However, if I'm completely honest, part of me was relieved. There was another woman in my life. As with Sarah, she and I had weekly, intimate conversations. Unlike Sarah, I had to pay by the hour. Hey-hey, it wasn't like that. Back to my therapist.

Mary got excited, "Oh, a yoga teacher?"

"Yeah, she has a boyfriend, though."

"Aw, okay. Anyone else?"

"Nope. Besides, I think it would be good for me to focus on a friendship with a woman I'm attracted to. No manipulation. No games. No hidden agenda."

"I still think you should start dating again."

"I still think I shouldn't."

Here you can rest easy, because this isn't the part of the story where a wounded person projects all their baggage onto some innocent bystander. Been there, *unfortunately* done that. And this isn't the story about a selfish bro infiltrating a relationship. That was twenty-three-year-old me, not thirty-three-year-old me. Though I didn't enjoy it, I embraced the friend zone purgatory. Sarah and I continued to get to know one another in the confines of her workplace. Mop. Sweat. Chat. Crush.

The obliquity of the Earth makes the seasons, and spring was filled with the internal storms of growth, then summer's sun bloomed its flowers. By the time I finally mustered up the courage to ask Sarah if she wanted to connect outside the yoga studio, March had turned to September, Sarah was now single, and I no longer felt broken. I wasn't back to my old self, rather, I was anew. A transformed man who had cultivated yet another ring of growth in life's complicated tree trunk. My friendship with Sarah was evaporating from the surface level, and a heavy thunderhead of hope waited to rain down love.

It wasn't a date, but it wasn't *not a date*. Before her evening yoga class, Sarah and I met at our local beach. The sandstone cliffs reflected the final day's light. Sarah spread out a blanket across the sand, then sat cross-legged. I turned my back on the ocean, and looking into her eyes, wasted no time, leading with the question I had contemplated for six months.

"In class, you said yoga saved your life. Tell me more."

She began, her eyes fixed on mine. "Well, I was married."

I nearly spit out my fizzy water. "You were married?"

She laughed, "Yeah, hard to believe, huh?"

"Ha, yeah. I wasn't expecting that. You're so young. How old are you?"

"I'm about to turn twenty-nine. I was married when I was twenty-one, divorced by twenty-four." She took a heavy breath, then went full disclosure. "We met in high school. After, he joined the military. He cheated on me while he was deployed. I thought I had the strength to leave him, but I was codependent, so I tried to forgive and move on. Then it got worse. He was a crewman on a helicopter. It crashed over the Atlantic Ocean. More than half the crew died. He survived, but barely. I became his full-time caregiver while he recovered."

"Geez, Sarah."

"Yeah, then things really spiraled. He started to abuse his pain meds and had horrible PTSD. One night, everything fell apart. He was drunk and pulled out a gun. I didn't know if he was going to shoot me or himself. Turns out he was having another affair. I decided I had to get out if I was going to live. The next morning, I told him our marriage was over …" She paused, her eyes drifting away. "Then he assaulted me."

"Oh my God."

"I'm sorry. I feel like I'm trauma-dumping on you."

"No, no. Not at all."

"Honestly, you're one of the few people that I've told."

"Sarah, don't apologize. I'm honored you trust me with your story."

"Thanks. Anyway, it was around this time, when I was at my most broken, that I found yoga. It was the only hour of my day when I did something for me. At a time when I was completely shattered, yoga was my saving grace. After our marriage ended, I packed up all my stuff and took this long road trip across the country. When I arrived in California, I enrolled in a yoga teacher training program."

"Sarah, I never would have guessed you've been through so much. It sounds like a Lifetime movie. I mean, we've been friends for six months and I had no clue."

A soft smile returned to her face. "And how about you? What's your story?"

The golden hour morphed into the amber minutes just before dark. Lady Pacific took on the color of the sky, darkening to a shadowy blue. Pelicans and seagulls circled the shoreline, but few things fly as pure and pretty as lovebirds skipping the surface-level topics that fill today's conversations for the vulnerable stories that truly matter.

I told her about my journey with alcoholism. How brushes with death, tormented ex-girlfriends, and worried family members had failed to stall my addiction. After several sober years, I had become accustomed to sharing this story, and its happy ending. Sarah listened with her eyes as much as her ears. Pre-therapy me would have hidden the parts I wanted to, and how badly I desired to suppress my recent struggles with mental health. But I knew there was more that deserved to be disclosed. I stammered at first, then found the confidence that honesty conveys—the effortless momentum when you let the truth tell itself.

"So, yeah, I haven't dated in a while. I have a bit of … commitment phobia."

"Ha, you too?"

Her smile put me at ease. "Yeah. I didn't think much of it until earlier this year when I was diagnosed with panic disorder. I was having panic attacks from dating. Well, not like asking women out or being nervous on dates. But the deeper stuff, the emotional intimacy. Anytime things progressed or I needed to set some boundaries, my anxiety worsened. I would try and have the difficult conversations, but that only made the panic attacks worse. Even after I stopped dating, the panic never went away. Eventually, it got so bad that I thought I was going to quit my job. So, I started going to therapy earlier this year."

"Really?" Sarah lit up. Apparently, admitting you go to therapy is more of a turn-on than a turn-off.

"Yeah. It's kinda crazy to admit, but even after all the 12-Step work I did to get sober, I was still oblivious to how my past really affected me later in life. Especially my relationships."

"Did it work?"

"Ha, I hope so. I haven't had a panic attack in a couple of months."

"That's amazing, Andrew," Sarah said as her phone alarm sounded. She stood up and brushed the sand from her legs. "I've got to get to work. But you're coming to class, right?"

"Yeah."

"Good, I'll see you there."

I went in for our first hug. No mop, no sweat. Her short frame snuggled up against my chest. With the physical space between us gone, I couldn't help but feel the overwhelming depths of the crevasse that remained. The timeless riddle that has plagued man since before Moses: *How does a dude get out of the friend zone?*

Two days later, I uncovered the antidote when I arrived at a packed concert venue in downtown San Diego. The sounds of electronic indie music reverberated in every direction. Intoxicated youngsters filled the dance floor. I scanned the crowd—and oh, my lucky stars—there she was. *Fate.* Sarah stood across the room, wearing a black top with matching shorts and high heels. We made eye contact. Her smile widened. We met near the bar.

She yelled over the music, "I didn't know you were going to be here."

"Likewise! Are you alone?"

"Just with my one friend. You?"

"Same."

She took a pull from her gin and tonic. "We're gonna head deeper into the dance floor, wanna join?"

My sliding door moment. When *no* meant nothing and *yes* began everything.

"Sure," I said. And we were off, forcing our way through the thick crowd.

We started dancing. Sweaty, radical, expressive. Like a tropical bird of paradise, I flapped wildly and rhythmically, as if the fate of my legacy teetered on the brink. The woman I had crushed on for the better part of a year was used to seeing me covered in sweat, and soon she began moving with me.

We danced. Hard and heavy. Laughing and glowing. A group of people not old enough to legally drink formed a circle around us. We danced some more. Hours went by, moving and grooving. Then our faces got closer, and closer. I bent my knees so our eyes could level, my baby blues and her jubilant jades. We kissed.

Sweat. Lips. Electricity. *Bullseye, bingo, touchdown, hallelujah!*

The friend zone riddle was solved. The answer: dance. Not synchronized tango, waltzing, or West Coast Swing. No—wild, sporadic, don't give two crackers who is watching, let-it-all-out dance.

For each person who crosses the crevasse of the friend zone, a thousand angels get their wings. That night the heavens celebrated as I drove home as high as a sober person can possibly get.

On our next date, Sarah asked, "Do you see yourself settling in San Diego?"

"I love it here," I replied, "but I would much rather put my money into a camper van than into a house."

"Really?" she said. "That's on the top of my bucket list!"

She even had it on a vision board. Of course she did.

Rudy cruised at a steady pace of 65 mph. Our van had no back windows, so the rearview mirror proved useless for watching traffic. Instead, Sarah angled the mirror so we could make eye contact and share a flirtatious glance.

"Do you have an intention for the trip?" she asked.

"Yeah, I do. I want to jump in the lakes."

"Oh yeah?"

"I mean really jump in them, not just sit on the sidelines wondering and debating. It's, well, I know I'm not gettin' any younger. I feel that part of aging I hate. All the overthinking and worrying. Talkin' myself out of things instead of into them. So yeah, I want to jump in the lakes."

"I like that."

"How about you?"

"It's something I've been thinking about a lot. I'm just so burned out after working three jobs, then going straight into building Rudy. I want to work on my book, but honestly, I know I need a break. I can't remember the last time I had this kind of freedom. My intention is to really seize this opportunity. To see how our relationship will grow now that we're sharing a home. To see what the road has to teach me now that I can slow down."

"You mean you don't want to get in a fight about where to store the Tupperware?"

"You know my idea was better."

"Ha. Yeah, yeah."

Our eyes met again in the rearview mirror. Sarah blushed. If the fear of leaving everything behind was on her mind, it didn't show. Reluctant to go all in, I had kept my car and closet of clothes at Papa Herb's, while Sarah took the leap. She terminated her lease and sold her car, furniture, and most of her wardrobe. Overly clean, doggedly determined, and impractically optimistic—a good balance to my anxious, messy mind. I envied her ability to dive in, to cut the anchor and see where the current leads.

The music played, Rudy steadily churning ahead. Only the horizon knew whether van life would be fruitful or destructive to this romance. Either way, love was on the run.

Chapter 4
The Road as a Teacher

EVEN GLOBAL PANDEMICS can have silver linings, one of which was the ability to actually test the speed limit on Southern California's freeways. News articles claimed that working from home had cleaned up the air. Unfortunately, my eyes concluded that the Inland Empire, LA's suburban expanse, needed more than a few traffic-free months to eradicate the pollution. The usual thick layer of smog wrapped around the San Bernardino Mountains, leaving the tops of the peaks protruding above the gray haze.

Every so often, I glimpsed into the side-view mirror to make sure a solar panel had not flown off and decapitated a biker. I also kept a close eye on the engine temperature gauge and listened to Rudy's rumble. Until now, the furthest we had driven the van was the day we brought it home. We originally planned to do a test run, but the longer the build took, the less necessary that seemed.

The diesel Ram ProMaster had a reputation for breakdowns and expensive repairs, but of course, I hadn't discovered this information until after we purchased it. Combined, Sarah and I could probably name five parts under the hood. Hell, we were so mechanically handicapped that only one of us could drive a stick, and by one of us … I mean Sarah. While we were both ignorant, at least *she* was optimistic. I departed with the incessant trepidation that something would break. After all, it had to—we had built it.

Even without traffic, my road trips never felt entirely underway until I exited the interstate and accelerated on my beloved CA-395. After the traffic lights of Hesperia and Adelanto, past the truck stops and drive-thrus, it was on to the high desert and its many pleasures: Mojave magic, Death Valley delights, and Sierra surprises.

The first Joshua tree appeared, guarding the lands from urban sprawl. Night arrived; overzealous and underprepared, we had no clue where to sleep. Sarah drove on, with glowing head beams and squinty eyes. With the satellite view on Google Maps, I found a vacant lot outside of the town of Aberdeen, California. The GPS did the work until Rudy illuminated a dirt plot next to a fenced-in electrical transformer. No signs prohibiting camping, only the night which concealed the landscape but not the sentiment that something beautiful awaited under darkness's duvet.

Despite my exhaustion, I awoke every other hour. My city-wired nervous system was hypersensitive to the softness of the rural night. I jumped up with each passing truck (three in total). When the refrigerator kicked on, its soft whir lifted my eyelids. The van felt foreign, and it would take a few blinks until I remembered where I was, and why I was there. What a strange sensation, to be in a home— a home we had built—yet feeling as if I was in a stranger's room, awoken by jetlag on the other side of the world.

A heavy *thump* on the roof of the van. I jolted up. Sleep fell from my eyes. Daylight had arrived, as well as our first neighbor. *Thump. Thump.* Out the window, I watched a roadrunner hop off Rudy and run under the chain link fence.

"What was that?" Sarah's voice croaked.

"It was a roadrunner. *Beep, Beep.*" I planted a kiss on her cheek. "You gotta check out this view."

Sarah peered out the bunk window. The sky was naked blue without a cloth of cloud. The eastern slopes of the Sierra Nevada mountains pointed towards the heavens. The rising sun emphasized the stone stripes of Earth's epochs. I hopped out of bed and slid the door open. A pleasant crosswind greeted my bare legs. With the cargo doors ajar, a more extensive view was unveiled. From north to south, rugged mountains stretched to either horizon.

Sarah looked left to the interior of our tiny home, then right to the majestic peaks. "I can't believe we did this. I can't believe we built this thing, that we're finally out on the road."

Her eyes grew watery, her gratitude present with each droplet that rolled down her cheeks. I crawled back into bed, welcoming Sarah into the nook of my right side. We simply lay there, wrapped in the views and one another. No plans, no decisions. Just two people discovering that routines were now optional.

Papa Herb had insisted on buying us a housewarming gift. Sarah and I chose something we knew we would use every day. As the new kettle reached 200 degrees, I smiled and thought of the old gaffer. I circled the spout over a funnel of coffee grounds and into Sarah's mug. The scent of dark, roasted beans filled the narrow walls of the van. We began journaling, frequently lifting our heads to enjoy the view. The pandemic had already robbed the things I would miss in the city; rural America came with the nature and quiet I had craved.

On the streets of Instagram, #vanlife worked the corner with the other floozies of hashtag whoredom. I never expected a filtered reality, but on that first morning I slowly savored the content in the flesh. How good it felt to cherish and not scroll.

Northbound, a federal sign off CA-395 caught our attention: ANCIENT BRISTLECONE PINE FOREST, NEXT RIGHT.

"What do ya think?" I asked.

"I'm down," said Sarah.

I turned Rudy right—after all, itineraries are for tourists. We enjoyed the empty lanes of CA-168. I yielded only to the tingles of going down a road I had never driven.

When I was employed, I had battled Inland Empire traffic on long weekends to experience the opportunities of eastern California, always opting for the Sierra Nevada and disregarding its smaller sibling to the east. The White Mountain range lies north of Death

Valley, near the Nevada border. Despite peaking at over 14,000 feet, it's a range overlooked by many merely because of its proximity to the more dramatic Sierra Nevada.

Miles of cement switchbacks traced the dry and rocky spine of this geological force. The flora told the story of elevation gain—sage to juniper, pinyon to ponderosa, fir to bristlecone. The scent of natural pine aromatized the cab better than any hanging cardboard Christmas tree could.

California is the Kingdom of the Trees and home to several world record holders. Reaching heights of 380 feet (equivalent to a 30-story building), the redwoods of the northern coastline are the tallest in the world. The sequoias of the Western Sierras contain the largest, with trunk volumes over 52,000 cubic feet and weighing over 6,000 tons. Further east, the White Mountains produce the neglected scholars of the land—the Great Basin bristlecone pine—possibly the oldest trees in the world.

These species grow at high altitudes and have evolved to withstand dry summers, snowy winters, and 70 mph mountain winds. As a result, the wood grows gnarled and twisted, compact and dense, creating a tree that looks mystical and spooky. The oldest trees here age close to the 5,000-year mark, meaning that the saplings sprouted before the Giza pyramids.

Sarah and I spent the day hiking amongst the ancient sages, applying lip balm every hour to combat the aridity. Sarah pressed her hand against a bristlecone that knew of times before Jews and Jesus, Moses and Muslims. Beyond the trees, rows of desert mountain ranges lined the longitudes like shark's teeth.

We saw a dozen other hikers on our walk, and even a forest 10,000 feet above sea level—an hour's drive from any town, and a day's drive from a city—is not safe from the shortcomings of humanity. Here, the Forest Service does not allow off-trail hiking, ensuring people don't vandalize or try to steal pieces of Methuselah, the eldest tree in the grove and considered to be the oldest living tree in the world (which remains hidden at a secret location). If that seems like an excessive safety measure then know this: the park's Schulman Visitor Center burned down in 2008 by a suspected act of arson. *Oh, humans.* If these old trees could talk, what would they say? The rebuilt visitor center looked beautiful, but—like most visitor centers in 2020— remained closed due to the pandemic.

Dirt roads and washboards took us to our second resting place of the trip. On the ridgeline of the White Mountains, we parked Rudy 11,000 feet above the sea. With a front porch view of the mighty Sierra front, the opened slider door unveiled the aggressive, snow-traced stone that rose not towards the sky, but into it.

Life was a dichotomy of emotions: slow and quiet, yet exciting and invigorating. Sarah read a book aloud while I cooked dinner. The sun fell behind the tallest peak, and the lights from the town of Bishop twinkled through dusk. We read until our eyes couldn't stay open.

I awoke in the night to empty my bladder, sliding the door open then untying my sweatpants. My eyes adjusted to the shadows of the mountains. I looked up at the moonless sky, then stumbled back into the van, nearly wetting the floor. The stars overwhelmed my senses. To see so many, so quickly, put my brain in a peculiar state of shock. Semi-recovered, I gave another look, then summoned Sarah.

"Check out the stars," I whispered. She crawled out of bed and made her way to the door.

"Oh my God!" Sarah, too, lost her equilibrium.

The Milky Way churned a thicker cream, streaking the sky with a billion sparkles. The sheer quantity gave me an inauspicious feeling. I'm unsure why, but I was afraid to look for too long, feeling like a computer without enough CPU to process a complex equation.

I guess it didn't matter that neither the bristlecones nor the constellations offered teachings about what we humans were doing wrong. We probably wouldn't have listened anyway.

The sky was a flirtatious blue, delightfully contrasting the gray granite of Laurel Mountain, which towered above Convict Lake. In 1871, the lake earned its English name in true Wild West grandeur, a story replete with fugitives, posses, shootouts, and lynchings. Convict Lake made the news again in 1990, when three teenagers and four attempted rescuers drowned after the teenagers fell through thin ice.

Despite my internet search yielding stories of death, the setting felt serene and far from haunted. A mighty wind gusted down, pushing the water across the pebbled shoreline and creating a calming melody with each crashing wave. We set up for the day, basking in the peace of the place. Two elderly couples to my right were Hispanic and of an age that grew more salt than pepper.

"Are you all early retired?" asked Julian, the man closest to us. A fair question on a more than fair Tuesday.

"Ha, no. We're *temporarily* retired," I replied.

I smiled at the idea. When I got my first job at the age of sixteen, Papa Herb said, "That's great, now only fifty years until you get to retire." Ole Herbie's statement took the wind right out of my sail. He had done it the traditional way, working for decades, saving, investing, then traveling the world as a senior. Now, with retirement still a far-fetched idea, the pandemic's forced hiatus was delivering some reprieve from my fifty-year grind.

Julian was less amused. "What does that mean, temporarily retired? You're not workin'? What did you do before?"

I turned my camp chair towards him, then told the story I was destined to repeat a lot on the road. "Well, I was a business teacher before the pandemic. I worked at an international school, so all the students were forced to return to their native countries. At first, we taught online, but it didn't work out with all the different time zones. So, the school shut down temporarily, then permanently, leaving me unemployed."

Telling fellow Americans you lost your job receives the identical response if you tell them your Great Aunt Susie died. They usually cock their head, start with the prolonged *"Aw,"* followed by the gently spoken, *"I'm so sorry to hear that."* Well, maybe ole Aunt Susie was a sadist, and maybe I was overworked and underpaid.

Julian followed the script. His head tilted and his *aw* blew like the horn of an ocean liner. If time holds more value than money, then I'm wealthier now than I was before. But I didn't say this, allowing the man to grieve a lifestyle I did not miss.

What do you do? The real American anthem. Often a signal to prepare for a lame conversation, or worse, an identity crisis. Even when I loved my job, I still hated this question. According to the book *Happiness At Work* (Price-Jones), Americans spend approximately 90,000 hours of their lifetime working. Must we spend our free time talking about it?

"How long you in the area for?" Julian asked.

"Not sure, maybe another few days. Do ya'll live nearby?" I asked.

"We live in the Central Valley and come up here a couple times a year. Fishin's bad this year, though. The hatchery had their own outbreak, a bacteria or something. So they had to kill all the trout. This lake usually has good fishin'. Guess it's not the best year for a lot of things."

Julian didn't have a line in the water, but the entire shoreline of Convict Lake was saturated with optimistic anglers. They appeared to have a stricter code than the Center for Disease Control, with a dozen feet separating each person. They all sat quietly, careful not to disturb the water.

"Is it always this crowded?" I asked Julian.

"Never seen it like this on a Tuesday. This weekend was crazy, we couldn't find any parking."

Sarah and I had already gotten in the habit of relocating to trailheads as soon as we woke up, where the early bird's worm came in the form of a parking spot. Every campground we saw had "FULL" posted at the entrance, but on the boondocker's east side of Highway 395, finding space and solitude was never a problem.

Despite the weekend craziness, the weekday crowd was lighter, friendlier, and moved with the gentle pace of retirees.

Julian fell silent. I turned my chair and went back to admiring the lake.

"Check it out," said Sarah, pointing above the water.

A bald eagle swooped down to the lake's surface, dunked its feet in, and flapped up, back into the mountains with empty talons. *Did the eagle curse the hatchery like the bored fishermen?* Either way, I sat in awe of the poster child for American liberty. For once, the bald eagle served as the reward of free living, rather than a symbol of it.

Sarah and I might have been experienced travelers and road-trippers, but we were newbies to van life. Driving away from Convict Lake, a passing van-dweller waved from the left lane. The wave said hello, but I felt it expressed so much more. The gesture acknowledged the unspoken respect that van life is not always about a photo, caption, and a hashtag. That this lifestyle is a commitment to a way of living that is not always easy, and does not always come with the support of friends, family, and society at large. Though you gain so much, you might have to surrender certain things—not just your belongings, but your sense of community too. I waved back, though I felt a salute would be a more worthy gesture.

Behind the wheel of most vans is a person who has heard the ill advice of an employer, the concerns of a parent, or the loaded questions from friends who hate their jobs. *What will you do about money? Your career? Retirement? How can your relationship survive such a small space? Aren't you scared of bears, mountain lions, and meth heads? What happens if you break down and don't have cell service? What will you do without WiFi?* (Oh, the horror!)

My own family and friends covered the spectrum of reactions to our setting forth. Some bit their tongues so hard I could feel the toothmarks on my own. *How irresponsible and immature,* I imagined them thinking. Others mastered the art of simultaneously expressing encouragement and envy, admitting, "I wish I had the guts to do what you all are doing." I had always associated courage with struggle and bravery, not travel and freedom. Are day-to-day obligations the present-day prisons that so many fear to escape?

These self-prescribed pressures were my fences, my prison guards holding me back, keeping me trapped. I wish I could say I had always honored my love for travel and my desire to live differently. That I cruised over those judgments and warnings as if they were tiny speed bumps in the road. The truth is I spent decades consumed by the torment of wondering what other people thought of me. I, too, feared the repercussions of not living life by society's script. I had spent so many years trying to fit in, thinking that would make the discontent go away, but this only added another layer of unhappiness.

Oh, the paradox of the road—its ability to take you back while moving you forward. Amid these thoughts came that day's conversation with Julian. The label *unemployed teacher* interrupted the smooth tarmac with a bumpy memory. The memory of the last time I cried.

I was eighteen years old; many years after my father's alcoholism and infidelity had led to my parents' divorce. While I was living with my mom throughout high school, my father always kept tabs on my academics, and now, with the end of high school approaching, he called me up.

"Have you thought about what you want to study in college?" he asked.

"Yeah," I replied nervously, "I … I want to be a teacher."

"A teacher? What? Why?" His inquisitive tone shifted. My father never hid his mood. Occasionally he was charming, usually he was serious. At his worst, he would grab the dog by the neck and beat it senseless. He had been off alcohol for many years, yet his recovery never fully reached his unhealthy affairs with rage, women, work, and money.

And with that shift in tone, I knew the conversation about my future was inciting the reaction I had feared.

"I, I was just thinking about all the people I could help," I replied.

"Oh, well that's cute. Give me a fuckin' break! How the hell will you make enough money to live?" he yelled.

I mumbled, "I don't know. I hadn't thought about it."

"Well, you better start thinking about it! Because I won't pay for you to go to college to be a teacher. You're my son. I'll be damned if you're going to be a teacher when you can do business, or law, or engineering."

I went silent.

"Hello, hello? You there? Earth to Andrew."

"I heard you," I growled.

"And?"

"And I want to be a teacher."

"Jesus Christ."

"Dad, I don't need your support or your money."

"Ha, yeah right! That's what your mother said. Maybe she can use all that child support to pay for your education."

He hung up.

I slammed the phone down and punched the wall. A welling from my chest heaved out a desperate sound. The tears began flowing. I cried hard. Not the gentle tears that come from a good movie or from installing a working light switch, but a true, cathartic cry. If I knew that it was going to be my last release for sixteen years, I would have savored it, letting it last longer than necessary. But hearing the commotion, my mom knocked on the door. Like the man I was trained to be, I forced those final tears to stop and wiped them away before anyone could see.

I told her what had happened. She reached out to her father, and Papa Herb said he'd foot the bill for my education. I know, the privilege. It makes me cringe to admit. Not just one family member who was willing and capable of keeping me out of student loan debt, but two. Sadly, I can't say eighteen-year-old me acknowledged the silk safety net I was blessed with. I was naive, entitled, and hurt. I appreciated Papa Herb's offer, but it did little to scab the father wound.

Six weeks went by without me speaking to my dad. Six weeks where I stewed and doubted, grappling with the reality of his rejection, until the day of my high school graduation, when a letter came in the mail. The university my father had wanted me to attend had accepted me off their waitlist.

Nervous, I picked up the phone, breaking the silence between father and son. "Meet me at Starbucks," I told him. "The one on Champions Drive."

It was the serious Starbucks, the one where big conversations happened. The last time we met there I was fourteen years old, when I told him I was moving out of his house. The tumultuous two years under his roof had left me suicidal and depressed. Four years later, we sat across from one another at the same table. I handed him the university's letter. He pulled it out of the envelope and read the contents.

Looking up with a straight face, he said, "I thought you were going to tell me you got your girlfriend pregnant."

He pushed the letter back across the table. No congrats. No reconciliation. It would have made a funny joke if that was his intent, but it wasn't. He was serious.

That afternoon, an eighteen-year-old boy made the most significant detour of his life. A turn that took him off the path of callings and passions. One that took him the long way round, through the soul-sucking traffic of conformity. Auditioning for my father's approval, I accepted the university's offer and changed my major to mirror what he had on his bachelor's degree. A lengthy era began that day, characterized by emotional suppression and not speaking up. Decisions around education, careers, and relationships were all in the pursuit of external validation. But, like most familiar routes, I drove on as if automated.

If my life was a car, I had spent most of my adulthood in the passenger seat. Occasionally, I'd be a backseat driver, but I rarely had my hands on the wheel. It wasn't until my thirties that I buckled up where I belonged. At the age of thirty-two, after a variety of failed business careers, I finally pursued my dream and became a teacher. Despite supporting my sister's long tenure as an educator, my father still held me to a different standard. He would say, "I hope this is a stepping stone to a *real* career."

The pandemic had other plans, and my career in academia was taken away before I could say goodbye. Though he never said it, I knew my old man would rather see me miserable in a cubicle than happy in a van.

I drove on, my eyes forward and my mind in the past, trying to remember what that last cry felt like. But I couldn't fully recall. Sixteen dry years had passed. So much had happened, many moments worthy of tears. The road didn't care that a dude reflecting on his daddy issues was grounds for cancellation these days. No, the road was doing what it always does: taking me to school and teaching me lessons.

When would I be able to stop caring about what others thought? Could I fully commit to an alternative lifestyle without having to justify it at every opportunity? Was I finally ready to live for myself— wholeheartedly, unapologetically, authentic, and free?

On the long-distance road trip, decisions come and go like street lights and exit signs. When the light turns yellow, do you hit the accelerator or hit the brake? The scenic route or the direct route? Drive-thru or walk-in? With each turn, the opportunity to change our story exists. The people we meet, the experiences we have, the lasting impact of a beautiful view or an endearing person all have an effect.

Turning left or right might be as simple as following your GPS, or as meaningful as following your gut.

On a road trip, a turn can change everything. Wrong turns and right turns, wide turns and sharp turns, hairpin turns and smooth turns, but *never* inconsequential turns. The turn can be prompted by a sign, a backseat driver, or a deep voice from within. Some call it coincidence, others call it fate. Either way, those who connect the dots of life's chronological atlas, who view the road to the present moment as something special, know the added value of an assessed existence.

The driver of this tale no longer barrels towards hedonism, nor does he shortcut around the painful detours of adulthood. After all, I have arrived at many dead-ends in my days, and thankfully I now know the cosmic power of a U-turn.

So, let us turn. For in a book, a turn brings a new page, and the road still has much to teach.

Chapter 5
The Shit You Don't See on Instagram

MANY BUSHES CAN be found in the high fields off CA-395: sage bush, juniper bush, and the hippie's bush. The last, having no genus but surely concealing a species, is mainly sighted around the habitat of natural hot springs, especially near Mammoth, California. At least that's where Sarah and I had our first sighting. The hippie's bush startled me more than the black bear we had encountered earlier that day. Sarah took out her phone to film the bear, she did not take it out to film the bush. I glanced at the bush, then quickly looked away. Still, I could not avoid the sensation that the bush kept staring at me, pleading for my attention.

Standing on the steps of a rusty motorhome, a nudist sipped from his mug, enjoying the view and the breeze on his bush. A naked couple set up chairs next to the rig, their bushes rustling in the wind. The sun gave the three nude bodies the final UV rays of the day as I pondered the situation. *Were the three friends or lovers? Had a fourth nudist gone missing during their full-exposure double date? Do even nudists have to play third wheel?* I didn't have the balls to ask, pun intended.

The hippie bushes moved inside the RV. Sarah and I walked to the hot spring. There are many sounds in the Eastern Sierras: birds chirping, shimmering leaves of quaking aspen, running reels of caught trout, and early 2000s rave music. The sound of thumping bass filled the valley floor. Two men stood next to the man-made hot tub. The area outside Mammoth Lakes is one of the few places you can hike pristine trails all morning, enjoy an alpine lake in the afternoon, soak in a natural hot spring in the evening, then camp with a million-dollar view—all without spending a penny. However, free still finds its costs, which usually come in the form of the characters you share the experience with. Like people who play club music in nature. People you'd crop out of a photo but shouldn't crop out of a story. People like Javier and Christian.

"Water's too hot," said the shirtless and pudgy Javier. A rusted pipe fed the steaming water into the well-crafted tub.

"Summ azzholez left da hot water on," Christian, Javiers's friend, slurred, a tall can of booze clinched tightly in his palm. Like Javier, Christian had caramel skin and straight, black hair. Christian wore glasses and his soft face sagged with his speech. Perhaps an opiate in his system, white pills with his White Claw, which never left his grip.

"Got it. Ya'll like Gabriel and Dresden?" I asked.

"Who's that?" said Javier.

"The music." I pointed at the speaker that played "As the Rush Comes," an old favorite.

"Oh, I dunno man. Juss some crap we put on." *So much for bonding.*

Javier, Christian, and Bluetooth speaker trance music actually served as an upgrade after discovering how crowded the other hot springs in the area were. With the nudists back at their RV, only the four of us occupied the hottest, cleanest, and prettiest tub Sarah and I had tracked down.

Slowly, I entered the water. Steam infused with the scent of sulfur lifted from the surface. Sarah waited another minute then joined me. Our bodies basked in comfort while our eyes drank in the sights. The sun slipped behind the mountains as the clouds stretched swaths of pink and purple across the darkening sky. My tight muscles relaxed in the heat. I sighed a long, "Hahhhh."

Javier joined Sarah and I in the tub. "Whew, that's hot. But do-able," he looked over at his friend, "C'mon bro, just get in wearing your boxers."

"Nahhh, man." Christian took a gulp then looked at me. "Forgot my trunxsss. Didn't forget my drink, though. You guys not drinkin?" He took another guzzle.

"No," I said. "Did ya'll see the nudists?"

"Oh, yeah, man. Nudists are always out here," said Javier.

"Lothss of nudiths bro," slurred Christian.

The other tubs we had tried out contained strange mixtures of families and the intoxicated, yet everyone's bush was covered like a freeze was coming.

Speaking of families, our rave-music-hot tub-double-date was about to explode in population. Two couples in their thirties arrived, along with a five-year-old, a toddler, and a newborn. One man was without his right leg, the other man without both legs. The two amputees used high-tech prosthetics, walking unassisted with ease. Hellos were given, smiles were shared. One woman removed her top and began breastfeeding.

"Did ya'll serf?" Christian asked the two men.

"Huh?" The men gave quizzical looks.

"Like Iraq or tha war?" said Christian.

"Oh no, we didn't serve. We're uh, not vets," said one of the amputees.

An awkward silence consumed the prairie. The tub was small and my desire to escape the heat outweighed my curiosity if Christian intended to pry into the story of how they lost their legs. Sarah and I exited, making room in the tub for the new arrivals. We said goodbye to Javier, Christian, the amputees, their wives, the children, and the burping baby.

Back in the parking lot, Sarah and I decided that sulfur isn't a sexy scent. In house life, "shower" is a ubiquitous term. You take a bath or you take a shower, done deal. In van life, the term shower or bath refers to a variety of things. For the fancy and well-equipped, bathing involves a thorough spray-down from a showerhead connected to a specially designed water heater. Simpletons, like Sarah and I, use the word "shower" more broadly. Typically, we hop in lakes, rivers, or creeks with some eco-soap and swim trunks. When we don't bathe in nature, our ten-dollar weed sprayer comes to the rescue.

While the hippie's bush had gone public, my bush had yet to make its Initial Public Offering. My swim trunks stayed on. Despite my nudist riffs, I envied their boldness. Had they stopped fearing what others thought of them? Or was it their way to go towards the fear, to find liberation in full exposure?

I loosened my trunks but not my societal conditioning and cleaned the goods while Sarah did the service of spraying me down. After I soaped up, Sarah took round two of treating me like a barnyard animal. A northerly breeze gave me a chill. I reached for my towel.

Sarah's turn, and God bless her, she incorporated shaving her legs and armpits into the same routine. By Texas standards, we're "eh couple uh hippies." By California criteria, we're too groomed and clothed for the title. I sprayed the soap off her body. She reached for her towel as goosebumps marched across her legs. The Sierras blew a roaring gust of alpine wind. The breeze picked up the dark dirt of the road and blasted it across the parking area. A wall of dust flew into us, clinging to Sarah's wet skin, making her significantly dirtier than she was before the shower.

"Son of a bitch!" she yelled.

My laughter raged with the wind—uncontrollable. Sarah looked at me and rolled her eyes, then realized her best option was to join in, so she did, and we had one of those laughs that I vowed to never forget.

Showering wasn't the same, but there's a Yiddish proverb that says, "What soap is to the body, laughter is to the soul." At least I could say we had clean souls.

❖

Don't shit where you eat—a note of caution, a warning of backfire, and a useless expression for van-lifers. After moving into a van, defecating where I ate became not only a daily occurrence, but a luxury. That's right, a luxury—and we didn't even have a bidet. Our alternatives as off-gridders were to dig holes or depend solely on public facilities. Imagine this: a cold and rainy morning, an hour from civilization, and you ate small-town enchiladas the night before.

Various self-contained portable toilets exist for the DIY RV'er, sailor, and van-dweller. Ours, a cassette toilet we named Vladimir Poopin, uses a chemical to combat the scent during decomposition. Unlike your home commode, this potty is all plastic and seals shut like a large Tupperware container. We hid this science experiment underneath the bed, concealed behind a small door.

Above the potty, the MaxxFan (praise be to its creator) purred softly on exhaust mode, pulling fresh air through the windows and out the ceiling. We chose the fan's central location thinking of its primary function—temperature control. Little did we know, the MaxxFan has more functions than a Swiss Army knife. The fan kept the van cool, the closest thing to A/C we had. Living in a vehicle means moisture, and the fan also kept the windows from fogging up. Overcook a pancake, no problem, the fan worked as the kitchen hood as well. And, most important of all, the fan could suck out a fart faster than Sarah could scream.

"Okay," said Sarah, her eyes sparkling large after draining her first cup of coffee one fine morning, a week into the trip.

The word *okay*, without context, can mean a variety of things in couple speak: *okay*, you win; *okay*, you can have the last eggroll; *okay*, I don't want to talk about it anymore. Sarah's *okay* implied a sense of bashfulness. However, the slight raise of her eyebrows indicated relative urgency. The time, 9:03 a.m., also told the tale that other organs and bodily functions had awakened. I cannot say I learned everything about Sarah in the first week of van life, but we were nearing that line that separates intimacy from an invasion of privacy.

I stepped out the passenger door and shouted back, "Leave Vladimir out for me when you're done, *okay*?"

Outside, the late morning sun forced my eyes into a tight squint, but my sunglasses sat captive inside the van. To retrieve them meant a violation of personal space, a boundary I intended to uphold with the utmost respect. Instead, I welcomed the glare by pulling off my hoodie and wool socks. Rudy was tucked into a setting that didn't quite qualify as a forest, nor did the terrain resemble a desert or a prairie. Here, the roots of small pine trees overlapped with sage and juniper. Prickly pear cacti guarded the pathway to a creek. I followed the sound of flowing water, trying to locate the stream that came down the nearby mountains. Before I reached the water, my ears perked up when *the word* returned.

"*Okay!*" Sarah's shout glided out of the van like a seagull on a windy day. Like the seagull, Sarah requires little effort to release her poo. I, on the other hand, sit for stretches longer than a sculptor's figure model.

Sarah stepped out of the van. Our eyes locked. She forced herself not to smile. The space between us was filled with words unspoken. *Goodbye to the past life of unknowns*, I thought.

Dating a girl with six brothers sounds intimidating, but in actuality, it proved to be the appropriate training regimen for Sarah to share a small space with a flatulent man. I stepped into Rudy. A small candle burned from the countertop. The much-appreciated scent of burning lavender waged war in the invisible battlefield of molecular gases. The white throne occupied the center of the van, inviting me to take a seat.

I did, and recognized that scrolling an iPhone while defecating for the past decade has given my sphincter some strange new muscle memory. After, I arose lighter, then pumped a blue liquid that flushed my substance into a deeper compartment. I sealed up Vladimir Poopin and slid him back into his dungeon. I was under the impression, according to some bloggers, that the magical blue potion would deconstruct everything into an easy-to-dump liquid.

I blew out the candle, leaving a burnt herbal scent wafting through the van. No evidence remained of what had transpired a moment ago. Convenient, seeing as in the same spot I just went number two, I could trade the toilet for a retractable table, converting the bathroom into the dining room or office. In an hour, I would eat my cereal in the same spot, and in one month, I would start typing out the words to the book you are reading right now. *Don't shit where you eat*—balderdash! *Don't write where you dookie*—hogwash! What's worse: constipation or writer's block? Answer: it doesn't matter, neither produces shit.

But would the blue potion make this chore feel as insignificant as taking out the garbage? Today, we would find out.

The tiny tourist town of Lee Vining, California, sits above Mono Lake, a beautiful yet uninviting body of salt water surrounded by limestone pillars and dormant volcanoes. Various long-necked birds basked in the sun, their bellies filled with brine shrimp and alkali flies. A handful of restaurants served tourists. I watched them, with their pampered, porcelain-imprinted butt cheeks, dining on their gourmet burgers. I took my righteous pity and plastic potty as I rode the high horse of self-sufficient living right through the town's main drag. I was ready, ready for dookie duty.

Our chore required a certain type of public facility and Lee Vining seemed to have been designed with the nomad's needs in mind. The Gus Hess Community Park became the testing ground for the newbie van-lifers' experiment. The layout was ideal, with an outdoor spigot of free potable water and a private restroom with a flush toilet. The park was simple with a slide and swing set. Across the lawn, two women shared a picnic table while their daughters took turns on the slide. One could only hope our week's worth of excrement would move down the chute as easily as the kids did.

Dating in your thirties makes firsts much harder to come by. Sarah was not the first girlfriend to join me on a road trip, nor was she the first girlfriend I have ever lived with. In fact, I didn't have the heart to tell Sarah that she wasn't even the first girlfriend I had who claimed to have invented avocado toast. (Yes, the other girlfriend was also a tattooed vegetarian from California ... at least I know my type).

Despite our relationship being short on initial experiences, I can state unequivocally that pouring out my partner's waste was a first I reserved exclusively for Sarah. I didn't ask Sarah if I was also her first, after all, bad questions might have worse answers. Though I was raised on traditional southern etiquette, I have been trying out the 50-50 couple split: expenses, carrying the hiking pack, and driving the van are all responsibilities Sarah and I shared. However, no gender norm sets a precedent for the disgusting chore of emptying the van's toilet.

We played good ole rock paper scissors to see who went first. My paper hand covered her rock fist. My victory came with no glory, only guilt. Our love story started with Sarah mopping up my sweat, now she is to dump my fecal matter? Perhaps this isn't what you had in mind for gender equality. She pinched her nose, masked up, and prepared to spill our poop soup.

After disconnecting the toilet seat from the cassette, she headed towards the restroom with the box of sludge. I put my chore, refilling the water jugs, on hold. Fueled by guilt and curiosity, I trailed behind Sarah.

Ah, the mask—a multipurpose tool. Helpful in preventing the spread of germs *and* just as vital in restricting the sense of smell when entering public restrooms.

Sarah turned Vladimir Poopin's release valve and unscrewed the cap. She gave me an anguished stare. We paused before crossing the van couple's Rubicon, the point of no return.

She tilted the case. A putrid green purée poured into the toilet. Chunks sent splashes along the upper rim of porcelain. I looked away so I wouldn't vomit. Sarah gagged. Somewhere in the depths of my vile ego whispered a devilish voice that said Sarah's turds, not mine, had struggled to disintegrate.

Sarah pulled the case up before the park toilet overfilled. I gave it a flush. Time for round two. She gave our package another tilt. This time a chunk came out with fierce momentum, sending a splash of green over the rim and onto my flip-flop. I looked down at the coarse drops of waste coating my bare foot. I looked back at Sarah. Our eyes locked yet again, that same unspoken sentiment, that farewell to the old times.

Don't splash toilet waste on my feet must be the van-dwellers' equivalent of *don't step on my toes.* And that, my dear reader, is the worst part of van life and the literal *shit* you don't see on Instagram.

Each generation, American writers have described life on the road during their time. Kerouac chronicled hitchhiking and hedonism. Steinbeck gave us the comforts of a camper and a furry companion. And my personal favorite, William Least Heat-Moon's *Blue Highways*, imparted on us that to gain the interstate is to lose the story. But have you ever wondered which of our classic writers, had they been born in this era, would have been on social media and which would have shunned the apps entirely? Would Thoreau own a selfie stick? Would Whitman care how many people liked his post? Would Muir vlog about his top ten things to do in the Sierras? And lastly, would Twain be twerking on TikTok?

After all, none of these writers had electronic devices that helped them navigate, answered the hundreds of questions that floated around in their heads, played any song they wanted, or took professional quality photographs. Let alone a single device that does all these things and still manages to fit on the dashboard without blocking the view.

The smartphone has forever changed travel. Gone are the days of pocket maps and asking strangers for directions. No longer do you throw the dice on a random restaurant or make a decision on a whim. It's a daily scroll-a-thon of reading the same reviews and tips that other travelers are consuming. Now everyone goes to the same place, at the same time, to take the same photo. How much we have progressed at capturing the moment; how horribly we have digressed at being in it.

This damn mindless scrolling seems to threaten the very happiness that I have worked so hard to obtain. While I have recovered from a multitude of addictions over the years, it's this all-knowing slot machine that I've struggled to moderate. I had dialed in the ability to abstain, but *balance*? I do not know this word. Heaven knows, I have deleted and redownloaded my social media apps more times than I care to admit.

Here are some methods I have tried: Deleting the apps and only using social media from my laptop. Setting a timer. Clearing my history. Airplane mode. Digital Detox. I know, I'll use it as a tool for connection. No, it's a marketing apparatus, share work stuff only. Look but don't post. Post but don't look. Unfollow those people. Follow these people. Guard yourself. No, be authentic, share it all. Give it up for Lent. Wait, I don't practice Lent. On it. Off it. This time for good, I swear. The list goes on, ad infinitum …

Before buying Rudy, I shared some of my mental health struggles on social media. While the blog reached a couple of people in need, posting about mental health on a platform that I knew worsened my own never felt right. Though I couldn't bring myself to delete my accounts entirely, I got off social media again, anticipating that this decision would make road exploration a more immersive experience.

However, it would be irresponsible (and unrealistic) to write a book about living in a van during 2020 and not talk about the sensation that is #vanlife. The hashtag was coined in 2011 by Foster Huntington when he quit his job, moved into a van, and began posting photos of the lifestyle on social media. A viral sensation was born, but Huntington never struck me as a like-thirsty egotist. His words in a 2017 interview with *The Inertia*: "You know, humans are originally nomads. And the whole living in a vehicle thing, well, people have been doing that since cars have existed and been a viable living situation. So, really, there's nothing new here."

But something is new: the exponential rise of how it's documented. Sadly, like most things on social media, #vanlife evolved from an inspiring movement into a filtered highlight reel designed to keep you looking down. Surely you've seen the many envy-inducing photos on Instagram. Picturesque mountains with perfect weather. Burning campfires under shooting stars. Yoga poses in front of still lakes. Crop out the crowds and force a smile. Like, share, comment, compare.

What started as a minimalist movement has evolved into a content competition, leading to clickbait thumbnails next to dramatic titles. You know the type: a bikini butt shot, some bro with toned abs, the caption, "How I Shower on the Road!" At this point, if Sarah and I wanted any relevancy on social media, we'd have to take it to the next level. Open up a subscriber's page and get pornographic—we'd call it OnlyVans.

The hypocritical irony is that Rudy wouldn't exist if it weren't for the follower-obsessed culture that I'm knocking. I'd wager that most influencers would admit that travel documentation is still a job, and like any job, it has its pros and cons. Good ole American over-glorification.

I suppose it doesn't matter what the classic writers would make of this insatiable appetite for content. What *does* matter? That being on the road is an invitation. To be present. To pause the premium subscriptions. To welcome the unplanned. Go find out for yourself— buy a road atlas, pick a place on the map you know nothing about, put away your phone, and pack only your curiosity. Discover if travel is more rewarding through a windshield or on a screen.

Or don't. After all, this book is filled with a rushing river of shallow wisdom that originated from a dude who lives in a van and went through 2020 without health insurance. Continue with caution. The settings will sound sexy at times. Other times, life's toilet water will splash. *That* I can guarantee.

Chapter 6
Tiny Home, Giant Backyard

OUR DAYS ALONG CA-395 were coming to an end. Northbound towards Lake Tahoe, the sun scorched through the driver's window, cooking my bare arm and evaporating my poise. Sarah and I switched spots. No amount of sunscreen or A/C spared her the same fate. Between the crinkled pages of my atlas, I searched for an oasis to break up the drive as the thermometer approached 100 degrees.

A short detour into Nevada brought us to Topaz Lake, whose color is implied. Somewhere out on the shiny water, fish pass back and forth under the Nevada/California state line, unaware of where gambling becomes legal and gas more affordable. From the Golden State to the Silver one, Sarah steered Rudy down an incline and into a small neighborhood of modest homes. The sound of our flip-flops pit-patted past signs: PRIVATE LAND – NO LAKE ACCESS.

After moving away from Texas and later Florida, I had acclimated to Southern California's softness. The Nevada heat penetrated my positivity, turning me into a sweaty and irritable mess. Down the street, two middle-aged women unloaded groceries from their sedan. California might have exaggerated my heat index, but my Texan manners still played it cool.

"Scuze me. Ya'll know if we can get'n the water real quick down here?" (Pardon my twang, I'm not proud to admit that it usually comes out when I think I can sound charming.)

Chances are my exposed pecs and Texan manners seduced not even my own feverish girlfriend. A smile shined naturally out of both women.

"Oh, sure thing," the older of the two said. "Just go on down the sidewalk right there. No one's living at that house and you can get to the lake right past it."

When lakes become bathtubs, you judge them differently. Sure, some are deeper, bluer, colder, and prettier. However, it's the landscape of the bank that matters most. Ideal lakes offer sandy beaches and easy access to pristine aqua. Unfortunately, most bodies of water come with a cost: funky-smelling mud or obstacle courses of jagged rocks, maybe some strange insects or a school of tadpoles.

After the sidewalk, the shoreline gave way to sinking wet mud. My foot pressed into the muck, and the ground gripped my sandal. Over the shallows, swarms of little flies buzzed. I stepped from the soil into the water. The topaz disappeared into a murk of sediment not even the scalding sun could penetrate. A foul smell of fermented earth boiled up. A few steps behind, Sarah crinkled her eyebrows, showing no desire to document the lake on her social media.

"Whewww!" I emerged from the water, cleansed of my heat-induced sins. Sarah tied up her hair, secured her Crocs, and splashed her limbs with the filthy water. Heat can make you do crazy things, like swim in murky lakes (or wear Crocs).

Before reentering California, we decided to fill up the tank for nearly a dollar per gallon cheaper than we paid a few days prior ($2.89 vs $3.85). Sarah entered the expense into her budget app. I calculated the miles per gallon on my phone. Anything over 23 mpg, we cheered. This pump we rejoiced: 27 mpg, our best yet. While fuel-efficient for a cargo van, the diesel ProMaster had been discontinued by its manufacturer. I said a quick prayer that Rudy wouldn't leave us stranded one day.

God bless you, CA-395. Other roads await, and I can only hope they'll be as pretty as you. A rare turn south brought us to our first route junction. A crank of the wheel and a new highway, CA-89, which would take us to Lake Tahoe and beyond. The road grew steep; Rudy roared loud but moved slow. The tarmac swung right, then left, then back right, up and up, towards peaks and passes. In the left-wing mirror, Topaz Lake shrunk until it became a memory. Above the timberline, dirt roads led to tempting boondocking spots, but we drove on to cover ground. Americans have many ways to justify their addiction to distraction. Most say they keep busy. I recited the road-trippers' version, "We're making great time!"

We had no address or itinerary, only the pestering indecisiveness of a million possibilities.

"I love your plants!" exclaimed Jan as she peered in the open side door.

Jan owned her nerd. A Star Wars-themed mask covered her face, big black glasses squared around her squinted eyes, and patches of anime characters were stitched across her shoulder bag. Behind her stood a pimply young man, maybe her boyfriend or travel companion—I will never know because he never spoke. Instead, he blinked behind his glasses, never smiling, never frowning. Behind him, Lake Tahoe showed more emotion—renewed and assured, classy and serene.

Sarah and I had scored the last parking spot at the end of the road in D.L. Bliss State Park. The park's surname earned its adjective, granting us a blissful front porch view. The sun glittered in the crater-sized clearing of turquoise water. Dozens of tourists walked by Rudy, sneaking peaks and whispering opinions. If you can imagine living on a busy street with no wall to conceal the front of your house, then you can imagine what it feels like to have your van doors ajar on a beautiful day at a popular place. I opened the slider door for us to enjoy the view and the fresh air, but as people kept looking in, I couldn't help but feel like a busty woman wearing a low-cut top to a sports bar.

Jan was the sixth person in two hours to compliment the plants. I forced out some fake laughter. It took over four hundred hours of labor to build the van, but the fifteen minutes it took Sarah to arrange her greenery received the most compliments. The plush green leaves of four potted houseplants tickled the back wall from the kitchen counter. Near the slider entrance, a fifth plant hung from a hook, allowing gravity to dangle the drooping neon blades of hanging ivy. Sarah had asked if a sixth plant would be too much. I told her yes, if she wanted to live in a van; no, if she wanted to live in a jungle.

"Thanks!" replied Sarah.

"Oh! And is that amethyst?" asked Jan. Between the plants were two large crystals, favorites of Sarah's collection. The crystals ranked second in the van's rankings of most received compliments.

"Yeah, and that one is quartz," Sarah replied.

"Want a tour?" I offered.

"Uh, yeah!" said Jan. Behind her, the statue blinked.

Jan was the third tour that morning. In order of appearance, an RV salesman from Oregon surveyed and his compliments sang the gospel of validation. Then, teenage girls from the Bay Area said, "You guys should start a YouTube channel!" I spared them my business lecture on the profitability challenges of an oversaturated market-place. I learned that morning that only one-third of gawkers ask for a tour. Most linger and ask questions, hoping you offer. Sarah and I loved doing it. The tours led to new acquaintances and passing recommendations from fellow trampers. Furthermore, when your living space is the size of a walk-in closet, a tour takes less than five minutes.

Even by tiny home standards our space was condensed, resembling a shrunken-down dorm room. Jan stuck her head inside to look at the full-sized bed and two upper cabinets, one for Sarah's clothes and one for mine.

"Oh my gosh, that's all your clothes?" Jan asked.

"Yup," Sarah lifted the cabinet door to show her the collection of decorative bags that contained a finely organized wardrobe. Aside from the jackets and sweaters stored above the cab, and a bag of "city clothes" we kept in the back, our entire wardrobes each fit inside a cabinet the size of a gym locker.

"And this seat swivels. It helps open the place up," Sarah took the three steps that covered the entire walk space and sat on the passenger chair. Even 72 square feet can be deceiving. After the bed, seats, and counters, there was only 15 square feet left you could actually stand on.

"Wow, you guys are legit minimalists. What's it feel like? I mean, I've always wanted to do it, get a tiny house or something, but could never take the leap."

"Ha, I wouldn't go as far as saying we're minimalists," I replied. "I've still got a closet of junk back home. And we've only been on the road for a couple weeks. We're still learning that we packed a bunch of stuff we don't need."

The statue appeared unamused by the admission, though he did blink, proving he was alive.

"Tell us about your trip," I said.

"Well, I started in Portland, heading back to San Francisco now after spending a week in Oregon. Ugh, it was the best."

"We're heading towards Oregon. Any recommendations?" Sarah asked.

"Hmm, Crater Lake was awesome but depends what you're into. I choose which towns I stay in based on the quantity of independent bookstores they have."

"Really?" My eyebrows met in the middle, my mask concealed the rest of my intrigue.

"Yeah, it works most of the time. Like, I loved Ashland! You should definitely check it out. *Great* bookstores and *suuuper* cute town. Not everything is open, but it's still worth a visit."

"I think we can fit that in, thanks. Enjoy the rest of your trip."

"Thanks for the tour! Wish I could keep going like you guys. I mean, *now is the time to do it!*"

Ah, *now is the time*. Like an eager disciple in the pew, I always felt the words were intended for me. *Now is the time* is the road-trippers' mantra, and I've heard it more times than I can count. I've heard it from a widower in Northern Georgia, and from an overworked man in the basement of a Brooklyn church. I've heard it from the tops of mountains yelled into the wind by retirees, and from immigrant families across crackling campfire flames. As I got older and spent more time working, I endured lengthy stretches without hearing the expression. Whenever the words found me again, they sounded like that old favorite song—that tune you played too many times, then went a couple of years without hearing, only to rediscover how good it still danced years later.

Yes, Jan—now is the time, alright. Time for dreams that need no waking, and breaks that need no stopping.

On the shores of Lake Tahoe, the scent of secondhand marijuana replaced the smell of dry pine trees. The morning sound of playing kids devolved into the afternoon sound of strangers' Bluetooth speakers, forcing me to consume Justin Bieber. The water glistened Caribbean clean and I regularly jumped in to wash away my judgment.

In the evening, we prepped Rudy to go rogue and headed deep into a neighborhood of millionaire mountain mansions. On a dead-end street, between a lightless house and a vacant lot, we parked for our first night of stealth camping (giving the appearance that the vehicle is empty and not being lived in while in residential areas). The alternatives—an hour's drive to public land or an outrageous $50 per night camp fee, provided us opportunities to gripe instead of legitimate considerations.

Stealth camping highlighted the in-between classification of van life. Similar to the homeless, we often fit in the same legal box of unhoused and unwelcomed. Like those with addresses, we had locking doors and a comfortable bed, our next meal was guaranteed, as was our ability to dial 911 in an emergency.

I woke up anytime headlights pierced the windows, wondering if criminals or the neighborhood cop would bother us. After enough nights in the wild, I know it's not the animals that disrupt sleep but the fear of people. Particularly those people who count crimes, not independent bookstores. Cops or robbers, our home was an exhibit by day and a perceived threat to property value at night. We left Tahoe the next morning, undetected.

I pulled Rudy off the tarmac and onto the dirt trackway of the Plumas National Forest. Darkness creaked so close that I could hear her whisper. My eyes adjusted to the moon's glow, piercing through the trees and casting silhouettes of the swaying forest canopy. The wind carried the sounds of night, stormy and haunted. On the left, a vacant gun range. Empty brass shells littered the shoulder of the road. Holes dotted used targets where trees once stood. Something spooky hung in the air. I sensed it through the windshield. Maybe death, maybe destruction, maybe the encroaching dark and its mental mockery.

The forest was telepathically saying, *I feel creepy because I am creepy.* Sarah assessed her sage inventory and concluded that there was not enough to smudge away the evil spirits of this place. She asked if we could go somewhere else to camp, and I was relieved when she did.

We had prepared for these moments. Before hitting the road, we established a golden rule: if both people don't feel comfortable camping somewhere, we leave.

Further north, with only the light of Rudy's eyes, we rode under the thick overcast of pine-woven branches. Sarah parked us on the side of a wide, sloped, logging road. Too exhausted to further our search, we settled on sleeping there. I grabbed my headlamp and went to face the shadows. I scanned the land. No red eyes from bears or

70

murderers, only trees and their uncanny ability to go from daytime delight to nighttime ghouls. Later that night, fast asleep, the realization bellowed that we had camped a stone's throw from a hidden railway. The locomotive's horn blasted as a long line of cargo roared through the forest in the middle of the night. Rudy shook from the train's momentum. *Always set up camp before dark*—a rule we broke too often.

The next day, Rudy rumbled ahead. I suppose some are born to navigate. I say this because at age three, I informed my mom from the rear child seat that she had missed her exit. On my first day of kindergarten, the school put me on the wrong bus and dropped me off on the other side of a massive suburban neighborhood. To an illiterate five-year-old, a mile of replicated homes and dozens of street signs should be as overwhelming as the streets of Delhi, but I got my bearings and found my way, no big deal. Sure, I've gotten lost in my life, but usually in the esoteric sense, never on the road. As Sarah drove, I got excited as I resorted to my old ways of analyzing maps to locate our next backyard.

Fifteen minutes after sunset, we began the squinting game. Our next twelve-hour home hid somewhere in the thick foliage. Shadows lengthened to touch the peaks of mountains that glowed with the final feet of day. Bridges took us on either bank of the same creek. Entrances for campgrounds came and went. Sarah spotted a dirt ramp and gravity slid Rudy down the mountainside to flat ground. An adjacent rushing creek drowned out the sound of zooming cars from the highway above. Mountains fortified our view on either side.

Life's low points had taught me to fully appreciate those rare times when my plans and God's overlapped. Bad camp spots had imparted the wisdom that when boondock doesn't go bust, go celebrate. I let the water's flow lull us to sleep, and celebration came in the form of uninterrupted and dreamless slumber. I awoke the next morning with a smile.

Sarah and I now had the tan lines and chapped lips of the liberated. However, my personal experiences didn't permit me to depart with some expectation that things would always be idyllic. In 2013, I lived in my SUV for three months. That experience taught me to be ready for dirty days in re-worn clothes, cold mornings with colder thoughts, and rainy afternoons trapped in a tin box.

Past experiences also taught this important lesson—when things get good, the good get present, for this sensation never lasts forever. The first days in the Sierras deserved glorification. We journaled, read, hiked, and jumped in many lakes. Enthusiastic to see more, we moved to a new campsite nearly every night, often awakening to deer dining outside the bunk windows. The weather was warm and sunny during the day, brisk and refreshing at night. Every meal had a view, every night a full heart. I experienced such a consistent abundance of gratitude that it reminded me of the pink-cloud days of early sobriety. I was so grateful to be alive. To smell the trees, see the mountains, and cuddle with Sarah. I still blushed every time one of us said, "I can't believe we built this thing." It was full-throttle honeymoon syndrome—love for each other, love for our home, and love for the lifestyle.

We had nature, freedom, and time. We had possibilities, ponderings, and the open road. We had a tiny home and a giant backyard.

Chapter 7
Zero Days

BACK IN HOUSE life, every day had a label: long days, weekdays, free days, and holidays. Van life days came with tags too: drive days, hike days, errand days, and my favorite, zero days. There was only one rule on a zero day: no driving. Thus, activities became fabricated distractions from one's own emotions. Zero miles but a million thoughts.

Further northbound on CA-89, we drove over the line that separates a vacation from a lifestyle. Perhaps it was where the Sierras ended and the volcanic soil of the Cascades began, into new territory and beyond the timeline for when I would typically head home after a weekend getaway. There was no dread of return, no contemplations of what if. Only forward to whatever new experiences lay ahead.

Trees covered every vista on either side. I had never laid eyes on so many conifers in my life. Rudy was an ant meandering through a grass lawn. Occasionally we drove through a curious little town or past a field with a few cattle. Little bridges hung over dried creek beds. At 8:00 p.m., the thermometer read 82 degrees. The forest seemed to wheeze, thirsty for rain, ripe for a blaze.

In the cloak of branches and under the veil of night, we camped in another pine forest until a deep grumble vibrated me awake. *VRUMP! VRUMP!* I jolted hard enough to wake Sarah.

"What was that?" she groaned.

Vrump! Vrump!

"Damn," I said. "We forgot to turn Ursula off."

"Ugh."

I got up, opened the cabinet under the sink, and flipped a switch that turned off our water pump. Ursula was the yang to our yin. A wet and angry beast, she was the loudest and most punishing water pump ever manufactured, a constant reminder of who built our home. Made in China and sold by Amazon, Ursula was one of those replicated products with an 80 percent discount, but what we saved on money we spent on sound. Anytime we ran the faucet, it sounded like a lawnmower was revving under the sink.

Back in bed, I closed my eyes.

"Did you empty the water line?" Sarah asked.

"It'll be fine," I grunted.

In the morning, we had a leak, a wet cabinet, and an amused forest that heard me sing the couple's opera, "You were right, I was wrong." Sarah contorted into the tight confines of the cabinet and fixed the line. Rudy's first blunder lacked any real drama.

An hour later, we arrived at our first national park of the trip, the "less visited" Lassen Volcanic National Park. I signed away eighty dollars for an annual national parks pass. After three park visits, the pass would pay for itself. The accountant genes in me intended to take it further and utilize our new lifestyle to get our cost-per-park as low as possible.

The only indoor facility open was a restroom. A young, friendly park ranger greeted us outside the visitor center, guarded by a mask and two big tables. His long, wavy blonde hair bounced under his brimmed hat as he whipped out a large map. The topographic master-piece took up the entirety of both tables. He pointed to the spots in Lassen National Forest of his favorite boondocking camps, circled the best hikes, and handed us a free map.

On one of our earliest dates, Sarah met me for a hike. She showed up at the trailhead having forgotten her boots. "I'll just go barefoot," she insisted. On top of her left foot was a phoenix feather tattoo that rose with each step. Her feet were clean and feminine, yet underneath she had the conditioned soles of a mountain girl. Unlike my soft city feet, hers had been toughened from a barefoot childhood living on a farm. Later she lived in the woods of a Western Sierra town with a population under 1,000. Trailing behind her, I watched as my shoeless girlfriend beat me up a mountain that I had hiked a hundred times. I didn't mind—I had finally found someone to keep up with. This pacing became commonplace in our relationship. The harder the hike, the further her lead.

Now, gaining altitude up Lassen Peak, my glutes contracted as I pushed to keep up with my mountain gal. The 10,457-foot volcano protruded well above the tree line. A littering of scree traced the slopes, evidence of previous eruptions, the most recent only a hundred years ago. I sucked in the thinning air, surprised at how populated the trail was. Sarah and I were not the only ones who justified hitting the road after five months of isolation. We added two more to the 120,000 people breaking the record for the busiest August in Lassen history. The previous month, July, had been the busiest month in park history, and in 2020 Lassen recorded its busiest year ever, despite having closed down for two months due to the pandemic.

On the peak, the most spotted wildling was the selfie-taker. While I ate my sandwich, I watched an adult woman step over a wire, past a sign that said, "FRAGILE HABITAT, PLEASE KEEP OFF," to get her ideal photo. Teddy's bravado and Muir's mission channeled through my bark, "Hey! Read the sign!" I yelled. The woman shrugged her shoulders and took her photo anyway.

I scanned the clear horizon, hoping the view would overpower my judgments. Instead, I found Mount Shasta, the magnificent volcano with its mystical white saucer cloud hovering above. Shasta's climate makes for one of the best places to view this weather phenomenon, known as lenticular clouds. In the other direction, steam rose from Lassen's various geothermal vents and pools. Trees connected every landmark and lined every lake. I spotted my next bath. Two hours later, a cold plunge in Helen Lake roused the wild within.

One of my favorite sounds is the light ping of falling rain on the roof of a four-wheeled home. Another—making Sarah laugh so hard she snorts. That night I heard both overpower the continuous gush of Mill Creek; I slept like a man without a worry. In the morning, we celebrated our first zero day with Sarah's hot flapjacks. Drizzle came and went, as did two anglers, otherwise it was only us and the trees.

A zero day without a bar of cell signal brought up all the emotional squirms that movement and technology prevent. Next to the creek, as I watched fallen leaves float downstream, I closed my eyes and tried to let my thoughts drift away with the same ease. Once upon a time, I attempted to impress others with my alcoholic drink count. Now I try to impress myself by tallying how many minutes I can sit with my feelings.

With life so simple, so surrounded by Earth's organic beauty, a foreign serenity settled gently on my shoulders. As I sat, the reason for this struck me: I hadn't had any panic attacks since we moved into the van. In fact, I hadn't experienced even the slightest symptom. During the build, the old sensations had returned, but on the road, I felt like I did before panic disorder. The only thing that was different: I didn't take it for granted.

The story of my panic disorder didn't stop in the spring of 2019. If it had, the message would be short and clear: struggle with anxiety, go to therapy, and all will be better forever. You'll even fall in love and live happily ever after. How badly I wanted that to be my story. But life, like a panic attack, is unpredictable.

In November 2019, Sarah and I were two months into dating when the chest pains returned. I was at work, standing in front of a small classroom of students like I had done for the last two years. Before I knew it, my legs were wobbly. I couldn't stand, the fear of fainting too strong to risk it. So, I sat in a desk and attempted to continue lecturing. My thoughts were jumbled, but my attentive students seemed oblivious to my state. How easy it was to conceal my struggles.

If March 2019 was a tornado, then that November was a hurricane. Even after cutting my work hours, I felt too unreliable to teach in my current state. I warned my boss that I may need to resign.

"Really? But you're so healthy! You're like the poster child for wellness with the yoga and meditation. You don't drink. You eat healthy. I don't get it."

I took a hard swallow and lowered my head. *Is healthy living a hoax?*

I was learning a painful lesson: anxiety doesn't care. It doesn't care if you're privileged or impoverished, fit or fat. It doesn't care if you're triggered by dysfunctional relationships or by healthy ones. It just doesn't care.

I was scared. On several occasions, I woke up in the middle of the night with a panic attack. Multiple times I had attacks while sitting on my surfboard in a still ocean, alone, on a perfectly beautiful day. Sometimes the symptoms would be short and intense, other times I could go *days* with chest pains and no reprieve. I wondered if this might be my new normal.

The more I thought about it, the more I worried. The more I worried, the more intense my symptoms. The vicious spiral of panic made me feel like the mind I loved had betrayed me. I rarely laughed that entire month.

It is said in addiction recovery circles that pain is the greatest motivator, for it gets us to do things we'd otherwise be unwilling to try. Yet recognizing the benefits of pain didn't make it any more tolerable. I felt all the suppressed emotions swirling inside me, pumping unwanted cortisol through my nervous system. The body was at its capacity; the emotions needed out.

A holistic approach meant journaling daily, cutting caffeine and sugar out of my diet, and giving up social media (again). I went to the boxing gym and unloaded all that suppressed anger. I began doing breathwork while my therapist and I honed in on the triggers that worsened my symptoms. I wanted more than to patch the ship, I wanted a better boat.

I didn't care which of the activities would fix me, I just wanted relief, to feel like myself again. To feel the sunshine after a cold rain. To make my girlfriend laugh. To not see Sarah so worried.

Sarah had a front-row view of the entire ordeal. We had already had *the talk*, and were monogamous, falling deeper in love. How painful it was, to see the concern on her face. She was desperate to help but unsure how. She often placed a hand on me, saying, "I'm so sorry you're going through this, bubs. I hate seeing you like this. I wish there was something I could do."

I wasn't the only one being triggered. In her past, codependency had taken Sarah to the darkest of places. She had done so much work to undo and reshape how she showed up in her relationships, and now I could viscerally feel her fighting the urge to try and fix me. Our relationship had its first true challenge. To endure, our communication became paramount.

One day, Sarah asked, "How can I support you? What do you need?"

It wasn't the first time she had asked. Usually, my response reflected my brokenness. "I don't know. I don't even know how to support myself right now," I would say. But that day, something shifted.

A supposed byproduct of the style of therapy I was doing was that I would find myself reacting differently to familiar situations. This must have been one of those moments. My response to Sarah's question wasn't something I had consciously dwelled on. The answer seemed to emerge on its own.

"I don't need any more sympathy, Sarah," I said. "Feeling bad for me isn't helping, it's fueling my pity party. What I need is accountability for the things I'm trying. Call me out when I put off something that could be helping me. Remind me that this is all temporary. That it *will* get better."

Wow, I was communicating my needs. It felt as if, all of a sudden, I was fluent in a foreign language. What a positive impact it had, not just for me, but also for Sarah. Now she knew how to show up effectively, something she was eager to do.

Everything shifted. I began having days without chest pains. Sarah and I grew closer and closer. We had regular check-ins to have the icky conversations. I had no foresight then, that what we were doing to endure this difficult time was setting us up to thrive later on. That it was preparing us to not only share a tiny space, but to allow that space to bring us even closer together.

Despite the zero day's tranquility, by nighttime a unanimous vote brought out some electronic distractions. We connected a DVD port to my laptop for our first movie night. A case of old DVDs had gone untouched in house-life but proved worthwhile on the road. *The Shawshank Redemption* on a thirteen-inch screen turned Rudy into a theater. Not until the credits rolled did I remember where I was.

The next day in the park, we hiked past the stench of boiling earth and swam in alpine lakes. Another home and another waterfront property, though Hat Creek deserves its own classification as creeks should never flow so fast. Just north of the national park's boundaries, I kept on its bank, and the mixing bowl used for pancake batter made for a pour-over shower. Oddly enough, the shower method many would consider a shortcoming to our van's design was becoming the thing I loved most about the lifestyle. Oh, how fervently the turbulent snowmelt rid my bare body of its grime and awakened the spirit within.

That night dragged on, not because of laughter snorts or sink grumbles, but because of thunder and lightning. Then the rain, thick and relentless, pelted the roof. I woke up every other hour, turning on my headlamp to scan the windows and fan, checking for leaks. We had tested them in San Diego with a hose, but I knew nothing could simulate a real mountain storm. Each inspection passed the test, and Rudy kept us warm and dry. I thought Mother Nature was testing my

DIY insecurities, but only my ego could think such thoughts. Mother Nature certainly had much bigger plans.

Sarah slept through the night while the forces of nature battled— great booms of thunder and flashes of electricity. San Diego and its idyllic climate felt more than a state away. I lay awake, loving the reminder of what a real storm sounds like.

Naivete is closing your eyes to consequences; stupidity is enjoying it. I lay there, foolishly grateful for my home, with its sealed windows and roof. I should have added trees and clean air to the mix, because thousands of lightning bolts moved through the Kingdom of the Trees and changed the world. This was no ordinary storm, for 2020 was no ordinary year.

Chapter 8
Volcanoes

I'M NOT SURE what gives our species the inspiration or bravado to distinguish one mountain as more sacred than the other. I suppose we have been doing it for eons—which stars to pray to, which rivers to baptize in, which moons to manifest with. An active stratovolcano in northern California, Mount Shasta last erupted in 1250 and often finds itself next to famed peaks like Mt. Fuji and Mt. Sinai on the shortlist of the world's most sacred mountains.

Most people remember the first time they laid eyes on Mount Shasta. I know I did—after all, I was many miles away on a different (supposedly less spiritual) mountaintop. If you told me Shasta was Tolkien's inspiration for the Lonely Mountain, I would ask no further questions. It stands isolated, powerful, and visible from many miles away. Something about Mount Shasta became a source of intrigue for me, and with intrigue came those cursed expectations that compounded my interest as I read about the tales of the volcano.

To the indigenous Shasta people, the mountain stands at the center of creation, where The Great Spirit stepped down from the skies to create the plants and animals. The New Age contingency believes Mount Shasta is a geographical power point and a source of cosmic energy. The Rosicrucians claim Shasta houses a group of spiritually advanced humanoids. The "I AM" movement founder, Guy Ballard, gathered over a million followers after he claimed to have met Master St. Germaine on the slopes of the mountain in 1930, and received the lessons of "ascended masters" like Jesus Christ.

UFO portals, a land of magic crystals, a gateway to the fifth dimension—Mount Shasta mysticism, spirituality, and occult beliefs

81

seem to know no bounds. Over a hundred sects hold Mount Shasta as a sacred place, and as the lonely mountain got closer, I longed to discover for myself if it would deliver fantasy or prophecy.

In the realm of the redneck, you got your hicks, hillbillies, and the country bumpkin—trucker caps and gun racks. In the harem of the hippie, you got your tree huggers, New Age spiritualists, and surf bums—tie-dyes and peace signs. To the outsider, it's easy to scoff and stereotype. To the trained eye, it's a game of *Guess Who?* If the South has every kind of redneck, then California has every kind of hippie. And the breed of hippie in the wooded north personifies its own niche, with the town of Mount Shasta unintentionally acting as its headquarters.

It would be impossible for me to describe the hippie in the town of Mount Shasta without sounding judgmental. It would also be inauthentic, for at the base of said spiritual mountain, I judged like only the sinful and incomplete can. So, here we go, hippies: the town felt like someone put meth in the mushrooms; it was like Jerry Garcia was grateful to be dead; like the people went to Burning Man so many times that the man burned back.

In the town, Sarah and I parted ways. Sarah went to scour the many crystal stores; I went to seek out an encounter so I could write a story entitled: *That Time I Joined a Cult.* An hour later, we met back up—Sarah without a crystal, me without a story, and a shared conclusion that the town of Mount Shasta felt more like a spiritual pitfall than a godly vortex. Even on a sunny day, the vibe was low, and the energy dark. Here, the lead role didn't go to the kind towns-folk who settled in the area, but to the drug users and drifters whose eyes sank into a lost realm.

Perhaps the mountain itself wielded the power to turn discern-ment to delight. We drove skyward, up the mountain, to the last parking lot where the concrete ended, and alpine fields began. Old pines dropped needles in the wind. Wild weeds bloomed tiny yellow and purple petals. The grass grew green and free. To my left, the peak of Mount Shasta resembled cookies 'n cream with patches of soiled glacier clinging to its black rock. To my right, a sign unlike any other:

NO CREMAINS ALLOWED. It is illegal to scatter or dispose of ashes and cremations in Panther Meadows. Panther Meadows is a National Register property – Title 36 CFR 261.9(g). ASHES AND CREMATIONS WILL BE REMOVED.

On the southern slope of the mountain, we walked towards Panther Spring. The repetitive sound of our boots crunching on the trail brought me into contemplation. The path was well-traveled and even better marked: STAY ON TRAIL, FRAGILE ECOSYSTEM.

The fragility came in the form of a grassy meadow, dotted with wildflowers, and traversed by a flowing stream. The site was postcard perfect. The sound of running water and chirping birds became the real version of the YouTube video I used to play when I meditated on my work breaks. At the end of the path was a pool of water where the stream originated. At its shallow bottom, the earth bubbled in a soft boil as the cold water of Panther Spring came out of the ground. Two tourists finished filling their bottles and walked off. Sarah squatted down and cupped her hands for a drink.

"Oh my gosh! This is the best water I've ever tasted. You gotta try it."

I took a handful to my mouth, swished, and assessed. The water was cool as jazz and clean as gospel. I bent down, carrying several loads from hand to mouth until I lost my thirst. We removed our packs, found flat rocks, and slid our shoes off. Attempting to meditate, we crossed our legs and closed our eyes. Minutes melted away with the gently bubbling water daring my mind to slow down with it.

"Hey! Read the fuckin' sign!" A woman shouted from behind me. I jolted up and turned around. Unbeknownst to us, she had been there the whole time, hidden behind a tree. The lady went from meditative to manic in a millisecond. "Get off the grass now! You idiots!"

A burly bearded man, a German Shepard, and a heavy woman ceased their shortcut through the fragile meadow.

The man shouted back, "How do you get over there, then?"

The woman behind me yelled, "By walking on the path like everyone else!"

The man turned around and assessed how far they had come. "We're already halfway there," he grumbled, then continued trespassing across the meadow.

Tensions boiled over like the bubbling water. The woman behind me rolled her eyes and mumbled some profanities as the sound of the stream lost its rhythm to my own internal rumblings of silenced anger. I fled conflict as naturally as the stream sought lower land.

Sarah and I relocated to the forest, this time alone with certainty, and tried again to find the sacredness of the mountain. Two minutes into this meditation, I opened my eyes to a lone man in his late twenties standing on the trail. He was scented with days of dried sweat, his lips whitened with dehydration, and his black hole pupils lost in a substance-induced trip.

"Is it kuwwl with you if I taaake a nap herrre?" he croaked.

I looked around, as if I'd see the limited space to warrant such a question and not the entirety of one of California's largest mountains. Why here? Why us? Why couldn't he walk a measly ten yards and leave me alone? Before I could respond, he stepped off the trail and began a series of sweeping kicks, clearing the land of its sensitive habitat until nothing but dirt remained. He set down a tarp, lay on top of it, then closed his eyes to begin his motion picture of hallucinations. If the people here were in a cult, I wanted nothing to do with it. It was evident that my own magma needed cooling.

Back in the parking lot, we kicked off our shoes and prepped Rudy to leave, then rolled down Shasta to what the locals call, "the headwaters." Here, the source of the Sacramento River blasted out of the rocks with great ferocity. Surrounding the water was a spectacle of characters. A shirtless man atop a boulder blew a five-foot didgeridoo. An older woman in a tattered sundress spoke gibberish as she splashed on the edge of the riverbank. A young male in a white robe chanted *"Ommm"* into the surface of the water.

I soaked my feet as people came and went, filling water in jugs that once held milk or laundry detergent. Dilapidated buses, RVs, and vans consumed the parking lot's gravel. The people looked too far gone to blame ganja. If you wanted to escape it all, I'm sure this parking lot is where you could buy something sold with that promise.

Never have I yearned to escape nature and a small town so quickly. A turn of the key and we were off on a fifty-minute drive, down one mountain, across a valley, and up another, to the Trinity Alps. Campers dotted the shoreline of Castle Lake, whose waters were besieged with the deadfall of surrounding trees. A topless woman hiked barefoot along the same trail. I flopped over rocks, into the frigid lake, scrubbing my limbs while all those judgments clung to my mind. Around the bend, we scored an epic campsite with a view of Mount Shasta towering over the tree-packed valley we had driven across. As I finished cooking enough pasta to eat my feelings, Sarah went to grab our chairs out of the back.

"Where are our hiking boots?" she yelled.

"Damn it," I conceded. "They're on Shasta. I put them in the sun to dry after the hike."

Sarah groaned, "Ugh, nooo."

"I'm sorry. Let's just eat, then I'll drive us back. We can camp on the mountain tonight."

Steam rose from my noodles as I looked east at the grand Mount Shasta. I hoped this was the mountain's way of reconnecting, that she still had something to teach me. Or maybe it was the carbs speaking.

We arrived back on the mountain to punishing sounds. No birds chirping or streams flowing, only dubstep clanging out of a speaker, a genre of music that sounds like robots farting. The bare hands of partygoers slapped off rhythm and onto drums. People danced and yelled, sounding as if they were next door and not a quarter mile away. We parked in the designated overnight area. Above us, the party roared on in the Old Ski Bowl parking lot, beyond the signs that said no parking after dark.

I tried to count our blessings. Our boots were right where we left them, the stars were bright and plentiful, and Shasta's air breathed with the crispness of a clear night at 8,000 feet. I stared up at the glittering sky. I had much to be grateful for, yet every five minutes, headlights rounded the final curve and pushed past Rudy, up the last switchback, to the parking lot party above.

In my younger years, I would have loved the party, maybe even started it. But in those years, I didn't make it out of the city much, and my thoughts didn't go far from the bottle. In my intoxications, I surely littered empty beer cans and drained bottles of cheap vodka. Many mature adults must have lost sleep to the sounds of my hedonism. I used to say I was the life of the party; hindsight says I was just another drunken toolbag. Perhaps embarrassment supersedes judgment because my transformation has come with the awareness that I was once really obnoxious. Listening to the party, I felt my own karma punishing me, one dubstep bass drop at a time.

They say you hit bottom when you stop digging. When you hit the elevator's stop button, get out, and take the long, arduous staircase back up. My bottom was not a one-and-done event, more like a multi-month slide that began in November 2009.

While love is an extension for the well, for the broken it's merely a mirror. And my reflection bounced off the pain in Ysabel's face. My alcoholism was no longer taking a toll on me or the family I kept at a distance, it was punishing the very woman I intended to share my life with. I loved Ysabel. Her charisma and fiery Latina ways, her intellect, and of course, her shared enthusiasm to work hard and play harder.

I anxiously tapped my dress shoes on the hardwood floor of my condo. Ysabel was taking forever to get ready, *again*. "We're going to be late!" I yelled.

I might as well fix a drink. The same glass, the same substance, another day: vodka, some ice, a wedge of lime. One down, then another, and another. I heard Ysabel's heels clicking down the hallway. We were headed to a black-tie event with all my clients and coworkers present, an open bar with an awards ceremony in the middle. *Better bring some booze so my coworkers don't see me go back and forth to the bar so much*, I thought. I grabbed a plastic water bottle, emptied its contents, and refilled it with vodka. I placed the bottle in my coat pocket just as Ysabel rounded the corner.

How badly I had tried to keep my worlds in separate orbits—party life, work life, relationship life. But they were merely comets bound for the same cataclysmic collision. I downed the entire bottle during the awards. At the open bar, in the thick of the crowd, I took shot after shot, cocktail after cocktail. First the slurs, then the stumbles. Ysabel, concerned I'd do something regrettable in front of my work world, tried to cut me off and ordered me a water.

I stared at her dead in the eye, as if I'd been possessed. "Leave me the fuck alone!" I barked.

She turned around to walk off. I reached out and gripped her upper arm, yanking her back towards the bar. It was the way a man should never touch a woman. It was the way I grabbed my own girlfriend.

Ysabel spun around, reared her right arm back, and slapped me across the face. Heads turned. The music didn't stop, but it sure felt like it did. I let my grip go. Ysabel stormed off.

The following day, I came to. My eyelids stuck to the dry surface of my unremoved contact lenses. A few hard blinks until the fuzz faded into a sobering haze. My suit was still on. My phone was missing. Wallet, keys, dignity … all of it gone. Where was Ysabel? She was supposed to spend the night. Then the memories came rushing back. My stomach churned. I went to heave. Next to the toilet, a mirror.

In the reflection, I saw only myself: the bloated face and sunken, bloodshot eyes. But the reflection was more than visual, it was visceral. The mirror seemed to transmit the pain of so many. I felt Ysabel's torment and embarrassment. I felt my father's alcoholic DNA, his history and my history intertwined. I wondered how many similar drunken scenes had played out in my parents' failed marriage. There, in that mirror, was a defeated man unwilling to surrender. There, in that mirror, was the person I said I would never be.

The physical hangovers I had learned to live with, but the emotional hangovers were getting worse with each bender. This one was the whitewater of a crashing wave. Its turbulence took hold of everything I had, refusing to let me go, drowning me in shame.

I knew what was coming—the ultimatum. Ysabel would surely lay it out clearly: me or the booze. As much as I loved her, I knew I was going to choose the booze. A liquid over a person. A person who made my life better in so many ways.

There is a misconception that the addict is always oblivious of their actions. How untrue that was on that wretched morning. While my vision was short-sighted, I had this sickening awareness: I wanted a liquid more than I wanted love. It was the harshest reality I had ever faced.

A few days later, Ysabel agreed to speak to me. "The only way this relationship will work is if you stop blacking out."

Whew. I don't have to quit. The booze, and the relationship, had a fighting chance.

Thus began my experiment—could I control my drinking? And if so, would I still enjoy it? After all, I had always sought to blackout.

I attempted to keep busy, taking up exercise, working more, and studying to go back to school. I made some baseline rules: no hard liquor, no weekday drinking, never exceed ten beers in one night. To keep track, I would go out to the bar with ten pennies in my right pocket. Each time I ordered a beer, I'd move a penny to my left pocket. Sometimes this worked, other times I joined in when someone else bought a round of shots. The one thing that was consistent—I hated it. Controlled drinking, what was the point?

I began having withdrawals: itchy skin, restless nights, and runaway thoughts. My emotional equilibrium was nonexistent. I was never angry, only raging. Never sad, only depressed. I felt shaky and unstable, my metabolism went haywire. I lost twenty pounds in a couple of weeks. I made an appointment to get a checkup at the doctor.

My last drink came on a Sunday evening in March of 2010. A cold beer on a crisp spring day. Had I known it would be my last, I would have had another, and another, *and another*. The next day I was sent to a cancer center. I had been told to go there after my blood tests revealed some irregularities. My body was shutting down and my low platelet count raised alarm. Patients at the center were given chemotherapy and life expectancy rates; I was told to stop drinking.

"Three weeks. Don't drink, then come back. After that, we'll see if your blood improves," said the doctor.

Like seeing police lights flashing in the rearview mirror, I had that horrid feeling as if I'd been caught. It was another harsh realization: I was more mentally prepared to be diagnosed with cancer than I was to confront my addiction. Drinking had not been my problem, it had been my solution. My confidence, my coping, my escape. My relief.

The doctor walked out, leaving me in the room alone with my father. My dad's alcoholism had cost him his marriage, but he didn't let it take his kids. He'd gotten sober when I was young, and had stayed that way.

My dad, concern covering his face, asked, "Can you go three weeks without drinking?" His eyebrows lifted, his tone implying that he already knew the answer.

I looked him dead in the eye and did what I had done for the last eight years: I lied. "Yeah, I got this," I said.

I could have asked my dad for help, but I didn't want to give him any hope that I might actually give up drinking for good. The only thing I knew for certain was that I didn't want to die, not at the age of twenty-four, not because of some liquid. I knew I needed help, a lot of help.

After I left the cancer center, I took to the internet to find an alcohol recovery program. The only person I told was Ysabel.

In 1875, a few thousand vertical feet up Mount Shasta, John Muir, also known as the "Father of the National Parks," survived a blizzard by lying next to a gaseous heat vent for seventeen hours. He was thirty-six years old.

Now, at the age of thirty-four, I cheered at 10 p.m. when two US Park Rangers drove up the same mountain. Surely, they would enforce the rules and end the parking lot party. Surely, I would be sleeping to mountain silence in no time. Ten minutes later, the Rangers rolled back down the mountain. Similar to Muir's blizzard, the party, and my thoughts, raged through the night.

In my insomnia, I took to the web to see if anyone had similar experiences. I found a published report by the Forest Service entitled, "Conflicting Values: Spirituality and Wilderness at Mt. Shasta," about a man who "had been drawn to Mt. Shasta by its power and approached the Forest Service with a desire to serve the mountain." The agency, eager to find some way to minimize the ecological damage, brought him in as a volunteer. They hoped to eliminate, or at least decrease and control, the building of sweat lodges, littering of urns and ashes, trampling of sensitive vegetation, illegal camping, and unpermitted fires. For an entire summer, this volunteer served as the liaison and educator between the hippies and the conservationists.

The man set up where the concrete met the meadow, a short distance from our parking spot. The conclusion was a temporary success with a drop in destruction and illegal camping, as well as the beginnings of a communication bridge between the opposing forces. I wondered if it was a program still in place, so I scrolled back to the beginning of the article to check the date. It was written twenty-nine years ago.

The only thing that changed since 1991 was the absence of the middleman. At the core of it all was the theme of hypocrisy. New Agers angry at the Forest Service for developing the land for logging, trailblazing, and attempting to create a ski area. The Forest Service angry that people who claim to spiritually harmonize with nature proved unable to grasp the simple concepts of ecological preservation. Then there were the elder stewards of the land, local Native American tribes like the Winnemem Wintu, who had to deal with both parties to attempt to keep their sacred land from being exploited. (I later read on the Forest Service website that the tribe asks no one fill up bottles or place objects in the spring. Both discretions that Sarah and I were wholly ignorant about. Furthermore, a month after we left, the Shasta-Trinity Ranger District closed down dispersed camping for the remainder of the season due to illegal campfires.)

Morning came with silence and an eerie sight. A sunrise with no sun, a gray sky with no clouds. Rudy's solar panels collected no UV rays. Instead, a layer of ash piled on the roof as a plume of smoke condensed at our altitude. It wasn't the volcano, but rather wildfire exhaust from a nearby forest fire. If the mountain had its gods, then they had undoubtedly spoken. Now was the time for us to leave this land and surrender the thought that at some point my Shasta expectations of spiritual enlightenment would get met.

The road rounded and weaved. Rudy hummed on third gear, while intermittent braking at the curves kept us on a steady descent down the mountain. Through the gray air, I festered at the littered campsites and smoldering coals of illegal campfires. We drove past communal buses and New Age "shamans" charging who-knows-what for a weekend retreat.

Northbound on I-5, a view of the western ridge and the smoke that crept towards it. Clean air now cut through a cracked window, but the smell of wildfire smoke had found its way into Rudy overnight. We needed a laundromat, some food, and a change of scenery. I remembered Jan. I remembered Ashland, which was an easy ninety-minute drive away.

Every town and city has its darkness, and Ashland, Oregon, hid its ailments as well as Shasta's problems shadowed my every move. Bookstores aplenty, a grocery co-op I could live in, and friendly welcomes from all. The washing machines tumbled our bedding fresh, and travel gave me enough space from yesterday that my own volcano went dormant.

California had disappeared in the rearview. I welcomed Oregon with the realization that the sacredness of something resides more in how we treat things than how we label them. Little felt sacred in the treatment of the holy mountain of Shasta, and nothing felt sacred in how I judged others, lacked education about the indigenous people, and spoke only to criticize. All of it felt unsustainable, for humans are like volcanoes—contained heat only leads to bigger eruptions. And the road, too, is like humans. For without regular maintenance, one should expect a bumpy ride.

Chapter 9
Risk

FOR THE TRAVELER who must learn as much as they see, the return brings up a simple question: *Am I better now than I was then?* Maybe the place has changed, maybe you have.

Located in the Cascade Mountains of south-central Oregon, Crater Lake is the state's only National Park. A site to behold, the lake was formed after Mount Mazama erupted in 5,700 BCE, and its cone filled with rain and snowmelt. The lake's depth created one of nature's finest colors: a regal and heavy azure that took not only the cobalt of a clear sky but funneled it into a shade of blue as wealthy as a million barons.

Wearing swimsuits, Sarah and I made our way to an overhang above the lake's edge. Her bare feet gripped the cliff's cutoff. A westerly breeze blew through the shade, sending a charge of goosebumps across her legs. On a neighboring rock, my fear extended a yard-long gap from my toes to the precipice. I peered over and looked down. The deep end, but not just any deep end. With a depth of 2,000 feet, it's the deepest end in North America.

Sarah, entering the last week of her twenties, tapped her tough feet as she eagerly waited for the signal to jump. As for my feet, well, I once threw my back out in my early thirties merely sliding my foot into a sandal. The flip-flop had not been dangling on a slackline nor on a floating log. It was simply on my bedroom floor when I soberly stepped into it and immediately experienced the gift that has no receipt—the gift of age.

This gift now comes in the form of tight hamstrings and a mind that spends a lot more time calculating risk than it used to. If I let it, the older I get, the more energy I spend worrying, the less I spend living. That's why this cliff jump posed one potential injury—the one you do to yourself if you let the doubts take over, if you let fear convince you that the risk is not worth the leap.

This knowledge hadn't come from a blog post or Google search, it came from experience. This was my return to Crater Lake, and I had taken this exact jump in September 2013. And that jump was the pinnacle of a trip that sits atop my many mountains of memories. The freefall lasted a second or two, but the liberation and growth from that road trip, the one that taught me how to be alone, transformed me forever.

I took another look over the edge. My eyes went in and out of focus, trying to register the height of the drop. Five feet? Fifty feet? It didn't matter. My goal was to jump into lakes, and here was the most beautiful lake I had ever seen.

I looked over at Sarah. "If I wait any longer, I'll talk myself out of it!"

She counted us down, "Three … two … one!"

My rubber band legs fired forward. My arms flailed until the rush of cold water slammed against my body.

"Woo-hoo!" I screamed, smiling Texas-wide, my heart beating with the fervor of freedom yet again.

It had been seven years since my last visit. The passage of time had made the cliff higher and the fears louder, which were all the more reasons to jump again. Not to honor the first twenty-seven years of my life that brought me to Crater Lake the initial time, but to honor the last seven years that brought me back. Seven years with three "careers," a couple of wrong-way relationships, and the spiritual dead-ends that followed. There were glorious windows when I was confident and cheery, and the arduous months when I was panicked, clawing for an easier way. An ode to the self, I climbed up the rocks again, and took a solo leap.

"I want to jump in the lakes," was my poetic way of saying, *I honor the caution of an aging mind warning my every move, and the spirit of a man who*

94

wants it to shut up. While I live a more calm, quiet, and risk-assessed existence now, the same protagonist duels most of the same scoundrels. Trips are no longer about peak-bagging and cliff jumping, they're about being in nature and slowing down. The road isn't about how fast I drive but what I learn along the way. And the return isn't only about sharing a favorite place with someone I love, it's about reflecting on the person I was, am, and hope to be.

On the shore of Crater Lake, I admired the thousand-foot-tall gray peaks that once served as the frame to a unified mountain. With dry bodies, wet hair, and broad smiles, Sarah and I hiked back to Rudy. Up the third switchback, I spotted a man. He was broad, strong, and had a thick ponytail of licorice-black hair that swayed across his lower back. The hair looked like a rite of passage, resembling the locks of a warrior or chieftain. However, Oscar told me that he lived in Los Angeles and worked as an apprentice to a carpenter. The lake's energy brought joviality to all—Oscar, his wife, their four children, Sarah, and me.

We hiked past Oscar's wife and eldest daughter, who took up the rear and sucked heavy breaths up the incline. Oscar, flanked by the two youngest children, pushed on at a slow pace. Sarah and I caught up to his preteen son, and the three of us shared conversation as we finished the hike.

Mount Mazama's eruption proved that even the biggest disasters have the potential for the most beautiful results. All transformation needs is time and the willingness to change. Or, in Crater Lake's case, an empty hole to be filled with as much purity and as little pollution as possible. Everyone has their hole, some crater-deep, others shallow scoops. Holes get filled with muck, mercy, and scary tales—drugs, God, and everything in between. Lord knows I've tried filling my hole with all of the above, but it's travel's enduring newness that seems to be my filler of choice these days. And if there is a universal risk, it is this: that a life confined to a geographical bubble limits us to who we meet and what we learn.

Like the rest of us, I'm sure Oscar had his hole. However, his smile—like the lake—said he chose to fill that hole with something that made it worth looking at.

"Hey, can we see your van?" Oscar asked as they caught up to us in the parking lot.

"Sure." Sarah slid the door open.

Oscar gave some compliments, then his youngest child, Joey, spoke up in a quiet voice.

"Amzest."

"What?" I asked.

"Amzest." Joey pointed to Sarah's crystal.

"Oh, yeah. That's an amethyst, really good!" Sarah replied.

Little Joey, old enough to add but not multiply, stuck out his small hand to reveal his own treasured, chicken-nugget-sized amethyst.

"Oh, you have one too!" said Sarah.

He nodded. The deep purple points refracted beautifully, but not as beautifully as the words whispered from his soft, innocent voice.

"For you." Joey stuck out his palm and offered the crystal as a gift.

Sarah and I stared at his hand, our vocal cords paralyzed. I'm not sure how long Joey had carried his precious treasure. Maybe it went with him everywhere. Maybe his parents recently bought it for him to commemorate their big road trip. Perhaps he saved up his allowance for weeks to treat himself. I don't know, and I was too overwhelmed by the gesture to ask. I just stared at the rock, my lip quivering, as Joey held his hand without a tremble, waiting for us to take the crystal.

I looked over at Oscar.

"He wants you to take it," Oscar said, "go on."

Teary-eyed, Sarah stuck out her hand. Chills marched down my neck as Joey handed her the crystal.

Oscar's decision to drive his family to Crater Lake seemed to be one of many things he and his wife were doing right as parents. The crystal was a present, but it was nothing compared to the gift of knowing that Joey didn't need a gem to prove he had a heart of gold.

Little Joey gifted me more than a souvenir. That crystal will always be my reminder about how greedy and selfish I can be, especially with things that I'm attached to. I know life does not guarantee returns, but if I see Crater Lake again, I intend to return as generous as that outstretched palm.

Our time in the Southern Cascades was cut shorter than planned. The next day, the wildfire smoke from California rolled in and swallowed the views of Crater Lake. Before we rolled away, fellow van-lifers told us to check out an endearing town on the Oregon coast called Yachats. Sarah and I said goodbye to one of my favorite national parks, where I recognized that the trip would be best if it wasn't measured in minutes, miles, or photos, but rather in reflection, gratitude, and new intentions.

That's why Joey was my teacher that day. And I learned that the real risk wasn't in the adrenaline of cliff-jumping; it was in my shortcomings, where old ways threaten me never to change, never to grow. On the road, or in life, there is always the opportunity to appreciate the small gifts as much as the big leaps. Thank you, Joey.

DANGER
Remote Road System Ahead
DANGER
You Could Get Stranded and Die!!!
DANGER

The professionally made sign was an ominous warning at Bear Camp Road's eastern entrance. We were en route to our first destination on the Oregon coast, Gold Beach. I had followed the intriguing little line on the atlas that led to this route, which apparently had quite the reputation. I now understood why Google Maps had suggested a different way.

"Do you want to do it?" I asked Sarah.

"Umm, yeah, I don't want to turn around and drive a few extra hours. Do you think they are just being dramatic?"

I looked at my phone. No service. "I don't know. Maybe it's more for winter or maybe the locals don't want a bunch of people driving this way."

"Do you want to go a different way?"

"Nah. Let's go for it!" Is what I said. What I thought: *Sure, in a van we built that has a shoddy reputation, on a notorious road with no cell signal ... what could go wrong?*

I met my nerves in that place where curiosity and fear swirl into trepidation. The single-lane artery wormed around the forested peaks of the Klamath Mountains. We drove on, wondering when we would have the luxury of shifting out of second gear. Halfway to the coast, we took a break, camping off the road and enjoying its wild views of tree-covered peaks. When cell service returned, we read the stories of the departed, those who had gotten lost on Bear Camp Road and died in winter storms, never to drive another mile again.

The Pacific was a comforting sight as I breathed in the smoke-free coastal air. I studied the wind and waves from the warmth of my puffy jacket. The great ocean took on the look and feel of a stormy January day in San Diego, but this was summer in Oregon. Relentless gusts pushed whitecaps out at sea and sent waves to break on the rocky coast. It was the first time on our trip that I missed something from San Diego—my surfboard.

Second to emptying the toilet, the next most challenging part of our new lifestyle was the adjustment to not having an address. Not because I missed jury duty summons or Bed, Bath & Beyond coupons. No, because uncertainty and the human brain clash like rams during mating season. As our trip unfurled, time performed its magic and my mind evolved. The challenge of not knowing where we would sleep most nights eventually transitioned into feeling normal, even bringing an element of excitement. Would we find a beautiful spot or a drug deal? Paradise or a field of litter? Where predictability lives, adventure dies.

Boondock or bust, after a day at the beach, we headed inland along the banks of the Rogue River in search of a safe place to camp. Overdriven and hungry, we pulled into an abandoned lot a few miles from Highway 101. Rudy rolled over concrete overgrown with weeds and wild blackberry bushes. A spray-painted structure littered with molded mattresses and empty bottles revealed remnants of squatters and derelicts. A dirt road hid behind the structure. Adjacent was a murky pond, then layers of dark forest. Across the pond was a rusty old RV, its owners a loud couple. The volume of their voices was exacerbated by the intoxicants in their system and the sinister silence of everything else.

I backed Rudy in to hide from the road as Sarah and I hid our thoughts from one another: *This place doesn't feel safe.* We stuffed our fears away as we stuffed down dinner. Our typical nightly routine commenced: pajamas, card games, and books. The comfort of our home-on-wheels settled our nerves. The clouds went from white, to pink, to black. From bed, nature's symphony filled the forest. That night, the crickets headlined. I closed my eyes.

The sound of car doors slamming brought me to my feet. Headlights penetrated our windshield covers.

"What was that?" Sarah whispered.

The strangers blocked us in, our exit via the narrow dirt road now cut off. Wearing only boxer briefs, I cracked the windshield cover for a view. Thoughts of meth heads and *Murder Mountain* scurried across my brain. Their headlights shut off. Nothing could be seen. Harmless or hostile, they lingered, feet away, in the dark of night.

"We gotta get out of here," I whispered, slowly pulling off the windshield cover.

"But how? They blocked us in," Sarah replied.

Shadows and silence persisted as I thought through what to do. I flipped the headlights on and turned the key. Rudy roared as loud as he could.

Two worn-down sedans illuminated a few feet ahead. The drivers quickly turned on their engines and raced away. They gained ground as we trailed behind them until they disappeared in the distance. Though I felt they were up to no good, I wasn't quite sure who was more scared of whom.

Sarah voiced my current thought, "We shouldn't have stayed there, it didn't feel safe." We shared our theories on what they were doing while I drove us to the solace of a church parking lot for the remainder of the night.

Since Sarah and I decided to hit the road, risk had been on my mind. Sure, there were the day-to-day dangers of living without fences and going down unknown roads, potentially camping in unsafe places. But there was also the risk of nonconventional living. At first, I looked at it exclusively from the lens of the traditional American script, fearing that I would one day prove my naysayers right and not have enough money to retire or afford a medical emergency. However, you know what nearly every senior I've met on the road says to me? "Do it while you're young." And I hear it in their declaration. They've seen too many friends' dreams cut short. Every lifestyle has its risk. Van life felt like the scenario *I* would least regret.

Society glorifies its warning signs. A constant reminder of what can go wrong. But how about the support sign? The sign that says you can always turn around if it doesn't work out, learn from that mistake, and hang it on the wall—for those experiences teach more than most degrees do, anyway.

During our trip, family and friends continued pressing me about work, asking what was next. I found myself staging answers in my head before the question even came up. Afterward, I would stir a thick pot of resentment, often angriest with myself. When would I stop giving answers for others? When would I find the clarity that I knew the road could provide?

For many, work is an obligation; for others, it's an addiction. But beneath its vital economic role hides that drive, that sense of purpose. Whether it's the eighteen-year-old deciding what to do after high school or the entrepreneur who can't secure funding, the late-stage career changer or the aspiring artist overwhelmed by rejection, almost all of us are destined to confront this mental maze at some point in our lives. During this stretch of unemployment, I felt myself agonizing over it for what seemed to be the dozenth time. I looked to writing to fill that void as I said goodbye to the shackles of employment. Without writing, I worried that I would be free but lost. Wandering yet wondering. Would I look back at this break as time well spent or days wasted?

The next night, Sarah and I camped on a logging road in the Siuslaw National Forest. There, I did not what I wanted but what I needed, and revealed to her what was festering behind my eyes.

"Do you feel any pressure that you're not working?" I asked.

"Umm, I do and I don't," she replied. "I feel relieved to have a break. But I also thought I'd be writing more and making progress on my book."

"Yeah, I get it. I know some of my desire to write comes from my love for it, but some of it comes from this feeling that I need to have an answer to the question: *What do you do?*"

"I feel that, too."

My eyes trailed away. I took a drink of water. "Can I talk to you about something?"

"Of course, bubs, anything."

My dejected look must have said more than the words. Sarah made her—*yay, he's getting vulnerable!*—face. The one she makes when a guy like me, wired to "tough things out," begins opening up. Her eyes widened to full attention. She tried to look serious, but I could tell she was forcing herself not to smile, that having her boyfriend open up was like the grown woman's version of unwrapping Christmas gifts.

My eyes drifted from hers as I spoke, as I confided how insecure and lost I'd become. I had been trying to get my first novel published and, after receiving another rejection, I no longer felt clear about what I should write next. Sarah sat the same distance away, yet my confession made her feel so much closer. She placed her hand on top of my mine, and though she gave an encouraging speech, it did little to shake me from my pity.

"Can I ask you another question?"

"Sure," I replied.

"What is your heart telling you?"

Mic drop. Our eyes locked.

"I don't know," I admitted. "I haven't asked it."

"Maybe you should."

After dinner, I stepped out of the van and into the dark, bringing all my doubt with me. Shutting off my headlamp, I looked to the stars. Only a few shined bright enough to break through the thick web of treetops. Facing the proof of the universe's infinite possibilities, I asked whatever was listening for inspiration, guidance, and to be a channel for something useful. I placed my hand on my chest and asked my heart to tell me its desires.

I can't say I expected a response, or that I got one in that moment. But I did reach a point where the risk of not asking outweighed whatever part of me thought this exercise was futile. After all, these pleas often go unanswered; other times the answer is just a one-hour drive away.

Chapter 10
Intuition

IT WAS A spring day in 2015 and Jackie was thumbing the worn beads of her rosary. *God save us. God help us. God be with us.* She sat in the comfort of a plush captain's chair on the passenger side of a 2006 Gulf Stream Crescendo. Behind her was the remaining thirty-eight feet of Class A motorhome. The chair extended wide with soft padding and a firm armrest; its leather upholstery tilted to the perfect angle for posture support. But Jackie felt far from comfortable as she recited prayer after prayer, her thumb adding to the rosary's erosion.

"Sit down, put on your seatbelts, be quiet," her husband barked at their two sons: the youngest, six, and the oldest, thirteen. Usually jovial and full of chatter, the family went silent—the clue that something had gone terribly wrong. His white knuckles gripped the wheel of the twelve-ton motorhome; the speedometer needle climbed as the vehicle tilted downhill.

Their house-on-wheels tore southbound on California's Highway 89. A road that descends 3,234 vertical feet from the higher peaks of Lake Tahoe, over Monitor Pass in the Sierra Nevada Mountains, and down to the high desert surrounding Topaz Lake. The two lanes snake downhill, wrapping around mountains prone to landslides. Every few miles, a sign with a winding arrow warns of upcoming switchbacks and the speed limit to match their intensity—30 mph, 25 mph, 20 mph. Around one of the several hairpin turns, one could find patches of scorched trees, leafless and lifeless from past blazes. Through the bare trunks, vistas of over fifty miles spread to the arid land below. It's a beautiful drive, unless your brakes have stopped working.

The driver pressed the brake pedal again, hoping for a miracle. Instead, only smoke shot from the axles. Tears poured down Jackie's face. The brothers latched in tightly. Gripping their two Chihuahuas and Labrador, they peered towards the windshield to assess the situation. Their father's brow and back dripped with sweat. It was more than the longevity of their trip in his hands, it was the longevity of their lives. As the tires squealed, they all prayed it would not end here. Not like this. Not barreling down Highway 89.

"I have something for you," the man took on a gentle tone. It was the kind of enunciation that adults transmit when they speak to children. His voice sounded soft and serious, kind and captivating. Middle-aged, he wore glasses with a ball cap pulled tightly over his head. A thin layer of gray and ginger stubble lined his jaw. Across the counter, a little girl with knotted blonde hair leaned forward, her mother by her side.

"Now, this doesn't look like much," the man pulled out a bumpy black rock about the size of a grapefruit. "In fact, it's called the ugly face rock," he twirled the rock around so she could see the jagged sides, "nothing special, right?"

"Uh-huh," the girl nodded. Her little eyes bulged out of her head with suspense. He had her hooked. And from across the Styx, Stones, n' Bones store in Yachats, Oregon, I was hooked too.

"But what I want you to do," the man continued, "is pull this side of the rock from my hand."

The little girl did as he asked. The rock split into two parts. Inside, an array of bright orange crystals.

"Wow!" the girl, and her mother, glowed. I gushed too, as I eavesdropped in front of a tray of Golden Healer Quartz—a faded pink crystal with an intriguing sign stating its origin (Madagascar) and its metaphysical powers (healing).

"Now, what I want you to do is take this rock," he handed her a replica of the stone, "and I want you to find someone and show them this same trick. But you have to let them keep the other half and make them as happy as I just made you. Can you promise me that?"

The beaming girl nodded and took the rock. I turned my head back to the tray, wondering how many kids' days he had made with the same trick.

Friendliness is the norm when visiting Yachats, a town on Oregon's central coast that seems to breed kindness. A seaside village with a population slightly above 700, it's short on residents but long on charm. It's a place so inviting that the only challenge is to pronounce the town's name correctly (YAW-hawts).

Yachats had no bank or gas station. Only a handful of small streets intersected Highway 101. The wind blew hard from the rocky Pacific shore, across the long sandy beach, and into the dense forest. Though it was late August, I wore sweatpants and a hoodie to keep warm from the oceanic gust. Our first stop was the crystal store in the heart of the village.

Dare I group humans so simply? Group A: the ones who believe crystals have special powers. Group B: those who do not. Group A: the stones can heal emotional and physical wounds, help manifest love and wealth, and even open chakras that have been closed for this lifetime and the last. Group B: they look cool. Though I walked in on my own accord, holding Sarah's cold hand, you would find me in Group B. Sarah is all A, *all the time*. Another reasonable expectation—if you met your girlfriend in a yoga studio, and you don't already love crystals, it would be safe to assume that this will be one of those interests that you *do not* have in common.

On my entertainment scale, crystal hunting scored a touch above furniture shopping and just below the security line at the airport. I always left Sarah alone while she shopped for crystals. I occupied myself elsewhere, roaming the aisles of grocery stores, people-watching from a park bench, or calling Papa Herb to find out if I was actually somewhere he'd never been.

Yet that day, whether it was the power of the crystals or the threat of boredom, there I was, taken aback by the sheer volume, beauty, and range of geological merchandise. Massive amethysts from Brazil, shaped like butterfly wings, featured multiple shades of violet, and cost thousands of US dollars. Pebble-sized agates, harvested on the nearby shores, had been polished and cost less than a bottle of water. The fossilized remains of a dinosaur from Morocco retailed for the equivalent of my monthly expenses. Row after row of rocks, gems, minerals, crystals, and fossils, each with a placard describing where they came from and how they were formed. I tried to read them all: Nevada, Afghanistan, Australia, Arkansas, and so on. Tourists, ranging from tattooed millennials and traveling families to new-age healers and rock-hounds, roamed the aisles. Then, there was me—in a crystal store—amazed, amused, and somehow full of curiosity.

Once the little girl left with a new rock and a new smile, I made my way to the counter. There was a question burning in my mind's eye.

"Do you travel to all these places to source these yourself?" I asked the man I came to know as Marc Taylor, age fifty-three.

He grinned a boyish smile. "Yup, I've been to all fifty states and twenty-six countries," Marc leaned over the counter. A rock hammer about three times the size of what Andy Dufresne used to escape out of Shawshank State Penitentiary sat next to the register. I imagined Marc in faraway lands, his hammer chiseling away on a cliff, miles from civilization. I pictured him arguing over prices with devious swindlers and crooked bandits who spoke in strange tongues.

"What's your favorite thing in your store?" I asked.

He paused and gave it some thought. "Smiling children. It's important to me that when we're in this store everyone's having fun, having a good time. And kids need opportunities to do and see things other than just what they see on TV or read on their phones. In my opinion, they spend way too much time on their devices. And if you can cultivate an interest in something else, I think you've done your job that day."

"Is that why you do the ugly rock thing?"

"I like to call it The Ugly Rock Club. It kinda represents the way our world is right now: dark and ominous on the outside, but there is definitely sparkle if you look for it."

Marc set up his first business at seven years old, collecting agates he found on the nearby beach to sell outside his parents' antique store. His passion shined as bright now as it did then. Born and raised "where the forest meets the sea," Marc had traveled the world, moved away five separate times, and allowed the charm of his hometown to lure him back.

"Yachats is a little bubble. And as much as it's affected verbally by the outside world, it's physically disconnected. It's at the end of the county, you're twenty-five miles from a town with any real population. You have this amazing sense of energy here. I call it *the magic of Yachats*. And honestly, more of the coast could have it if you had people that are willing to live life. And I feel like living your life is a really important way to be. If you just *be*, you'll just have another little town. But if you *live*, you'll have a whole other experience. That shared thing is infectious. And all of a sudden, you have all these people who come to this little, tiny town and enjoy themselves at a level they didn't even know they could.

"We have good food, good stores, good people. Sure, we have the riff-raff and crap just like everybody else, but you have to seek it out if you want to see it. You also have one of the most highly educated communities around. You have people who actually think about what they are doing before they do it. And we want to represent the place that we love because, honestly, as a tourist-based economy, we have nothing else. We would never make it with 65 percent retirees living in this town. I mean, my local business is 5 percent of what we do. And we would never make it on 5 percent. None of the businesses would."

A few months prior, I was working as a business teacher, going over case studies of giant corporations, engaging students to extract lessons that weren't nearly as valuable as one small business owner's perspective in this humble town.

"Where you guys from?" Marc asked after he finished ringing up a young woman, a new chunk of amethyst in her bag, a smile on her face.

"San Diego, but we're livin' in our camper van now," I replied.

His demeanor said I had squeezed the trigger to an old memory. His glasses wiggled up and down as he recalled the story, "Yeah, we lived in a thirty-eight-foot coach. It was me, my wife Jackie, three dogs, two kids, one cat, and a goldfish. We were going for three years, but sixteen months in, our brakes went out coming down the mountains from Tahoe."

"Yikes," my eyes lit up. "I have a hard enough time picturing myself steering a big motorhome when everything's working. You were drivin' down the 89? Near Topaz Lake?"

"Yeah, that's the one," Marc replied.

I flashed back to when Sarah and I drove up the road. I could still remember the nervous sensation I got when we wrapped around the fifteen miles of cliffside highway. I imagined coming down it, without brakes, in an RV built on a bus chassis.

Marc recapped the rest. The image made me shudder, hearing how he threaded the needle passing trucks and cars, doing everything in his power to keep his family alive.

"How'd you get it to stop?"

"When the road started to flatten out, I could get the rig on the gravel shoulder to slow it down. Once it slowed enough, the engine brakes started working again."

"Geez. I imagine something like that changes you."

"The scariest thing I've ever done in my life. And I had my family with me. And having my family with me on something that *spooky*," he gulped back emotion, his tone grew serious, "I didn't want to do it anymore. I was literally shaking when we got out."

The family gathered around at the end of the ordeal. The kids sang praises of their father's skill. Jackie held the family together in a group prayer. For them, it had become another adventure, one of many in their cohesive unit. The family wanted more. However, for Marc, the fiasco represented the turning point.

"I wanted to be done in a big way. I wanted to sell the coach and move on. And my wife wasn't happy with me, my kids weren't happy with me. Bottom line is, we had to do what we had to do." Marc sold the rig, moved the family back to Yachats, then opened up the crystal store that filled him, and so many travelers, with joy.

"What was your favorite memory from the trip?" I asked.

"We really had a lot of good memories. Just sitting as a family while I was barbequing, and everyone would just be looking around at wherever we were. Our favorite was Central Nevada. We spent so much time there that the wild donkeys would come in and the kids named them."

"How did the trip change your lives?"

"Well, we still talk about the trip quite a bit. If we didn't believe in God before, then we certainly did after. And though we definitely believed before, something like that will make anybody believe in the power of *grace*."

The word *grace* clanged emotion's bell. I thought back to when I gallivanted young and reckless, selfish and delusional, drunk and negligent. When I almost lost my life behind the wheel, not by the malfunction of a machine, but by the malfunction of my own human frailty. I thanked my own Higher Power for my grace, and for sparing Marc and his family. Marc had a notable presence about him, the kind a person carries when they pursue the most out of life. Marc's road trip might have ended, but his influence was far from over.

Like many people chasing freedom on the open road, Marc had not been prepared for the complexities of motorhome life. Driving a three-room home-on-wheels is not easy; keeping all the engineering functioning is even more difficult. But, more than that, is the challenge of adjusting to the stillness of nature, and about facing the combative thoughts that arise when life lacks income and a prevailing sense of purpose. Marc's vulnerability around freedom struck me, his sentiments timely, echoing my thoughts from last night.

"I feel it's my duty as a man to take good care of my family, both financially and emotionally. And I got myself in a weird spot mentally. I wasn't making any money. I became disappointed in myself. I didn't feel like I was living up to my potential."

When we do what is counterintuitive to our culture, the feelings that come up are often as difficult to navigate as Highway 89. So, while Sarah and Marc began discussing crystals, I went inward, cherishing the serendipity of what was unfolding.

Fifteen hours earlier, when I said my prayers, Marc Taylor was merely a stranger. Now I was in his store, in a town I would have never come to had it not been for a recommendation from a fellow traveler. The dots were connecting. As Marc told us his death-defying RV story, I felt the background noise of doubt fade away. One clear, distinct voice remained. I knew what I was destined to write. A book about the road. Any reason to second guess myself vanished. I was committed. To my future. To my journey. To this story.

I'm not sure what the antidote to that destructive emotion of feeling lost is. Maybe it's prayer, journaling, quiet time in nature, or getting vulnerable with another human being. Or perhaps it's fate, when you simply meet the right person at the right time. Either way, the fog lifted off the Oregon Coast that day. Not the kind of fog that blocked the views of windblown trees growing out of ancient sand dunes, but rather the kind of fog that blocked off the God-given gift of intuition. The kind of fog that now cleared and revealed the future's horizon, setting the path not only for a new chapter, but for a new book.

❖

"You bought a T-Rex?" Sarah asked Marc. The question brought me back to the present moment, standing mid-conversation in the crystal store.

"Oh yeah, that was a fun one to explain to the wife," he grinned.

Marc gave us the rundown on the upcoming renovations, including where the fossil from Montana would be on display. He worked his way behind the counter to ring up a customer. Sarah and I sought out small gifts, hoping to make someone as happy as little Joey made us.

Marc returned and placed a crystal inside Sarah's palm, a single point of thick quartz. The spire had strength and flawed beauty, a pink base that dissipated to an opaque point. Sarah squeezed her hand closed and brought it to her heart.

"It's a Golden Healer Quartz from Madagascar," said Marc. "It's a gift, for your trip. It's powerful, and good for strengthening relationships."

I put my arm around Sarah and gave her a loving squeeze. We exchanged an unspoken, soulful recognition that made us both smile. Another lesson. A lesson on what happens when you trust your intuition. When you ask your heart what it wants.

After our conversation with Marc, we left Yachats and drove inland, following a satellite view on Google Maps to a potential camp spot for the night. Just before our turn, a pullout revealed itself right along the Yachats River. We backed the van in. The sound of flowing water replaced the grumble of churning pistons. I chased behind Sarah as her love for the forest drew us deeper into the woods.

Old-growth conifers, dressed in moss, reached the sky. Ancient stumps decayed while new life rose in its place. Plate-size mushrooms grew from fallen relics. The only animals in sight were singing sparrows and curious squirrels. It was a boondocker's Shangri-La.

"This place is magical," Sarah whispered.

Our feet left the soft soil of rotted fir needles for the pebbles down at the river. We walked along the river's bank, scouting for a place to get in. The air was crisp and the water fully shaded, the evening sun unable to penetrate the thick canopy above. Two streams trickled over rocks to merge with the river, creating a sandy entrance into deeper water.

"If we're gonna get in naked anywhere, this is the spot!" Sarah yelled.

It had been three weeks without a traditional shower. Our cleaning rituals had covered sixteen lakes, two creeks, one river, and some ever-awkward hose downs with our weed sprayer. I eagerly stripped off my clothes and stumbled into the river, where the cold water washed away dirt, fatigue, and stress unseen.

"This is our life," Sarah said softly. The bumps of cold skin traced up her legs to her bare torso.

As a couple, Sarah and I were deepening our relationship in every sense of the word. We had dialed in an organic teamwork that kept Rudy clean and cozy. Sure, there were little discoveries. As the nights grew quieter, her snoring grew louder. The more settled we got, the more frequently I couldn't find things. Not because I misplaced them but because Sarah would relocate an item to "a better location" without telling me. I'm sure she had her own observations, too. But most importantly, our alternative lifestyle was providing hours of opportunity for relationship growth that conventional dating did not. And as we shrieked with each naked plunge in the river, I couldn't help but smile wider at the realization that I had just experienced a day I would cherish for the rest of my life.

While life was in alignment, home was becoming a confounding word. Yet I had never gone to bed so many nights in a row feeling so properly placed. Each day was new, free, somewhat sustainable, and undoubtedly simple. Sarah and I still went to bed most nights looking at the ceiling, repeating, "I can't believe we built this thing."

The magic of Yachats had done its deed. In that quaint town, I experienced the Great Shift—when I stopped *recognizing* intuition and started *following* intuition.

Van life was changing me, but it was more than the parks and the views. It was the moments when Sarah felt closer and more accessible than any human I had ever known. It was in the serendipitous events where I could viscerally feel my life taking a different turn.

Chapter 11
Smoke

THAT SOUND. THE sound I had been dreading. The sound of spinning tires, flinging sand, profane language, and thumping hearts. The sound of getting stuck.

I slammed on the brakes before Rudy's city tread tires dug deeper. To my left, Mount Hood, Oregon's tallest, climbed to a height of 11,249 feet. To my right, Sarah's eyes widened with alarm. Beyond her, the real threat.

Smoke. Not the smoke we had been dodging the last few weeks. No, this was fresh smoke. The kind that smells of flames and destruction, the kind that alters landscapes and requires aircraft to extinguish. Oregon was burning, and the White River Fire was blazing nearby. And the winds shifted too—40 mph of blow-dryer heat—right in our direction. How much space between us and the flames? We didn't know, but the stifling gray wind didn't bode well.

We had no cell signal and no neighbors; not a soul knew where we were. It was how I wanted things after returning to the Central Cascades. I haven't driven an ugly highway in Oregon, and OR-20 had taken us from the coast's dense forests back to the state's central mountain range. To think we had left the city of Bend only the day before because of the air quality, predicting that it would be better at Mt. Hood. Now yesterday's air seemed the better option, as Sarah and I pondered how to escape our precarious situation.

To try and not scare her further, I said little, but inside me sheer terror pulsed with each rapid heartbeat. I shifted into reverse, and thankfully physics played hero. God bless gravity; Rudy rolled out of the rut and down the sandy slope.

I pushed on the gas with a heavy foot and a hard head. Rudy roared back up the hill. When we reached the same spot, we got the same sounds. The tires squealed. Curse words spewed from my mouth; any false poise purged along with them. We were stuck again. To my left, more smoke. Mount Hood had already vanished behind the thick haze. To my right, a thicker hollow of smoke, the entire forest enveloped by this ashy fog.

Sarah hopped out of the van. I put Rudy in reverse. She patched up ruts while I rolled the quarter mile back to where we had camped. When we had arrived the day before, the spot was everything we wanted. A delightful subalpine meadow with a panoramic view of the volcano. Seclusion, on Mount Hood, on Labor Day Weekend, felt like a van-life victory. The popular areas around Mount Hood National Forest were beyond crowded. Portlanders had come by the thousands.

We had stumbled upon the area used in the winter for snow-mobile trails and thought it the perfect strategy to avoid the masses. We drove down with no problem and no second thoughts. *Hakuna matata*. After all, we had our one-year anniversary to celebrate. We had our ideal date—dinner with a view, the solitude to converse, and the memories to reflect. I never could have predicted that my yoga studio crush would become my partner-in-life, and that within a year we would have bought a van together, built it into our dream home, and got said home stuck on a snowmobile trail that was about to catch fire.

The ash in the air thickened, so dark that I could stare at the sun with my naked eyes. One option remained if we were to make it out safely. Despite not being four-wheel-drive, if Rudy gained enough momentum, maybe Lady Luck would see our cargo van to paved roads and safer grounds.

I put Rudy in first gear. *Pedal to the metal* became more than an expression. I was another millennial in a camper van, but in my mind I was a rodeo cowboy steering a wild beast. Like the cowboy, the next eight seconds would determine my fate. Up the hill, with sweaty palms and crossed fingers, Sarah watched from the sidelines near the worst stretch of road.

The needle fought to ascend. I bounced like a wild man, guiding the machine over rocks and around sandy curves. Sarah's pupils swelled with anticipation. I drove past her and hit the rut. The tires stalled. Then, with a fiery spin of dust, Rudy broke free, churning further up the hill to safer ground.

Oh, 2020, a year so undeniably crazy you could have easily overlooked the historic wildfires. After our time in Lassen Volcanic National Park, the lightning storm that had kept me awake threw down over 10,000 lightning bolts. As I stupidly enjoyed the show, each bolt exploded trees and ignited entire forests. Days later, the winds that blew the fire towards our campsite near Mount Hood belonged to a different rare weather alignment that created the worst-case scenario across the Pacific Northwest: high temperatures, dry air, drought, and offshore winds that blew faster than the interstate speed limit.

Oregon went on to record its second-largest fire season. Washington fought its largest fire ever. Colorado chronicled their three largest fires ever. And California burned five out of six of its largest wildfires ever. All in 2020. In total, over ten million acres burned in the United States, the most since record-keeping began. This equates to a land mass larger than the entire country of Switzerland.

Of all the reported fires in the American West in 2020, only 16 percent were ignited by lightning; the other 84 percent were from human causes, including: downed power lines, improper fire protocols, disregarded burn bans, and an alleged arson to cover up a murder. There was even a gender reveal party where a smoke machine malfunctioned, sparking a Southern Californian blaze that burned

22,744 acres and left one firefighter dead, Thomas Morton, age thirty-nine.

Van life delivered us to the vulnerable reality that we were at the mercy of the elements. What was once news consumed on a screen now became haunting images we saw for ourselves. With no air filtration in Rudy's living quarters, our tiny home relied on whatever we breathed in through our windows. The air quality index lingered in the 400s in much of the Pacific Northwest. In these areas, each day exposed to the elements was the equivalent of smoking at least twenty-three cigarettes.

But our home had the ability to move away from flames. Others were not as fortunate. Thousands of homes and structures became ash, including Sarah's hometown. One of her brothers escaped with his family, but they lost their house and everything inside. Fires across the West claimed the lives of at least forty-three people, along with countless pets and wildlife. Further deaths and health complications from the smoke tallied in the thousands, but the actual impacts are impossible to measure accurately. According to NOAA, the fiscal damages across the country were estimated at $16.5 billion. The smoke expanded outward until it covered most of the West. Currents took it as far as Europe.

I loathed seeing smoke, breathing it, and losing the battle to avoid it. I had to remind myself that my inconveniences were trivial compared to those facing the flames. Eventually, we surrendered and I quit agonizing over wind predictions and NOAA satellite images. We joined millions of others and hoped for rain.

The story plot was nature's tie-in to an apocalyptic American year. Yet, the destruction was nothing new to other parts of the world. South of the equator, the 2019-2020 fire season merely foreshadowed what the Northern Hemisphere could expect. The world's largest tropical wetland, the Pantanal in Brazil, lost a quarter of its land to fire—another record. On the other side of the globe, Australia recorded its biggest fire year on record (46 million acres, four times that of the US losses, and the equivalent in size to the entire state of Washington).

Not even van life proved to be an escape from the troubles of 2020. Like many other things that year, the wildfires left me with a cocktail of emotions. The road was my hangover, where I painfully pondered it all.

OR-35 took us down the mountain and into the Hood River Valley. Under a skyless canopy of burnt air, we bought fresh fruit and lavender-scented souvenirs. Tourists and locals engaged in commerce, but I overheard no one voice concerns about the dark sky. Across the Columbia River and into Washington, we lost sight of Oregon. The visibility was only a couple hundred yards, the smoke so thick that the lush hills of the river's gorge hid behind a curtain of hovering ash.

Along WA-14, the Lewis & Clark historical markers emerged. Beginning in 1803, the three-year journey took them across the Louisiana Purchase, over the Continental Divide, and down this section of river to eventually reach the Pacific Ocean. In 1903, a hundred years after the Lewis & Clark departure, the first automobile crossed the country from San Francisco to New York City. And now, how different the West was. We connected with I-5, the same interstate I used to commute to work pre-pandemic. We were 1,100 miles from my old classroom, heading for the furthest tip on this corner of the contiguous United States.

At Olympia, Washington, we left the interstate for Highway 101. Rudy cruised north on the eastern side of the road's lasso of the Olympic Peninsula. Sleepy fishing docks splintered on our right. On our left, abandoned trucks decomposed in the thick foliage. Interesting signs and searches taught us that the mollusk, geoduck, is pronounced "gooey-duck." Believe me, the "clam that will make you blush" is a disgusting sight you can't un-see. (Go ahead, google "geoduck.")

As dusk settled, our journey led to another lesson on surrender. A roadblock stopped us nineteen miles shy of our intended crash spot outside Olympic National Park.

"Road's closed," said the cop.

"For how long?" Sarah asked.

"Don't know."

"What happened?"

"Fire. Turn around, Hoodsport is a few minutes back. You can wait it out there."

A downed power line had torched a patch of trees along Highway 101. We spent the night parked outside the Lilliwaup Post Office.

Our time on Highway 101 in the Pacific Northwest took boondock or bust to new lots and wooded lands. In a small Oregon town, a drunk parking lot attendant, in his slur, admitted he was too lazy and didn't care if we overnighted next to the no-camping sign. Further up the coast, we found free and quiet sleep in a casino's parking lot. In Washington, we parked behind a small-town high school, where we were awoken by screeching bugles in the middle of the night. Out the window, shadows of regal elk marched by Rudy. The next night, we crashed at a cemetery parking lot (no nightmares were had). And in Port Angeles, Washington, we welcomed Walmart into the wheelhouse of options, grateful that some still allowed RVers to crash for a night, even if it meant shoving towels over our bunk windows to block out the overnight glow of streetlights.

Since Mount Shasta, Sarah and I committed to leave every campsite cleaner than we found it. On a river bend in rural Washington, we cleaned up every damned beer brand and fast-food wrapper known to Uncle Sam. Michelob, Miller, Modelo (and those were just the M's). The Chik, the golden arches, the bun monarchist, the creep in the cube, and the $5 foot of something. Used diapers, stained Styrofoam plates, napkins, plastic bottles, toilet seat covers, cigarette butts, and bullet shells. All told, it was eight full trash bags from thirty square feet of riverside forest. With it I threw away my crooked idea that littering was a twentieth-century problem. If only this case were an anomaly, for picking up litter became the first kind of charitable work that never made me feel good.

Sarah's birthday arrived and we closed out her twenties in the best way we knew—a nude plunge in the milky gray glacial waters of the Hoh River. Her thirties started with a shiver and a *woo-hoo!* Despite smoke blanketing the sky, Sarah found much to be grateful for. She was living in that special place where one journey was merely the chapter in a much bigger story.

Chapter 12

Grace

OH MY GOD. The guns.

Sarah ran to the door. Locked.

"Nick?"

Click. Click. The sound of the gun case opening.

"Nick!" she screamed. "Let me in. Please, Nick!"

Nick, drunk and suicidal, had locked himself in the bedroom, now armed with a loaded pistol.

An enlisted man, Nick's military service had been traumatically altered by a helicopter crash. He was one of two survivors, three had died. The burden was immense. And it wasn't his alone. So much of it fell on his caregiver. His wife—Sarah.

Other relationship problems predated the crash. Married at twenty-one, it wasn't long until Nick had an affair, then another. Devastated but dedicated, Sarah sacrificed more and more of herself in hopes they could overcome, hoping one day they could love harder than before.

"Nick, please. Please, don't do this!" she pleaded through the closed door.

"Shut the fuck up!" he yelled. "I don't want to hear you crying."

Sarah squeezed the doorknob with all her might. Nothing. She kicked it. Nothing. Desperate, she ran and grabbed a hammer, then aimed it at the doorknob. WHACK. WHACK. WHACK.

The door broke. She pushed it open. There he was. Nick, her husband. Holding a gun, pointed at his head.

Sarah spoke calmly, "Put the gun down, Nick."

Nick's hand trembled. Time froze. Them standing, staring. Eventually, he lowered the pistol.

It was March 15, 2014. A significant day for Sarah. And an important day for me. Three thousand miles away, I was an unknown stranger. On the same night Sarah's drunk husband could have turned the gun on her, I was out celebrating. It was my sober anniversary, four years without a drink.

When Sarah left her husband, she was twenty-three years old, broken, and barely hanging on. While Nick's demons continued to haunt him, Sarah set out to heal her own. She packed her car and hit the road—that trusted sanctuary for so many of us. She hiked the Grand Canyon and Angel's Landing. Sarah journaled, grieved, and filled the idle time, trying to understand how her life had spiraled, how she not only endured the nightmare but ended up in it in the first place.

Growing up, her parents were in the depths of their own challenges. High school sweethearts who wed young and went on to have eight children; Sarah was the sixth. Then: addiction, infidelity, and rage. Everything worthwhile and precious nearly lost. Sarah just a child overshadowed by her parents' pain.

Sarah's road trip ended in 2014. She was a divorcee with little to her name when she arrived at her parents' floating home, a liveaboard sailboat. They embraced her, and she moved in. Her parents had done their work, recovered, and were more in love than ever. They reached a place where they could offer more than physical space, and they loved Sarah unconditionally until she, once again, could love herself.

Now, Sarah was thirty years old, back on the road and once again heading to visit her parents, who still live on a boat. Only her marriage seemed like a lifetime ago, the scene with Nick and the gun a distant nightmare.

Rudy rolled south of Brinnon, Washington, parking across from a floating stretch of wooden planks. If Sarah and I are rubber tramps, then her boat-dwelling parents, Dale and Molly, are varnish vaga-bonds.

"My mom has the loudest laugh," Sarah warned as we walked towards the marina.

The unmistakable, high, reeling-in-a-big-fish, burst of a laugh was heard before she was seen. The cackling gasps sent schools of salmon scurrying across the Hood Canal. My ambition, as the new boyfriend, was to hear that laugh as much as possible over the days that followed.

Due to the smoke, we had arrived two weeks ahead of schedule. Dale and Molly greeted us with excitement and joy. Maybe it was our stench, or simply good emotional intelligence, either way Molly sang my hallelujah, "You two must want a shower after such a long drive. Here's the code to the marina's bathroom, take your time."

Thirty-two days without a traditional shower or bath. Sarah and I took our sweet, sexy time under the hot heads of endless water. We earned that scrub, Sarah especially. One week prior, I watched her on the edge of Elk Lake, attempting to shave her legs when a swarm of long-bodied mayflies decided it was the right time of evening to invade the shallows. They covered her entire body, sending her shrieking across the shoreline. I laughed, until the bugs swarmed me too, clinging to my wet skin.

Sarah came out of the bathroom with smooth skin and conditioned hair. "That was the best shower of my life," she grinned.

Just as Rudy had its naming story, so did Dale and Molly's home-on-water. The trail of floating wooden planks took us to *Grace*, their 1977 trawler. The scents of varnished wood mingled with the slow decay of salt air. I had met Sarah's parents only one time, a week before we bought Rudy. Sarah still had her apartment at the time, and we were losing hope that the right van was out there. Dale and Molly said they would pray every night that we be graced with the perfect vehicle. I guess God had listened.

Dale, Molly, and I built a great rapport during our brief first encounter. The three of us had a shared love of the 12 Steps. They said the Steps had saved their marriage, I said the Steps saved my life. They asked big questions and wanted the details. There was no hiding, and within minutes they knew the specifics of my story's darkest parts.

Dale prepped the boat and we set out to sea. Life on a boat mimicked life on wheels: a confined kitchen, low-voltage appliances, propane stove, and limited storage. We went up the canal and into Jackson Cove. Seals circled the boat all day. Bald eagles flew over the cedar-tipped mountains. Starfish waited for high tide on the sands of Camp Parsons. I took long swims in the cove's cold saltwater, treading near baby seals and floating jellyfish.

As it does when on such a journey, the banters of the road cruised across conversations. Dale and Molly shared stories of their honeymoon in a 1968 Volkswagen van, and they laughed about the adventure of taking six of eight kids in a thirty-six-foot motorhome when Sarah was a ten-year-old, traveling from California to Key West, up to Maine and back. Needless to say, our excursion across the West and away from desks was met with interest and approval.

The sharing of *Grace* led to many more deep and enjoyable conversations. The four of us huddled around a small collapsible table, sipping coffee, and opening up. Once codependent and suicidal, Sarah had been married to an abuser and manipulator. Now she shared a van with a man who knew his demons and worked diligently to keep them in the past. We were each in awe of one another's transformation. On *Grace* and in grace, living one day at a time.

It was in the simple witnessing of how they spoke to Sarah, asking her questions and expressing encouragement, that I learned a new standard for what support looks like. How strange it felt to be in the presence of a happy marriage. And without knowing about their painful past, how could I truly appreciate their effort?

We said our goodbyes, and as we walked up the steps, a weeping sound echoed across the marina. This time it wasn't Molly's laugh but her wailing cry. Was she sad to see us go, or was it her gratitude that couldn't be contained? Perhaps it was both. After all, her marriage had survived, gifting her these precious moments. Her daughter had survived too, finding love again.

Grace—what a great name for a boat, what a great word to capture it all. (For the full story, read Sarah May's memoir: *She Journeys*.)

Perspective met purpose while traveling in 2020, and things like clean air and hot showers took on new appreciation. Life on the road, free from airline tickets and TSA timelines, also blessed us with the extra minutes to go beyond the surface and into the depths of our pasts.

Smoke, trees, and sweet salt breeze, north was getting as high as the latitudes allowed. The friendly neighbors above put up their own proverbial wall, and the border to Canada remained shut since March 21, 2020. (It reopened August 9, 2021 for fully vaccinated Americans only.)

Off I-5 again and onto two-lane sweetness, WA-20. Our time to head east had arrived, or so we thought …

Chapter 13
World War Flea

I HATE THE smell of anti-itch cream in the morning. You know, one night I got eaten alive for eight hours. When it was all over, I woke up. They were everywhere, every stinkin' bite. The smell, you know that hydrocortisone smell—the whole tube—smelled like ... (sniff) ... defeat.

Into the heart of darkness we went, through the shadowy forests of the Pacific Northwest, inland to North Cascades National Park. Droplets built on the tips of Douglas Fir needles that occasionally fell onto the van's roof. *Pit-pit ... pit ... pit-pit-pat.* It had rained all night, but the real lightning happened under the sheets. Sounds frisky, but I assure you it was *not*.

This wasn't the first morning of itchy despair. The war had been waging for weeks, first starting in Bend, Oregon. *Mosquito bites?* Nope, they kept coming. *Poison oak?* Maybe, but why are the bumps scattered? *Bed bugs?* Please, not bed bugs! *Fleas?* But how? We don't have any pets. (I know what you must be thinking: *Yeah, yeah. Big shock. The couple who lives in a van parked in the forest, and went a month without a traditional shower, got a pest infestation.*)

According to Central Intelligence (the internet), flea bites usually occur on the lower body. The even more dreaded bed bugs prefer the flesh of the upper body. We first tested the bed bug or flea experiment in Bend by trashing our pillows and comforter, then washing all our bedding and clothes on high heat, followed by extra spins in an industrial dryer. To my relief, it had worked, and my bites began to heal.

Sing some Hootie with me—*Tiiiiime ... why you punish me?*

The clock ticked and, unbeknownst to us, the fleas had laid eggs throughout our mattress. And time, well … it gave those tiny flea eggs room to incubate, and the larvae mined our mattress, setting the stage for one epic battle. Three weeks later, with a wounded man wrapped in an orange towel neck brace, they attacked. And they fought with the honor of Samurai avenging their fallen ancestors.

We traced our memories to the potential culprits: that one dog we befriended on the Simian River? Or was it the other puppy outside Yachats? Let me explain. It was 2020, I had hugged maybe seven people since March. (I used to hug at least seven people a day.) Loving on friendly dogs brought normalcy to an atypical time. Now, a few furry pets had led to weeks of struggle. And if it were going to end, we would need some weapons. Something destructive and toxic. Something nuclear and radioactive. Something like a four-dollar bug bomb.

Our van, which usually breathes the life of fresh plants and scents of pine, would have to be flooded with poison. Chemical warfare, a pest genocide. This posed an undesirable living situation for a couple that usually spends the extra ten cents per banana to get the organic.

It was time to retreat. To a … *hotel*. Gasp. The *h*-word meant bust over boondock. It meant more than dipping further into our travel funds than my tight fists desired. It meant defeat.

Surrender was only one of many obstacles. North Cascades National Park had no exterminator, hotel, or cell phone service. So, Sarah and I drove the ninety minutes back to the town of Burlington to score the weapons. We needed a hotel cheap enough so that I would sign the treaty, yet clean-looking enough that Sarah would approve. She did have a point. After all, the only thing worse would be trading the fleas for bed bugs. (Okay, maybe crabs would be worse. Actually, crabs would definitely be worse.)

But where does one purchase this chemical weaponry? Your best bet is from the arms dealers in blue vests. These dealers, or Walmart associates as they're usually called, come in various forms. There's the old, Velcro shoe seniors. The immigrants grateful for work but pissed at whichever forefather came up with *the customer's always right* doctrine. Of course, there's also the made-too-many-Cs-in-business-school-managers who run the place. And let us not forget the grunts, those still chipper teens who aren't yet jaded enough to begrudge the work. These young soldiers are the most concerning. They work hard and haven't been ruined by years of low-paying, monotonous, how-did-I-end-up-here labor. They still have ambitions, but they also have a desire to wreak havoc. I know because I was one.

You read that right, for two glorious years I did my time in the blue. I even held a few records. Like the youngest to win the Four Star Cashier Award. (A prize that came with a coveted maroon vest, which felt like winning the Masters.) I also recorded the most consecutive weeks with the highest IPH—that's Items Per Hour, a cashier's batting average which tracks the rate you ring customers up. I often remind Sarah what a decorated Walmart employee I was, though I wouldn't recommend this as a strategy to make a woman swoon.

Of course, there's a dark side to working for such an enterprise, and my own eyes have seen it all. I once watched a kid break free from a kidnapper in the parking lot. I've seen an infant take a poop on a register's conveyor belt. (The cashier washed it and people were placing their cilantro on top of it again within minutes.) My fellow teenage colleagues and I even created our own secret lingo, where we developed a system that involved announcing on the intercom, across the entire supercenter, "H.W.B. register 4. H.W.B., register 4." This meant an attractive young lady—or Hottie with a Body, as we called them back then—had been located at register 4. My fellow grunts and I *might* have stolen stuff too, a lot of stuff. But I can't emphasize the word *might* enough, because I'm not sure what the statute of limitations is on these sorts of things.

And despite my glory years donning a blue vest that was pinned with medallions like a Four-Star General, Sarah still thought she knew it all. Anytime we walked past the sliding doors, she always held firm that she knew her way around Walmart better than I did. Our bug bomb purchase proved no different.

"I think it will be this way, near the home goods," she said.

"No, babe, trust me. I know Walmart. I bet it's in the garden center," I said.

"No way," she argued, "follow me."

Now came the real test. You know, the who-is-right, make-matters-worse, test. Sarah and I separated, only to learn that Walmart, of course, was the real winner. We met back up five minutes later, both with the same product. What kind of mind games have these Walmart generals been up to? Same product, two different locations. We avert the *who is right* conundrum. We were both right. Now, we both love Walmart more. But back to those dern fleas!

In the hotel's parking lot, I gripped the bug bomb tightly in my sweaty palm. Sarah, my honorable comrade, had volunteered to detonate the bomb. We discussed it at length, strategizing who should take the leadership role in such a historical military operation. Heck, Sarah had devised the strategy. Yet, for some reason, I insisted that *I* press the button. And once I did, there would be no going back.

Hesitation is the luxury of more stable men. Any more thinking and I would talk myself out of it. After all, who wants to bomb their own home?

Do it. Just do it, I told myself. The skin covering my lower legs blazed with an intense fury. This was no Cold War. No, this war was hot, and the tensions had escalated. My enemy had mastered the art of stealth warfare, and I had paid the price. Vengeance is not the finest of intentions, but it gave me sufficient motivation. There must be retaliation. There must be blood.

I held my breath and pressed down on the top of the bomb. It started to hiss violently. I set it on the floor in the center of our home, then darted out the side, and slammed the door shut. Toxic chemicals filled Rudy's walls. On the outside, I kept my poise. On the inside, I yelled, *"DIE YOU BASTARDS, DIE!"*

Into the heart of darkness. Into the hotel.

The horror. The horror.

Watching a couple with a reservation for one night bring in two bell-cart loads of stuff, ranging from pots and pans to coconut oil and a coffee grinder, must have given the receptionist some theories. *"Welcome to Burlington, Washington. Come for the meth, stay because you sold your RV for the meth."*

Navigating a hotel in times of COVID was one challenge, but ethically ridding ourselves of fleas without spreading them to others was even more complicated. If you ever find yourself in such a predicament, here are your marching orders:

1. *Acquire appropriate armor.* (Our "city clothes" were uncontaminated because they had been secured in a different area of the van's storage space.)
2. *Surround the enemy.* (Place contaminated clothes/bedding in a sealed laundry bag. These will either need to be nuked, or simply washed and dried on extra-high heat. The laundry bag will need to be sterilized as well.)
3. *Establish a safe house.* (Place the contaminated laundry bag in the laundry room. Start the washing process. Hot water, extra hot dryer.)
4. *Secure barracks.* (Go to the hotel room and immediately take a hot shower without sitting on or touching any furniture. Place the clothes you were wearing in a plastic bag.)
5. *Counterattack.* (Clean, and in your uncontaminated clothes, bring the outfit that you were wearing to the battlefield. Finish washing all clothing.)

6. *Minimize civilian casualties.* (Prep for the bug bomb by removing all food-related items from the van including spices, dishes, and cooking ware. Any dishes not removed should be thoroughly washed after. Remove anything else you don't want exposed to the toxins like toiletries.)
7. *Prepare for detonation.* (Disconnect all electricity. For us, this meant shutting off our solar charge controller and opening the circuits from our battery bank.)
8. *Take no prisoners.* (Seal all ventilation by closing the windows, doors, and fan.)
9. *Get ready for the launch.* (Detonate the bug bomb.)
10. *Improve troop morale.* (Enjoy cheap Mexican food whilst watching recycled blockbusters on cable TV like *Point Break* and *Tombstone*. Try not to think about the chemical fallout occurring in your living space.)

Five applications of anti-itch cream, four loads of laundry, three hot showers, two neck rubs, and one continental breakfast later, we moved back into Rudy.

Thank heavens, it worked. Yet, everyone knows the battle doesn't end when you leave the war front. I developed what I coined: FLEA-T.S.D. I lost sleep every night for nearly a month, scratching at any sensation on my legs as I lay in bed. I even had dark dreams about bug infestations. In this paranoid state, I avoided using certain pillows, thinking they might still be infected.

Adventure occurs in many forms, but it rarely happens when everything goes as planned. But what is a trip without some extension out of the comfort zone? Answer: a vacation. And to make van life a vacation would be the worst strategy of all.

Long trips had prepared me for times like this. Those rare windows when I wanted to be *Home*, or my old home I should say, in a broader bed, away from the bugs, smoke, and rainy days. This stretch—roughly four days out of five months of tramping—was the only time I wanted to be *somewhere else*. Considering all the pre-Rudy days I dreamt of traveling, they're odds I'll take. After all, the cost of freedom has justified many wars.*

*An enormous amount of fleas were harmed in the creation of this story.

Chapter 14
Sights, Sounds, and Selfies

THE SKY WENT from gray to black to blue. A vibrant, brightening blue. A blue that expanded irises and lifted spirits, a blue that should never be neglected.

Bombs had rid bugs, the rain had extinguished fires, and something Almighty made the clear sky oh so precious. Our hiking boots skipped with the glee of humming wings. We stripped off layers of raincoats and sweaters, peeled back strata of gloom and longing, and cast aside desires for old places and tempting comforts. Another mile, another vow: *Appreciate the blue of a smokeless sky, even when heat wants me to curse the sun in my eye.*

Atop Cascade Pass, visibility opened up, revealing a neon valley with lines of snow-tipped peaks. Worthy of the nickname, "the American Alps," the Northern Cascades were order-less yet commanding. In the Sierra Nevada, the western slope is vastly different from the eastern. And the Cascades had their own duality, with the southern volcanoes standing isolated and lonely, while the northern peaks huddled together like breeding emperor penguins, innumerable and congested.

The clean air delivered a natural high, and we hiked on. Charcoal-colored marmots, plump and fearless, poked out from scree fields to screech. A black bear pulled weeds and flexed with each saunter. Pika squealed and disappeared. Millennials staked out the best views from

Sahale Glacier and crunched granola bars and crackers dipped in hummus. Indeed, life was bright again.

On the descent, another color caught my eye: Fightin' Texas Aggie maroon, the shade of my alma mater Texas A&M University. A quartet of new grads, two females and two males, bobbed down the trail ahead of us. Sarah and I were gaining ground on them, and I calculated that we would pass them in two minutes' time. Time to reflect on a town that I left behind. A place where I traded brain cells for booze and hours for a degree.

My first day there, I realized that most people looked like me but dressed like Chuck Norris. It left me strangely homesick for the diverse neighborhood I grew up in. A large percentage were from towns I never heard of. From these classmates, I heard time and time again, in that uncanny Texas tongue, "Yer tha first Jew I ever met!"

So, in college I was a lot of people's *first*, just not in the way I had anticipated.

Conformity is a parasite on a college campus. Perhaps the strongest example I've seen is Texas A&M, where Aggies claim to "bleed maroon." There, students actually hiss at the nonconformists. No joke, anytime you don't participate in the hundreds of school traditions they make a snake-like sound, as obnoxious and creepy as you might imagine. If the hissing isn't cult-y enough, it's also accompanied by a hand gesture. They call the nonconformists "2 percenters" (based on the theory that 98 percent drink the Kool-Aid).

Nevertheless, there are two things Aggies are not short on—friendliness and manners. Two traits I lacked in my four years there. I drank at work, at school, at bars, and in the shower. I bullied classmates and annoyed my professors. I'm still recovering from the three A's: alcoholism, atheism, and asshole-ism.

In the Northern Cascades, trekking not-easy-to-get-to mountains, I was actually excited to see some alumni. I promised myself I would say *howdy* and not tell any of my bro tales. After all, these Aggies were enjoying places I was too sick to see at their age.

"Hey, some fellow Aggies," I said.

"Hey! Yes. What year are you?" one woman replied.

"2008. What about ya'll?"

"2019."

"Ah, fresh grads. What did you study?" I asked.

"Mechanical engineering."

"Electrical engineering."

"Aerospace engineering."

"Petroleum engineering."

That's a lot of protractors. The six of us hiked out together, discussing their travels. Then, back at Rudy, I got my pop quiz.

"Hey, can we see the van?" one of the young women asked.

Sarah slid open the big side door where most people spent their time on the tour, talking about plants and crystals. However, engineers ask different questions. So, we moved the group to the rear cargo doors. Their questions came one by one, the answers found in the garage (the storage area under the bed).

"How is everything powered?" said the mechanical engineer.

"There's 300 watts of solar on the roof." I grabbed our giant backcountry packs that never got used and threw them to the ground. Behind them was an array of cords and devices.

The electrical engineer of the group chimed in. "How long can you go without any sun?"

"Well, this has been our longest stretch yet with the smoke and the rain. I guess about four days, depending on how much the fridge kicks on."

"And how about water?" asked the aerospace engineer.

Sarah pointed them to the left side of the garage, where five six-gallon jugs lined the wheel well. "So," Sarah said, "we designed it to be able to go off-grid for at least a week. We have two of these jugs inside under the sink: one for gray water, one for fresh. In total, we carry thirty gallons of fresh water when fully stocked."

"If you don't mind me asking," said the petroleum engineer, "how much did it all cost?"

"Don't mind at all," I said. "The van we bought used for $22,000, then add a couple thousand more for taxes and registration. For the build we spent about ten grand. All in, what you see is about $35,000. When we get back, if we have the money, we want to put some more into it. Get a proper propane system for the oven, install a heater, and figure out a better shower system."

We gave them some stories: the toilet, the fleas, the propane fiasco. I watched eight eyeballs drift off, engineers designing what they would do with their own build. Perhaps we left them with something to think about. I know they left me with the contagious vitality that the young transmit.

They wished us well on our trip. We wished them well in their new post-college lives. I didn't have the gumption to say, "Gig 'em," nor did I start bleeding maroon. But I did have a smile. I suppose maturing means not being the worst parts of our younger selves. Perhaps Aggies weren't the problem after all.

Let it be known that Rudy never played the Beatles or a country song, nor did he struggle through rural radio. More often than not, Rudy resembled a British disco or the best gay club you've ever been to. *That's right*, Rudy raves as well as he roars and rumbles.

The soundscape is a necessary sidekick to the moving landscape. As with most mornings, I felt like dancing. "You Make Me Feel" by Sylvester had Sarah's shoulders bouncing and my free hand vogueing. WA-20 was a route worthy of celebration as Rudy coasted down the eastern slopes of the Northern Cascades. My disco queen crown sat atop my house head as the eastern vista revealed the prettiest hills I have ever seen.

The town of Winthrop was worthy of a stay and a desire to return. WA-20 went as much south as it went east, following a river until our road merged with wider ink and the water merged with a broader flow. "Finally Ready" produced by The Shapeshifters and sung by Billy Porter, beat the next morning's dance party on the stereo. WA-97 had us bumping hips with the Columbia River. Livestock ranches gave way to sprawling orchards.

Roads on the east side of the Columbia lost variety. Though the highway numbers changed, the crop did not. Macintosh to Granny Smith, Pink Lady to Honeycrisp, apples for the whole world to crunch. A good audiobook makes the Earth spin at the right speed. The perfect narration for Washington helped bring interest to less interesting sights. *Boys in the Boat* played until we made it to the Walla Walla, Washington Walmart—good for alliteration and a night's rest.

A new day and a return to Oregon. Garfield Fleming's "Don't Send Me Away" pleased the ears while cattle farm after cattle farm seared the nostrils. OR-82 was our saving grace, Smokey Robinson the savored sound. We chanted, "Go Rudy, go!" as the low gears struggled to take our heavy home to higher grounds, up mountains and past pines, back to the highlands of the bearded and flannel-wearing. The town of Enterprise, Oregon, was good for maps and groceries. Leaving town, no tunes could drown out the jostling of our cabinets as we rode over washboard dirt. Miles into the dark forest, we set up camp in the Eagle Cap Wilderness.

With the engine off, nature played DJ. The gurgling Lostine River slid over rocks and under footbridges. That night the *ping-ping* of continuous rain went open to close and into the after party of the next day. Sarah and I shared the van, breathing in the clouds of each other's exhales. Fall had arrived, and maybe winter too. With cabin fever taking over, we set out on foot for a long hike. An unforeseen snowstorm found us on the way out and most of the way back. The call to go south was there, but I rarely listen the first time.

It was a cloudy and cold scene on a road with no lanes. Eastward, on the rural route to the Hell's Canyon Overlook, ID-71 proved that the journey is more important than the destination, for the canyon overlook was underwhelming, but the drive out reigned supreme. Brene Brown's *Unlocking Us* podcast played away, unless the occasional pause came so Sarah and I could discuss the vulnerable thoughts of the day.

In Ontario, Oregon, at the Pilot gas station, we experimented with our first truck stop shower, which sounds like a great way to get athlete's foot or a staph infection. However, for twelve dollars, we shared what resembled the bathroom portion of a Holiday Inn Express. It was one of the top ten showers of my life, and bathing was now some kind of aphrodisiac. (Bumper sticker idea: When the van shakes, hit your brakes.)

American journalist Charles Kuralt once said, "Thanks to the Interstate Highway System, it is now possible to travel across the country from coast to coast without seeing anything." Thankfully we had the oversaturated podcast industry. *The Joe Rogan Experience* played on, with UFO experts, comedians, and investigative journalists helping pass the time. I-84 took us to Boise, a municipality with laws prohibiting people from sleeping in their vehicles; Rudy went into stealth mode.

Back on I-86 to Rexburg, Idaho, where we stepped into a Walmart, and a mystery. Everyone looked twenty years old, mostly blonde and tall, shirts tucked in, and hair clipped tight. Locals smiled and said hello. I had so many questions, like why was everyone so tall, blonde, and kind? Wikipedia gave the answers. BYU-Idaho explained the big temple atop the hill, a university of 27,000 students in a town that is 95 percent Mormon.

Lastly, I must recognize one of the most beautiful sounds to life on the road—the absence of the stereo. I reserve this for those proper moments when the land is too beautiful, the air so clean, and the mind just as clear. When it's time to hit the mute button and lower the windows as far south as they will go. When it's time to welcome the irreplicable harmony of wind and open road. Such was the sound entering Montana.

"Take my photooo," said a high, whiney, female voice. She was in her early twenties, coated with enough makeup for the red carpet.

Her significant other wore khaki shorts with a can of bear spray fastened to his belt like a gun holster. She jammed the newest iPhone into his hands. He held it up, capturing the pose—arm bent, lips pursed, chin down.

This wasn't a gala or an award show. No, it was Yellowstone National Park. Behind her the Grand Prismatic Spring occupied the valley floor. A sapphire center, aquamarine border, sunshine-yellow ring, and an outer orange crust that bled into the gray ground. It is undeniably Earth's most beautiful boil. And now, the setting for a never-ending photo shoot.

The young woman stuck out her left hand. A sparkle from her diamond engagement ring caught the reflection of the sun. She took the phone to scrutinize the picture. Her glossed upper lip curled with disgust. She swiped right. Her lower lip coiled with rejection. She jammed the phone into her fiance's chest.

"Ummm," her voice whined like a toddler without a toy, torturing each vowel, "yuu haave to taake liike a buunch of umm! Yuu ownlee took wuun!"

"Okay," he mumbled.

He aimed the iPhone and started snapping away. The vowel killer moved her head to the left, to the right, and down. She shifted her arms, tilted her hips one way, then the other. She smiled, then got serious, then found a demeanor in between, contorting her face so hard she appeared to be holding in one righteous fart. The girl wasn't a model or a celebrity, nor did she have some type of mental handicap (at least none yet defined by the American Medical Association). And he wasn't a professional photographer or a servant of the royal family. Still, the photo shoot clicked away, and behind Mr. Saving-For-Divorce, a crowd of twenty people waited their turn for a chance at the same backdrop and the same self-absorbed souvenir.

I sensed Sarah's eyes in my periphery. She wanted to see my face *so bad*, to witness my judgments gurgling over like the geothermal vent. But I couldn't let that happen. I would lose it and say something that would make Mr. Better-Have-A-Prenup's life worse than it already was. Instead, I shook my head and rolled my eyes. Then imagined Teddy Roosevelt running up the trail and bull-rushing the crowd, yelling so loud that the girl stumbled back, fell off the cliff, and landed in the boiling sulfuric concoction below. And when Mr. I-Like-Them-Basic went to use his bear spray, he realized he didn't have enough time to finish reading the directions before the twenty-sixth president slapped the tighty whities right off of him.

To say I came to Yellowstone with the wrong expectations is an understatement. For this was my first visit to the first national park in the entire world. A place that has posted at its entrance: FOR THE BENEFIT AND ENJOYMENT OF THE PEOPLE. An asterisk should be added—*Should the people desire to benefit themselves.*

I read a rumor that 95 percent of the four-million-plus annual visitors to Yellowstone National Park stay within view of their car. Apparently, all the National Park Service needs to do to motivate the masses to walk more would be to put a mural of butterfly wings a couple of miles into the forest or paint the side of a mountain turquoise with an inspirational quote like, "Not all who wander are lost." Hordes of people would migrate. Photo shoots would capture every angle of one's face. Filters would eliminate every shade of honest lighting. And narcissism would continue its rampant plague across the globe.

Sarah and I had visited six national parks so far this trip. Simplicity and solitude amid a serene setting still survives, camouflaged and harder to find than the places exploited by the vanity economy. Parking lots overfilled, iPhones extended, drones buzzing, and stories getting uploaded with each brunch bite and deer sighting. Here, I go down the judgment rabbit hole until I remind myself that at least *some* of these people, who range from tweens to selfie-stick seniors, will find a moment in nature that will give the revelations that a thumb scroll cannot.

If this sounds like the ramblings of a critical and crusty old man, then at least I looked the part. Gone are the days of throwing on boots and recklessly meandering down the *very strenuous* trails. Hiking through the park I realized I resemble a dad, wearing zip-away pants with cargo pockets, a full-brimmed sun hat, and a knee brace (or two, depending on the day). A twenty-minute ritual now pre-games each hike: sunscreen application, hiking pole assembly, ample water and snack preparation, plus coating areas of my feet prone to blisters with Bag Balm—a product originally invented to stop cows' tits from chafing.

Furthermore, I'm not immune to milking the narcissistic nipple. This SPF-protected elder millennial takes some photos and watches his girlfriend do the same. Though thank God Sarah has dialed in the daily limit when I start rolling my eyes and begin griping. If I'm on good behavior, I find patience by reminding myself how many pointless arguments I got into with ex-girlfriends when they wanted a photo shoot and I wanted to hike or simply sit and stare. I wish I could say these arguments happen less frequently because I have grown so much, but the truth is it's because Sarah's photo-taking is just more time efficient.

Honestly, I don't know what's more narcissistic—posting a bunch of photos of your trip or writing an entire book about it. Hell, if I wrote something that got quoted on Instagram as much as John Muir's, "The mountains are calling and I must go," then I would probably fall asleep with a self-righteous smile every night. However, I can only wonder if Muir would be enthralled or disgusted by each national park selfie queue. In the meantime, one can hope for a world where people lead lives that are not centered around the idea that if *you* like my life, then maybe *I* will like my life.

Chapter 15
The Neighborhood

SARAH AND I cruised around Yellowstone National Park, taking long hikes to mountaintops, canyons, and waterfalls. The boondock or bust mentality took us through four of the five park entrances in search of free camping. Rudy's odometer ticked away. We camped up mountainsides, next to gutted buffalo carcasses, and in areas that prohibited tent camping (too many grizzlies). We had no cellular service except for our final night, tucked in the flat-forested land outside the town of West Yellowstone, Montana. There, we spent the post-supper hours glued to our phones, exercising our thumbs as we caught up on the news of the globe.

Armed with popcorn and chocolate chips, YouTube played the first presidential debate of the season. We watched it a day late, but a lifetime too soon. If I ever see a presidential debate more immature than that, tattoo George Washington's face on my ass, slap my butt cheeks commie red, and call me an ex-pat.

The following morning brought more drama. Trump had COVID. Big shock? Not really. It would be like finding out Joe Biden had erectile dysfunction. But how serious was Trump's condition? No one knew.

We said goodbye to cell signal and set off for our last day in the Disneyland of national parks. Old Faithful was true to form, underwhelming me right on time. Yellowstone Lake rippled with the late afternoon wind. I was the only fool in early October eager for a swim, but I had odor and judgments to repent. I resurfaced with life feeling far from numb.

Outside the park, we pulled down a dirt road. Campers overran each plot of land. Summer had ended, but America's rush to the road was still coasting in high gear. Yellowstone tallied almost 360,000 visitors in October 2020, the busiest October in park history (and more than double the amount of October 2019). One after another—RVs, trucks with toppers, vans, tents, and trailers—filled the boon-docking spaces. Sarah turned Rudy around and pulled us into a crowded clearing. The area was designed for four rigs, Rudy became the eighth. By nightfall, a dozen vehicles squeezed in, ranging from a forty-foot Class A coach to someone crashed out in the passenger seat of a Honda Civic.

Rudy settled in nicely with a remarkable view. A flowing creek separated the lot from lush marshlands and meadows. Beyond rolled green mountainsides with round, forested peaks. The creek water was mixed with the flow of geothermal activity, making it lukewarm. A mile away was a natural hot spring. It was the boondocker's bull market, and we had picked the right stock.

Turns out that even nomads have neighborhoods. We had found our kin. License plates came from far and near: Rhode Island, Utah, California, Texas, Oregon, and more. Sarah and I had been blessed with compatibility, but we spent most of our time isolated from others, longing for friends and social outings.

A nomad community shares some characteristics with the traditional neighborhood. Some neighbors over-talk, others want to be left alone. Some know wealth, others can't afford to keep up. Of course, the trampers' neighborhood has its differences. Attachments should be avoided because new friends come and go, as do the creepy characters you're not sure about. The most significant difference between a rubber and a brick neighborhood is the absence of the fence. Without the barricade, this nomad community flourished with the joviality people carry when they have wheels but no garage, when they have meadows, not lawns.

A circle formed outside Rudy. Millennials and boomers, Oregonians, Texans, and everything in between. Some owned gargantuan RVs, others slept in the bed of their pickup. All these people, with no bars of cell signal and no way to know who knew what, or how they felt about it.

"Did you hear the headline?" someone finally spoke up.

"Eh, I think Trump's diagnosis is just a show to make him appear tough," said the millennial from Oregon.

The old Texan quickly replied, his slow drawl hanging on to the end of each word, "I downt wan the president sick. I jus hope Me-lawn-yuh is oh-kay. I always thought tha best job woulda bin her bodyguard. I think I'da bin perfect for the role."

His wife rolled her eyes. Laughter eased the tension. Gone was the worry of the conversation going south. For up north, in the river-cut lands of Wyoming, Americans with divided political affiliations and varying bank account sizes discussed politics and news with the tones of mature friends. While the media attempted to keep everyone at odds, travel had created a safe space in a fresh setting. With no internet comments, people could look one another in the eye. I cherished the moment, as if finding something forgotten: people sharing land that did not share beliefs.

My biggest concern with so many neighbors in big rigs was the G-word. Not guns, God, or gonorrhea, but generators. Right on cue for dinner time, the sound of burning fossil fuels competed with the natural sound of running river. Generators buzzed through sunset until one by one, each household went to sleep. In the realm of the unregulated campground, quiet hours are etiquette and not enforced. So, relief came when the sound of crickets returned by 10 p.m. By 2 a.m., the hum of generators buzzed again, for it was October in Wyoming and temperatures rose to a mild 68 degrees during the day but dropped as low as 21 degrees at night. The next morning, my damp swimsuit was frozen stiff, as if it had been starched. Counting clouds of breath was like counting sheep, until hot tea and sunshine reminded us how worthwhile it all was.

America. No other nation has the history, the passion, or the revolving zeitgeist surrounding the road trip. Where else in the world can you find as many (or as massive) means to drive across a country? In our little neighborhood, you could find a young couple in a vintage trailer purchased on Craigslist for $3,000, or a luxurious fifth-wheel trailer that retailed for $120,000. The professional Winnebago edition of our van was parked two vehicles up and had been purchased for $110,000. Some rigs had giant antennas, which still failed to pull in any internet. Many generator-buzzing neighbors endured my sales pitch on the perks of solar power. Despite all my time on the road, it was an elderly neighbor (and first-time RV'er) who gave me the scoop on all the smartphone apps that had been created to help users find the best boondocking spots. To think I was so old-fashioned. Traveling should not be so easy, but hey, what roadie doesn't appreciate a good shortcut?

The economics of "camping" has always baffled me. RV parks ranged from $30/night to over $100/night. The closest one was charging $84/night. Most campgrounds cost $15 to $50 per night. And many didn't even offer real amenities like showers and flush toilets. Criticisms aside, without a reservation you were stranded anyway. Every campground was full, and would continue to be. With every reservation someone coddled with the security of having a place to sleep. Boondock or bust, why surrender the freedom that makes concrete flexible?

Our minimalist van was the best home we ever had. I couldn't imagine driving a Greyhound bus-sized RV, while the owners of motorhomes thought our van's small space was a great way to destroy a romantic relationship. Everyone had their preferences, and despite the equivalent of mixing mansions with shacks, no one seemed to care about property value.

The neighborhood was nourishment to the soul; Sarah and I got our social batteries recharged as one night extended into three. We didn't have exclusive ownership of the land, but I found it easier to trade my judgments for a generator. We had no fences to conceal our secrets, and no virtual firewalls to hide behind, but we did have community—and that felt more valuable than anything a mortgage could buy.

Fishing waders sagged off the old man's body. White tufts of hair poked out from his cowboy hat. His walking pole pressed into the river's bottom. His other hand held tightly to his son, who steadied the old man with his right arm and hauled the fishing gear with his left. Fly-fishing is mainly a solo activity: no talking required, adequate spacing a necessity. For some, the cast is as close to God as they get, a meditation of movement. The "tug is the drug," they say.

Fly-fishing seemed to be the cup of life for this senior, who refused to sit around in his old age. The elder moved one step at a time, through the river, up the sandy bank, and around the bend. My eyes blinked many times before the two vanished through the willows.

Hours went by with no sign of their return until I looked up from my book and found them in front of Rudy, sitting in their lawn chairs, staring ahead as if the meadow were a theater screen. The two looked nothing alike. The old man, Ray, was one month shy of ninety-two, maybe five feet six inches tall if you stretched his curved spine straight, and about as thin as his fly rod. His son, Darren, stood over six feet tall with lanky limbs and broad shoulders. Ray held on to a healthy amount of white hair and kept clean-shaven. Darren was fully bald with a bristly brown mustache and goatee.

Every neighborhood deserves a legend and Ray was ours.

"Heard you been comin' here a long time," I said.

"Fifty-three years," Ray replied. A sparkle of confidence shined from his blue eyes.

"Much change?"

"Gosh, everything was better—the fishing, less people, more elk, bear, and moose."

"He still caught seven fish today," his son gloated.

"Now the rangers can't keep up," Ray continued, "used to be four people in this place max. Often you could get it all to yourself."

Ray was born the same year as Papa Herb, with the same get-it-done attitude that made life long and interesting. I had called ole Herbie from the road a few times, checking on his health, sharing some travel stories, and surprising him when I said the van was still working. The more I talked to Ray, the more I missed my grandfather.

"That your RV over there?" I pointed to a small Class B Pleasure Way that looked to be about fifteen years old.

"Yup. It's my fifth RV. Downsized from a Class A after the wife passed away."

"Where did ya'll drive in from?" I asked.

"Two hundred forty-one miles away. Outside Logan, Utah. I used to be a farmer. I grew peas, sweet corn, and wheat. My son's an attorney."

"Took me twenty years of schoolin' to finally get my degree," he chimed in.

"Never thought he was gonna do it, but he pulled through," his father grinned.

Darren had been busy with van life. Not #vanlife—the post it, blog it, vlog it, like and subscribe to my channel van life. No, Darren was old school, a true predecessor, from the *Blue Highways* era of road tripping. And I gathered he thought the latest craze to be a bunch of, well, poppycock.

Parked in front of his father's small RV sat his 1978 Dodge Tradesman. The van was a strange shade of dark green, with a low roof and dark, tinted windows. Permit me some candor … the van looked creepy, like if it was parked outside your kid's playground, you would gather all the children and leave immediately. Darren offered me a tour, and I took my chances.

His van build occurred forty-two years before ours. Without YouTube or blogs, Darren took two years to complete the build. I ducked my head to enter, like Gandalf squeezing into Bilbo's hobbit hole. Surprisingly, the interior was not reflective of the exterior at all, in fact, the decor resembled a fancy old schooner with glossy wood lining the walls. A small sink, spice rack, and refrigerator took up the space behind the driver's seat. In the back, a full-size bed ran lengthwise with the van. Darren admitted needing to sleep diagonally to fit.

Now, Darren wanted to see what the kids who kept crowding his favorite fishing hole could pull off. We invited Ray, who opted to stare at the meadow. Darren followed me back to our van so that Rudy could undergo a thorough Boomer investigation.

Darren moved his bald head up and down, side to side, scrunched his bushy eyebrows together then spoke, "With this big door you gotta worry about the mosquitos."

I showed him how we fasten our bug screen with Velcro lining along the slider.

"And with that giant windshield you got too much cold air comin' in to keep it warm."

I showed him our window covers and the thermal curtain.

He lowered his head and gave it a little shake. The river sang its way over rocks as the attorney deliberated his closing statement.

"I wish I hadn't looked at yours. I didn't think I could be jealous, but I am. Ya'll did a really nice job."

"Thanks. I doubt it'll last forty-two years, but we're proud."

The tours concluded with an elder succumbing to the idea that the next generation might have something to offer after all, and a young admirer impressed by the resourcefulness of the pioneers who built with no technological crutches or look-at-me motivations. After all, what are generations without links of past and present, without hope and respect?

Jackson Hole is a great place to go if you like mountain towns with more facelifts than ski lifts. The town of Jackson, Wyoming, featured lots of traffic and lots of bars. The last time I was there, in 2008, I drank at one of those bars until I was told to leave. I stumbled to my family's rental, then threw up from the second-floor patio onto the lawn below. Hiking the next day was a nauseating experience. I blamed the altitude. Traveling while intoxicated just meant the same scene in a different zip code. Bars and beers, blackouts, then coming to. On these weekend getaways, little experience was had, no lessons were gained. Wherever I went, there I was.

Southbound on WY-89, the traffic lights disappeared. The highway curved and lifted, like the children's coaster at the amusement park: never too steep, never too sharp. South of Hoback Junction, near the Snake River, a giant moose ran out from the woods. Sarah slammed on the brakes, nearly colliding with the beast. The eight-foot herbivore awkwardly trotted off like a horse wearing sneakers on the wrong feet.

Sarah took a deep breath, I reached over and put my hand on her leg. She looked at me. Her emerald eyes swirled, making me blush. Between the two cabin bucket seats, an entire arm's reach separated the driver and passenger. I kept my hand on her side of the cab for several miles, palming Sarah's thigh or stroking her hair. We reflected on all the miles we had covered, not only as two roadies, but as two birds that had flown through many storms to find one another.

It had been over two months on the road. During this lengthy trek, checking multiple items off the bucket list, I hate to admit that I experienced a deep melancholy. The long-haul gloom, when not even movement and new experiences can brighten the inevitable— that every second of living doesn't feel euphoric. The cold posed a threat, but not as big of a threat as jaded thinking. Thankfully the driver determines their fate. They can keep on going, nose down and despondent, *or* they can take a turn and head somewhere different. Not a change in scenery but a change in perspective.

The year 2020 was full of change, unpredictable and complicated. Unlike those intoxicated trips with nothing gained, each sober mile of this journey offered an opportunity. After all, change is the great gift we all receive. Whether we open the package or not is our choice. Change has blessed my life over and over, yet I still default to resisting it. How can someone so adaptable be so stuck in their ways?

As the scenery and seasons transitioned, I felt that familiar resistance to change. The next morning, I chiseled a layer of ice off the windshield using a credit card. Below 7,000 feet, trees dropped dehydrated leaves. At higher altitudes, the branches swayed naked in the cold mountain wind. The sun worked harder to keep me happy. Rudy pointed south, towards the equator and the nearest city.

It was a three-state day thanks to WY-89's little dip into Idaho. We continued the latitudinal descent, to WY-30, into Utah, and through the Cache National Forest. We drove past barren hills speckled with wooly sheep, and ranches dotted with long-faced cattle. Magpies flew from fence post to power line, their white-tipped wings shining in the sunlight.

I had set out to jump in the lakes, to invigorate my vigor, to quell the overbearing mother of caution. I had kept my word alright, jumping in twenty-one lakes and many rivers. There were cold soaks with seals in the Northern Pacific, and hold-on-to-your-ankles baths in the rushing creeks of Northern California. Jenny Lake in the Grand Tetons marked the last cold swim of the year. As I reflected on this, the melancholy washed away, as did the fear of wondering what my life would be like if I failed to honor the commitments I make with myself.

Wyoming was gone, and the trip far from over. If I were going to head south with fresh wisdom, then a new intention would serve me better. To embrace the long haul, to truly evolve a vacation into a trip, meant not skirting around life's speed bumps. I could press the pedal, hoping the boredom would be left behind. Or I could put on a new pair of glasses, look out the same windshield, and see opportunity instead. Wherever I would go, there would be something to learn.

They say to be careful what you wish for, and intentions deserve that same caution, for you never know what lessons are around the bend.

Chapter 16
Salt Lake Pity

A MILE UPHILL, my chest panted with shallow breaths. The well-groomed Salt Lake City neighborhood had taken us past various signs, from VOTE TRUMP 2020 to rainbow flags that drooped in the warm, windless evening. A red light brought us to a halt. Above, a dozen college students packed onto a tiny apartment balcony. The sound of hip-hop blasted through the open door, a Black Lives Matter banner hung from the railing.

In front of us, a dozen vehicles ranging from small sports cars to a full-sized fire truck drove by with horns honking and banners waving: KEEP AMERICA GREAT, TRUMP 2020. We kept walking until we hit the cross streets of University and 200, on the University of Utah campus, where we spotted the demonstration.

A young Black woman wearing all black squeezed a megaphone, her voice rattling through the speaker. "Fuck Donald Trump!"

The crowd, also dressed mostly in black, masks covering their mouths, shouted back. "FUCK DONALD TRUMP!"

She repeated the chant. The crowd yelled it again.

I grabbed Sarah's hand, pulling her body in closer. After camping, coming to a big town always felt overwhelming, and cities felt downright oppressive. That described normal days. This was *not* a normal day.

I looked at my phone to check the time. In a matter of minutes, Vice President Mike Pence and Senator Kamala Harris would be taking their seats across the street in Kingsbury Hall for the Vice-Presidential Debate. I had read that twelve feet of space and two Plexiglass walls would separate the candidates, an unusual layout at an extraordinary time. Most political pundits agreed: this VP debate would be one of the most important in US history. After all, their bosses were the two oldest presidential candidates ever. Not to mention, President Trump was still recovering from COVID-19. Outside the auditorium, a different scene was unfolding.

"Respect the constitution!" A White woman in her twenties screamed into a megaphone. She wore a red shirt, with perspiration building on her upper lip.

"RESPECT THE CONSTITUTION!" a few supporters repeated.

I turned my head to the right, back to the crowd of liberal protestors.

"Justice for Breonna Taylor!" The woman in black chanted into her megaphone.

The protestors chanted it back.

Through the chaos, I read some of the picketing signs. There was the usual: DUMP TRUMP. And the more shocking: DON'T VOTE FOR JOE "CHILD MOLESTER" BIDEN.

Back-to-back, two rows of police officers separated team liberal from team MAGA. The stoic cops stood shoulder-to-shoulder, gripping riot shields, wearing helmets with clear face masks and bulletproof vests. Pistols, assault rifles, tasers, and batons at the ready.

"Blue lives matter!" The woman in red screamed into her megaphone.

The Republican protesters shouted it back. Though their group was about double the size of the liberals, their chants were disjointed and a fraction of the volume.

Standing in the center, I surveyed from side to side. Despite the barricade of cops, I could walk from the liberal side to the MAGA side with disconcerting ease. And I did, feeling the atmosphere and observing the people, until I retreated back to the undeclared spectator section. Then, I heard it. Music. My eyes scanned the crowd. On the corner of the street, a Black man in pressed jeans and a fitted navy blazer blew into his saxophone. He put his whole body and soul into the notes as the sweet sounds of soft jazz competed for attention. Had anyone else noticed? The evidence seemed to say no. But I took it in, getting lost in his music, allowing the melody to lift me out of my concerns, if only for a moment.

To my left, a drag queen in a sequin red and blue dress stomped with high heels through the throng of Trump supporters. The dress sparkled against the setting sun. Across her chest, a beauty sash read, "Lady MAGA." She stopped her procession and stood right next to me. With her selfie-stick extended, she recorded on Instagram Live. "And there's the liberals. Look at how few there are. It's pathetic."

Is there a word for when you experience culture shock in your own country? To put it simply, I was overwhelmed. Gone were the privileged days of off-the-grid living, jumping in mountain lakes, secluded from the troubled times.

A shouting match began, each command originating from either of the women gripping megaphones. They yelled like protesting was a contest and the winner would be declared not through logic or reason, but by the old metric of who could yell the loudest.

"Black lives matter!" "BLACK LIVES MATTER!"

"Blue lives matter!" "BLUE LIVES MATTER!"

The woman in red ordered a new chant. "Four more years!"

"FOUR MORE YEARS!" The right-wingers, now united, drowned out the smaller, liberal group. The call for Black lives faded into the background. My head swiveled from left to right, the air reeking of aggression.

Sarah nudged me. "We should get going. I don't think it's safe here. Look at all the cops coming."

Back towards Rudy, a fleet of large cargo vans emptied scores of police in full riot gear. A barricade of officers formed between us and our van. The megaphone and chants echoed through the street. It was a far cry from inside Kingsbury Hall, where the debate rules required the audience not to make any noise.

Sarah and I started walking, unsure if we could get back to Rudy. Following us was a dozen right-wing protestors, who picked up their pace, jogging towards the police officers.

The officers faced the intersecting street, riot gear clenched tightly in their fists. Racially diverse, the cops were all males, disclosing no emotion with their hard stares. Did they resent the protestors? Or did they hate the cops who abused their power and now put targets on their back? I assumed the one thing the officers didn't feel was the apathy they portrayed.

I turned to see what the police were anticipating. Roughly thirty people, dressed in all black, marched towards the cops, their banners printed with BLACK LIVES MATTER. Their chants grew louder and louder:

"WON'T START NO SHIT, WON'T BE NO SHIT!"

A White woman wearing a red MAGA hat jumped on top of a concrete barrier. "Get out of here, you hood motherfuckers! Who you gonna call when you're in trouble? Huh? Who the fuck you gonna call?"

A lanky college student to my left yelled back at her, "And who you gonna call when your husband can't sexually please you?"

Laughter awkwardly spread through the crowd.

The marching protestors continued getting closer, a standoff in the making. The group stopped face-to-face with the police barricade. The tension intensified, a palpable hostility. The one with a megaphone called for the next chant.

"BLACK LIVES MATTER, BLUE LIVES DON'T!" the group repeatedly yelled into the faces of the police.

My stomach churned. A nervous nausea took over as the chant continued echoing through the streets.

Sarah and I cut through the crowd, walking through the protestors and around the police. The rich scent of herbal smoke opened my nasal passages and slowed my progress. I turned to see what it was. A Native American woman was burning sage, her bare feet pressed into the road's black tarmac. She wafted smoke over the police officers, one-by-one, chanting, her prayers barely audible as the crowd roared on.

From crowd chaos to killer quiet, Sarah and I rolled Rudy across the darkening streets of Salt Lake City. Two sunsets ago, we had watched the sky change colors over the Grand Tetons. Stars came out one by one while we silently took in the grandiosity. That silence felt organic, peaceful, and meditative. Now, in the cab of our van, the silence felt intentional, contemplative, and heavy.

A mobile billboard drove by: COVID VACCINE MAKERS EXEMPT FROM LIABILITY. Closed bars and breweries flew rainbow flags. A radio station's billboard paid its respects to Eddie Van Halen, who had died the previous day. Down the hill, the illuminated Latter-Day Saint headquarters commanded the skyline.

The red and white lights of an ambulance flashed in the parking lot of a decrepit motel. I didn't question what caused the emergency; I questioned whether it was heroin, meth, or fentanyl, and whether the first responders had arrived in time. (According to the CDC: 93,000 people died from overdoses in 2020—a record and a 29 percent increase from the previous year. This record would be broken in 2021, and again in 2022.)

The emotion in the air engrossed us, grimy and raw. I hoped some respite lay ahead, across the threshold of the restaurant we walked into. I was hungry: for dinner, for dialogue, for a reprieve from my own emotions. A hostess took us to an isolated booth in the far corner. The scents of cardamom, chili, fennel, and cumin did the dance from the kitchen to my nose. There were a few things I had been excited for in the city, and at the top of the list—Indian food.

"How you doin', sweets?" I reached across the empty table to put my hand on top of hers. Sarah looked at the ceiling, then at our intertwined fingers. Tears built in front of her green irises.

She shook her head, the right words a runaway train. "Everyone was just so angry. There was so much *hate*." She took her hand from mine and used the base of her palm to wipe her tears away. I handed her my napkin.

What followed was one of those difficult conversations that many of us had in 2020. It was a discourse that ruined many relationships, tore apart families, and disbanded groups of lifelong friends. But the conversations were vital, and Sarah and I could have ours privately without the fear of cancellation. We discussed race, leadership, and our country's challenges, and it only took a couple of bites until I realized that no matter how savory the food, the discussion was too sour. Somewhere in 2020, I had lost my optimism and couldn't find it on a menu.

Watching the news or reading articles had not prepared either of us to experience the division of the nation. I observed the two sides of America, with indignation in their eyes and righteousness cloaking their hearts, pull even further away from one another. Must we be so binary? Black Lives or Blue Lives? Democrat or Republican? Mask or no mask?

I had more emotions than I could name, more questions than answers. Yet all I had done was stand there. Silent. In my head. Wondering, but not acting. Then eating Indian food, hoping to forget it all, only to feel more guilty than ever.

After dinner, we cozied up in the van to watch the replay of the Vice-Presidential Debate. By the end of it, we were too exhausted to drive. The parking lot was dark, empty, and as quiet as one could hope for in a city. We covered the bunk windows and got under the blanket.

It was close to midnight when a noise startled me awake. I jolted up. Something right outside the window collided with a bush. I peeled off the window cover, careful not to wake Sarah. A woman in a long white robe, with olive skin and knotted chestnut hair, stood right outside the van. She turned around to face the window. Her untied robe slid open, revealing a black bra and panties.

She was unaware of my presence through the tint of our window. Then her pipe came out. Tainted red glass, burnt from regular use. She put a lighter to the bowl. The smell of burning crystal meth filled the dark corner of the parking lot. She exhaled a cloud of smoke.

Few things are more unpredictable than a person in the darkness of a meth high. I watched as her paranoia deepened and a shadow consumed her eyes. The only thing predictable was the pattern: light the pipe, inhale, exhale, look around, walk in a small circle, squat down, light the pipe, inhale, exhale …

Sarah woke up, leaning against me while we waited for an opportunity to leave without terrifying the stranger. The woman took another drag, and as soon as she turned around, I went to turn the key. We took off, seeking our own escape from the tragedies of today.

I wanted the move to feel safe. Instead, I was haunted by yet more cowardice. Is there much difference between a soldier leaving behind a wounded comrade in battle than one addict leaving behind a fellow addict in the struggles of life?

No strangers to addiction, both Sarah and I were raised by addicts. I had every intention not to become one and failed. Since recovering from alcohol addiction, I have dropped any delusional theory that one addiction reserves the right to look down on another. Sure, some are cleaner, less lethal, more accepted by society, and easier to hide. But at the core, the only difference I saw in myself and the woman in the robe was the substance we chose as our means to escape. Perhaps that's why my soul ached, leaving her behind without acknowledging her. Addiction—an evil teacher—had taught me that intervening at the wrong time is risky, dangerous, and almost always met with backfire. Addicts, and their loved ones, face this tragic dilemma every day.

In the course of one day around Salt Lake City, traces of addiction were seemingly everywhere. At the In-N-Out Burger, attached to the register was an advertisement for a charity supporting those suffering from substance abuse. At the store, I watched patrons pile barrels of candy into their shopping carts. On the streets, people pointed their heads down, scrolling on their phones as they walked by, ignoring one another. We drove through the city, with the Wasatch Mountains faded by layers of smog. We cruised by countless "massage" parlors, windowless to conceal their sexual offerings. We rode past several plastic surgeon advertisements, with billboards proclaiming what is sexy and what is not.

The consequences of our addictions have destroyed our cities and ravished our smallest towns. Maybe at one point, demographics mattered—whether rich or poor, rural or urban. But the new normal has no bearing on geography, politics, or class. Addiction knows many faces; discrimination is not one.

We found a safe location to stealth camp for the remainder of the night. Streetlights pierced through the cracks in the windshield cover, creating a faint glow in the van. Similar to Yachats, I knew I had just experienced a day that would stick with me for the rest of my life. But unlike that fateful day in the crystal store, the preservation of this memory wouldn't be about intuition or purpose. It was about how I lay awake that night, analyzing the roles I played, replaying every single action I didn't take, tormented by all the ways I knew I could be better. Perhaps it's more sustainable not to grow overnight, but yikes, how cruddy it felt.

Chapter 17
The Look of Mormon

SALT LAKE CITY was not all division and addiction. In fact, there was a place where everyone smiled and greeted one another with cheer. A place where the hospitality was so endearing that even the air seemed to wrap you in a warm, uncomfortably long hug.

The Latter-Day Saints (or LDS, commonly called Mormons) occupy most of the real estate in downtown Salt Lake City. There is the main temple, a large white building topped with the golden statue of Angel Moroni; the Salt Lake Tabernacle, which seats 8,000 people; the LDS Conference Center, which seats 21,000; two visitor centers; the extensive Family History Library (the LDS claim to house the largest collection of genealogical records in the world, with even more archives found nearby in a secured cave called Granite Mountain); and lastly, the Church Office Building, the second tallest building in Utah, where the LDS manage many things including its billions of dollars, wide-ranging enterprises, and charitable outreaches.

Driving through small towns in the Mountain West brings questions to the Google search box: *Why do the LDS meetinghouses have big satellites? Are outsiders welcomed in temples? Why are Mormons so damn friendly?* I needed answers.

Sarah was dressed in frayed denim shorts that concealed *most* of her butt. I wore a tank top with sweat glistening off my arms. We stood out in Temple Square like the Amish at an airport. Every woman, from teenagers to octogenarians, wore either full-length pants with long-sleeve blouses or dresses long enough they could easily be converted into a teepee. And the men, well, I saw no men. *Where were the men?* We saw only women, always walking in pairs, with metallic nametags pinned below their left collarbones. Everyone, *absolutely everyone*, said hello *and* did it with a smile. Not the smile you give to Susan in HR, or to the neighbor who doesn't pick up after his dog. No, a genuine, flexed cheek, I-mean-it-because-I-feel-it, Mormon smile.

"Hi." "Hello." Two female LDS missionaries worked their way towards Sarah and me.

"Hello," we said, smiling back. As the young women approached, I read the nametags pinned to their floral pioneer dresses. Maria had thick dark hair and Pacific Islander skin. Next to her smiled Elizabeth, who looked corn-fed, with farm girl knots of light brown hair. Both nametags had flags, neither of which I recognized.

"How are ya'll doing?" said Elizabeth.

"Doin' great, you?"

"Wonderful," said Maria, layering a smile on top of a smile. "Do you have any questions?"

My opportunity! Questions? I have more questions than a first date. What's it like being a woman in the church? Have you seen the play, The Book of Mormon? *Is "soaking" fact or fiction? And why is everyone so damn friendly?*

My mind scampered, yesterday's cowardice returned for a bitch slap. "Ummm, what are the little flags on your nametags?" I asked.

"Well," Elizabeth looked towards her nametag, "this is for New Caledonia. It's an island east of Australia. I'm from Montana, but I was about to head there for my missionary trip."

"Oh, I thought only the men went on missionary trips?"

"No, women do too. The men do two years. Women do eighteen months."

My mind raced. *How does that extra six months for the men make you feel? What's the training and preparation like? Do they teach you how to be friendly or is there something in the caffeine-free cola I'm missing out on?*

But my only reply was, "Oh, I didn't know that."

Silence. Smiles.

"And your nametag?" I said to Maria.

"Oh, this is French Polynesia. I'm from Tahiti."

"Tahitian Mormons?"

"Yup, my parents are LDS. They converted before I was born."

"So, what happened to all the missionaries during the pandemic?"

Maria continued, "Well, it was pretty crazy, as you can imagine. Most missionaries had to return to Salt Lake to finish serving their mission or await reassignment."

Of all the unintended consequences of the pandemic, this one had eluded me. How many aspiring Mormon leaders had their hard-earned conversion rates plummet? Did they give up and move on with their adulthoods? Or did they return to Salt Lake depressed, rip off their neckties, slam some espresso, and think of Timothée Chalamet naked?

Smiles. Silence.

"Well, let us know if you have any other questions. Enjoy your time in Temple Square!"

The only person who heard my dire questions was Sarah, on our drive away from Temple Square, towards the airport. Sarah was on her own spiritual quest and had commitments to attend to back in San Diego for the weekend.

Rudy idled a sad hum as I kissed my partner goodbye. Sarah and I had spent more time together in the last five months than I had with any other person in the previous five years. But there was solitude to be had, and I missed my alone time.

Or so I thought. Driving back into the city, I looked at the empty passenger seat for the first time and was overcome with grave-deep sadness. The emotion of missing someone. It was foreign to me. I didn't know what to do with the feeling, so I drove on thinking about how strange it was that I had lived over three decades and hardly ever missed someone. Never truly aching at a person's vacancy, never longing this painfully for their return. Not a family member. Not a significant other. Until now.

Rudy felt like a good home does. Not because of the bed or the food, the plants or the crystals, the surroundings or the freedom. No, the person I loved gave it that pajama-comfy warmth where my heart went to sleep.

I pulled into Sugar House Park in search of the perfect grassy knoll. Many young families were congregated there. Each time I caught the eyes of one of the mothers, I was met with a protective glare. These were not the stares I was used to from women. The mothers scowled at me, armed and defensive; for the first time in Mormon country, I felt unwelcomed.

I rubbed the thick curls of my beard that had not been trimmed since we left San Diego. My head hair was chaotic and unkempt. I had the tanned hide of a drifter. Then, the light bulb moment: *Ah! A lone man. With facial hair. Driving around a park in a big white van.* The only thing missing was a sign on the door that said, FREE CANDY.

Seventy-eight hours went by until I got to tell Sarah how vacant home felt without her, and how creepy I appeared driving Rudy on my own.

The Costco parking lot had more vehicles in it than a car dealership. I pulled Sarah away from the traffic, took her hands, and looked intensely into her eyes.

"I need you to hold it together in there."

She smirked.

"I'm serious. We live in a van. Not a house with a garage. There's no storage closet or basement. A van! With a fridge the size of an ice chest and a pantry the size of a ... actually we don't have a pantry."

She laughed.

"Sarah, this isn't a game. *This is Costco.* Now keep your shit together in there."

The pep talk was aimed at me as much as it was her. As minimalists, we should loathe Costco, avoid it at all costs, but what can I say … I'm a sucker for free samples, good deals, and five-dollar genetically modified rotisserie chickens. We walked through the sliding doors that were wide enough you could tow a yacht through. A greeter in a red vest gave a good Mormon smile. I flashed my black Executive Member card. The greeter nodded; we were in.

Golden plates and special underwear—what in tarnation is going on? TVs the size of garage doors rotated images of mountains in 4k. Stacks of survival buckets rose two stories tall, each one containing over 200 preserved meals. Two additional cross streets intersected towering rows lined with jugs of mayonnaise big enough to swim in and tubs of ketchup that weighed as much as a ten-year-old. This was no ordinary Costco. In fact, this was the largest Costco in the world. The interior covered 235,000 square feet—that's over five acres and as large as four football fields.

I have been to many Costcos in my life, but none as puzzling as this one. When I asked a manager why this location was so mind-boggling gigantic, he told me the store served as the pilot center where corporate decided to test combining a business center Costco and a normal residential Costco. *But why Salt Lake City of all places?*

Mormons have their stereotypes and the demographics of Utah probably passed the test. Large families, doomsday preppers … what more could Costco want? After all, the LDS website recommended three months of food, water, and money to be kept in case of an emergency. The website stated, "He has lovingly commanded us to 'prepare every needful thing' (Doctrine and Covenants 109:8) so that, should adversity come, we may care for ourselves and our neighbors, and support bishops as they care for others."

That's right, the LDS Church possesses the reputation as the best-prepared organization in the event of a catastrophe. So, when it really hits the fan, it might be a descendent of Brigham Young's twenty-first wife saving your ass.

The end of days could wait. Van life lacks the space for proper prepping. Yet Sarah and I still managed to leave with enough almond milk to fill a kiddy pool; enough cheese I might not poop the rest of the trip; *and* enough of my acid reflux medication that I shouldn't have indigestion until we needed a new set of tires, which we would probably buy at Costco.

Rudy was road-ready for a few weeks in the Utah wilderness. With fully stocked provisions, the passenger seat filled with tenderness again, and the sweet tunes of Motown on the speakers, we said *goodbye* to the city and *welcome back* to the boondocker's rhapsody.

I pressed the pedal to catch up with the hurried pace of I-15. Our trip had begun on the same freeway, sixty-seven days earlier. We tore south, passing packed neighborhoods on our left, with the occasional golden trumpet of Moroni shining from the foothills of the Wasatch. On our right, large swaths of rolling farms grew plants that would be distilled into essential oils. UT-50 was a welcome relief. Less than a song later, we unwrapped the gift of Utah's country roads.

Every fifteen minutes or so, a car would travel past in the opposite direction. We entered the high desert with snow-dusted mountains in the distance. The layers of the West's geological delights came into view. Cliffs sparkled like cinnamon rolls. Boondocking lost the lakes and rivers but found enchantment in the open spaces. We settled on one of the many luring campsites. I had seen many juniper bushes over the years, but apparently no real juniper trees. The ones here towered thick and ancient, leafless with webbed extremities that smelled deliciously tangy. All the vegetation was spaced out, with endless opportunities to explore. No stars could hide, and no color could elude the hour after sunset when the coyotes began their yapping.

UT-24 brought us to Capitol Reef National Park, the least visited of the famous Utah Five (fact), and the most underrated (opinion). We hiked up stone mountains as bald as a baby's bum, around thick-trunked cottonwood trees, up washes with names, and some without. The night temperatures dropped to sweater chilly. The day's mercury climbed to a shirtless warm. The Fremont River tempted me to cool down. The park warned of the river's high levels of E. coli bacteria from nearby agricultural runoff (the Department of the Interior's way to word cow shit). It was brown, but I got in, my mouth zipped tight, splashing my limbs and torso.

One hike took us to Grand Wash Canyon, a high-walled, roofless tunnel with a sandy bottom. There I read a historical marker: uranium had been mined here before Americans built world-ending bombs with the stuff. People claimed the element had "medicinal" and "healing" purposes. Consumers wore it around their necks, crushed it into a "health tonic," and swallowed it. Now, yellow signs warned of radiation, and to not drink the water or stay in the area for long periods. *What imbecile would drink uranium?*

Then I pondered what current trends, in the names of living longer and looking younger, would eventually be considered ridiculous. Botox and lip fillers, testosterone therapy and cold plunges, face lifts and nose jobs. America, land of the manufactured, home of the insecure. God forbid we permit ourselves to simply age naturally.

Granted, I've fallen for the same social pressures myself, and these ponderings belong to a man who once took things too far. In 2004, the ladies preferred smooth chests and baby-faces, not the naturally hairy vest I had at age 18. Nair—the thick, ultra-toxic, hair removal cream—never warned me to avoid the nipples. After all, the cream was marketed to women as an alternative to shaving their legs. As I covered my chest with the stuff, my areolas burned like Hitler in Hell as the Nair disintegrated my nipple tips. They never entirely grew back, and are mostly missing to this day. But hey, at least I never drank uranium.

Chapter 18
The Van in the Mirror

ARCHES NATIONAL PARK, located in eastern Utah, had to temporarily close its entrance eight times in 2019 due to capacity limitations. In 2020, Arches closed an astonishing thirty-six times in September and October alone. As Sarah and I approached, the line to enter was over a quarter mile long. Our agenda needed a makeover. We skipped the turnoff, driving towards the Moab Information Center through a subdivision with a shellacking of political yard signs. One that stood out: KEEP PUBLIC LANDS IN PUBLIC HANDS!

A fitting proclamation, for surrounding the town of Moab, you can find nearly every public land classification: National Parks, National Monuments, National Forest, Bureau of Land Management (BLM), National Recreation Area, etc. These photogenic public lands are the gold to the rush, and are converting this town into a booming city.

Sarah, the captain, looked outside the window to a line of cars that wrapped around a Wendy's drive-thru. The line was so long that it went past the parking lot, and into the shoulder of the highway. A block away, each pump at the gas station had its own line of cars impatiently waiting their turn. I lost count of how many vehicles lengthened the queue as I tried to sort through the line that existed just to get into another line for one of the dozen gas pumps. The scene reminded me of 2008, when I fled Houston ahead of an encroaching hurricane and watched millions of people drain the city's fuel supply. But there was no hurricane or frantic evacuation here. Rain scarcely fell in these parts. The arid maroon soil was only occasionally dotted with sagebrush. On either side of the road,

167

towering crimson cliffs looked ready to crumble. The sky was a pale blue, with two drawn-out cirrus clouds. A warm breeze blew into the open windows of an idle and impatient Rudy.

On this Saturday in mid-October, we experienced traffic not seen since pre-pandemic times. There was no holiday or special event, yet this town with its population of 5,366 permanent residents (2020 census) was undoubtedly over capacity. The government of Moab estimates that it receives three to five million tourists per year, which puts the ratio at almost 1 resident per every 1,000 tourists. Not surprising given the town's proximity to the photogenic National Parks of Arches and Canyonlands. The only municipalities I have visited with more extreme ratios are Vatican City, with 6.9 million visitors and 825 residents (2019); and Springdale, Utah, located outside the even more popular Zion National Park, with 4.5 million visitors and only 629 residents. (Though Springdale is much closer to larger municipalities; Moab is not.)

Papa Herb and my grandmother stayed in Moab in 1954. They spent a night in the town when their car broke down, the mechanic making them wait a day because hunting season had just started. As soon as the sedan was fixed, they took off to drive the five hours to Utah's only national parks at the time: Bryce Canyon and Zion. Then, Moab was known as the "Uranium Capital of the World," and mining was its core industry. The population grew to nearly 6,000 as the Cold War raised the demand for nuclear material. Now Moab's major export appears to be Instagram photos.

These days, Moab is all about the public land and the activities they offer. The sandy roads extending from the town attract off-road enthusiasts, and one should never expect to camp in quiet. Dust flies off the tires of dirt bikes, dune buggies, quads, and Jeeps, with engines revving through the day and into the night. Further from town, each trailhead tells a different story. Hikers strap on their boots and don packs in search of views and unique formations. Mountain bikers click into their pedals on the internationally famous paths. River runners slide their boats and kayaks into the silty waters of the Colorado, eagerly anticipating rapids in the confines of canyon walls. Climbers clique together, sharing their gear and goals of scaling world-class rock faces. Professional and amateur photographers try to beat the rising sun for the perfect shot of an arch or canyon. Families cram into hotels, stores, and restaurants when they're not out horseback riding, ziplining, taking helicopter tours, or trying their hand at any of the above adventures.

Moab—a modern-day hashtag town capitalizing extensively on the obvious observation that Americans hate to be bored. Sarah and I didn't come to Moab for adrenaline, we came for the desert's solace—a commodity that appeared to be exploited. Good luck finding any silence at the more popular Island in the Sky district of Canyonlands National Park (you'll have a hard enough time finding a parking spot). Thus, we rolled south on UT-191, away from the hotspots and to the park's Needles district, a ninety-minute drive southwest from Moab. According to the park's newspaper handout, this federal land is supposedly one of the quietest places in the country.

We drove past a roadside arch luring tourists onto private land. Past the turnoff for Rockland Ranch, a polygamist Mormon community hidden in the cliffs to the west and made famous by *Three Wives, One Husband*—a docuseries on Netflix. Off UT-211, we camped on public land, next to friendly dirtbag climbers who flooded the dispersed camping spots to get their go at the famous red cliffs. It's hard to use the word dirtbag and not sound belittling, but to them it's usually worn as a badge of honor, not an insult. And hey, if there ever was a misfit that never got its due praise, it's the dirtbag. I envied them more than the lotto winner or the tech tycoon. To drop it all, to rough it so hard for so long. I lack the courage and boldness, which is why I respect them so much.

Inside the Needles District, we hiked to Chesler Park, put down our packs, and perched our bodies on a dried waterfall. Strange sandstone cliffs wrapped around pillars of time-weathered rock. Then the spirits called, silence thick enough to straighten the spine. Who knew nothing could sound so sweet? We crossed our legs and meditated. Unlike Shasta, no one dared to interrupt.

While the most famous national parks have their beauty, what makes Utah so incredible is that the places found outside of the park boundaries are nearly as breathtaking (and with much fewer selfie-sticks). God bless man's laziness, for all those "Top Eleven Things to do in _____" websites ruined some attractions but made exploring other places hidden from the hashtag all the sweeter.

On the other side of town, following the Colorado River up UT-128, we snaked through a shallow canyon as the rising sun began turning the sky blue. At the trailhead to Fisher Towers, giant sandstone cliffs climbed out of the desert floor. The hiking trail wrapped around spires of mud-dried monoliths. Distant hikers looked like marching ants. Climbers roped in and summited the main tower far above, posing for photos with their arms flexed. Post-hike, back in the parking lot, we met Eric.

Eric, a mountain guide, greeted us as jovially as anyone I had met on the road. He stood tall and fit, wearing a ball cap and white neckband that he used as a facemask. He had recently taken his client to the summit of a tower. Eric joined us at the van to have a look inside.

"How long have you lived in Moab?" I asked, leaning up against the kitchen counter.

"Fifteen years," he answered from outside the van.

"How much has it changed?"

"Oh man, the town has grown so much. The last five years especially." He stepped back from looking in the van and lowered his neckband. "This parking lot midweek would maybe have six cars, max."

I stuck my head out for a look. The parking lot overflowed down the dusty road with four times that amount. A vehicle idled for the next empty space. The wind blew the nasty stench of the overfilled outhouse across my face.

Eric continued, "I mean, it's good for business. Every other business owner I know is having a record year. And that's even after being closed until May."

"The traffic was crazy."

"Yeah man, you used to only see numbers like that on maybe Memorial Day or Labor Day weekend, but now it's every weekend because of COVID. Last weekend we had 100,000 people in Moab. On Sunday it took people three hours to get across town. I had friends who just pulled over, parked their cars on the side of the road, and walked home."

Our chat continued until we bid farewell and gifted our parking spot to the queue. Midweek, Sarah and I gave Moab another chance, waking up each day before sunrise to get into Island in the Sky or Arches National Park. By 8:30 a.m., the crowd to beat the crowd occupied every parking space. Sarah and I marched on, two more termites on the mound. We left Arches at 11:30 a.m. on a Wednesday, driving by park rangers serving as traffic controllers, passing a sign that read: PARK CLOSED, REOPENS IN 3 HOURS.

In the afternoons, we spent our time at Swanny Park, a manicured plot of city land lined with nomads. I counted fourteen vans around the perimeter on a weekday. One dirtbag joked, "It's the VAN-demic!"

If over-tourism was a plague, Sarah and I were contagiously coughing on everyone.

Chapter 19
The Dig

THE MOKI DUGWAY, a section of UT-261, is a road that defies logic, physics, and sanity. Like someone took a bulldozer, strapped it to a massive cliff, and let it dig its way from the plateau of Bears Ears National Monument to the iconic Southwest scenery below.

Sarah lifted out of her seat to peer out the window. "Oh my God! There's a car that went off the road down there. Look!"

"I'll take your word for it," I said nervously as I inched Rudy forward on the graded dirt.

She went on to describe the vehicle that had rolled off the cliff. I assumed it wasn't the Dugway's only casualty. I gripped the wheel tighter. A sharp curve approached, one of many. The road was wide and empty. Rudy drifted into the wrong side; the closer the wall, the safer the descent. I cleared another switchback and lifted my eyes to take in the view.

As the juniper trees disappeared, the whole drive became a vista. Between the immeasurable desert and a distant horizon, towered dozens of vermillion monoliths. Grasping their size was a fool's errand, but the closer we got, the more commanding and life-like they appeared. Freestanding, some mesas looked ready to crumble, like an old sandcastle. Some had wide bases that funneled into solid, flattened boxes, like giant crimson mausoleums. Others resembled stone statues: a woman twirling in a ballgown, a toy soldier guarding the land. Each rock tower was an individual—unique and flawed, yet adaptable and resilient.

An occasional RV parked between the posing rocks. To the right, brown tectonic plates pushed towards the sapphire sky; to the left, a thousand-foot drop off where the terracotta land gave way. Down in the distant wash, auburn leaves dangled from a lengthy trail of Cottonwood trees.

Bigger than the mesas and broader than the views, was the all-encompassing energy of the place. Even from inside the cab, I could feel it—a heavy serenity, a powerful sanctuary, a desolate shrine.

The Wild West of popular culture only exists in movies and magazines. Out here there were no tourist traps or mining towns, no cowboys or wagon trains. No, this wasn't the Wild West at all. It was the Wise West. A place where distractions go to die. A place that will dare your discomfort and antagonize your growth. Welcome to the desolate lands of quietude. Welcome to Valley of the Gods.

Rudy rolled across the dirt road, spraying caramel-colored dust in his tracks, until we found home for the week. Killing the engine brought knee-buckling silence. The kind of quiet that takes the subconscious mess inside your head and empties it out in the open. My mess was a splattering of emotional clutter. Sort it out or avoid it at all costs? The place felt too enticing. Not only to explore the land, but to survey the soul.

In the summer, the desert is deadly and uninviting—snakes, scorpions, heat stroke. But in the winter, the scariest thing is yourself. For seven winters I took solo pilgrimages to the empty lands east of San Diego. The first night camping was always the hardest, when the massiveness of the place overwhelmed my senses. Mentally, I would squirm, like trying to adjust in a wood chair, attempting to find comfort that does not exist. I fought the demons that arose from the cocktail of solitude and stillness. As my spiritual ancestors had done millennia before, I wandered the desert. Many lessons existed, but they weren't found in hallucinogens or prayers. I learned that the lessons of the desert do the finding; the seeker does the waiting. At night, I would pull my wool sweater over my body and lay in the sand, staring at the stars. The night sky: a great place to go with questions if you want more questions.

Sometimes I drove to the desert with an excited grin. Other times I bore the burden of a broken heart. I knew these trips would bring challenges and lack fun, yet I strangely looked forward to them. Thus, the desert became my sanctuary. My safe place to grow, to be, to deal with whatever came up. The place where I could sit in my skin long enough that it went from feeling like a corset, to feeling like my favorite pair of pajamas.

In the desert, life must adapt to survive. In the desert, thoughts wilt so a person can bloom. In the desert, you spiritually evolve or lose your mind—maybe both.

Sarah calls it digging, and the desert is the best place to dig. It's the excavation of what is under all those layers of distraction. It's the mining of the precious mineral of truth. It's about digging closer to the core, where pain and past can come up and evaporate their hold in the arid emptiness of the land that most people belittle. Desolate, nothing, wasteland—they say. I say dig. But don't be fooled, digging is no shortcut to spiritual growth. No, digging is dirty, laborious, and disobedient.

I always dug alone. After all, it is a solo activity. I watched Sarah as she fought her own calling to dig. First, she built a path with flat stones that led from Rudy to an open plot of sand. I watched her clean: sweeping, dusting, scrubbing, and polishing. She reorganized her wardrobe, checked her face for pimples, and clipped her nails. Then I watched her run out of things to do. She located a plot of sand, sat down, crossed her legs, and dug. This gave me the awareness that watching her was my version of avoidance. So, I closed my eyes, and I dug too.

It took time until the silence transitioned from a sound to a sentiment. There was no wind blowing, no flies buzzing. If there is a sound more powerful than a still desert, I haven't heard it. With my eyes closed, my bare feet pressed against stone, I listened to the electrical charge of my own nervous system. At one point a raven flapped overhead, the sound of its wings cutting through the void. *Woosh. Woosh.* Then all went dangerously tranquil.

Maybe the thing that makes silence so uncomfortable is that it reminds us about all the times when others robbed us of our peace; that the absence of distraction forces us to confront the noises we most want to forget.

❖

Bam! A tin dog dish crashed against the marble floor. Dog food pellets cascaded across the tile, echoing down the hallway. The yelling between my father and stepmother continued.

Tall, with platinum blonde hair, Karen was closer in age to my oldest sibling than to my dad. At first, I liked my stepmother. Youthful and fun, she said "yes" to things my parents often refused. But you can't put crystals on a wrecking ball and call it a chandelier. After they got married, my siblings and I never lived under the same roof at the same time again. When sixth grade ended, I moved from my mom's one-story house and simple lifestyle to the luxurious dysfunction at my dad's. Right away, Karen became different, making it clear she wanted to be called "Mom." Do it, and I would get spoiled; don't, and prepare for her to rage.

Next, Karen began the quest to cut me off from my real mom, using lies and manipulation to convince me that my birth mom was evil. Sadly, it worked. I stopped talking to the woman who raised me, only hearing her voice on the answering machine when Karen would play it for herself, then tell me my mother never called. My father watched it all happen, encouraging Karen from the sidelines. And though the two stayed united in the war against my mom, every night felt like their own marriage was under siege.

Bam! Whomp, whomp, whomp. Another tin dog dish hit the marble, reverberating as it spun on its side.

I went to the top of the staircase, the place where I eavesdropped when Karen and my father fought. I couldn't see them, but I could always hear them. And despite the grandiosity of the house, I was pretty sure the neighbors could hear them too.

"You psycho bitch!" yelled my dad.

"What the fuck are you gonna do, huh?" Karen yelled back.

"Shut the fuck up!" My father yelled back.

A door slammed. The screams muffled.

"Andrew."

I jumped. It was Jordan, standing behind me. Jordan was a step-cousin slightly older than me who lived in the adjacent room. The two of us shared more than a bathroom; we had a firsthand account of the chaos that was our household.

"Andrew, it's not safe. Come with me."

I got up and retreated to the sofa. We closed the door. Minutes lapsed as we listened to the muffled sounds of their screams until footsteps could be heard, coming up the stairs.

My dad opened the door, his polo shirt half untucked, covered in water. *The dog's water,* I thought. *She must have thrown the dog dish at him.*

"Get some clothes together," he whispered. "We're going to a hotel for the night. I'll take you to school in the morning."

My father looked different. The man who beat the dogs and had the disciplinary tactics of a drill sergeant wasn't there. He didn't look so scary, not so tough. He was wet, pathetic, beat.

Your own home, I thought, *you're leaving your own home.* I packed my bag for the first, but not the last, time.

A week later, I found myself at the mercy of another conflict. My father was away on business. Karen and Jordan were in the middle of a vicious argument.

"Andrew! Get down here!" yelled Karen from the master bedroom.

I walked in. Jordan and Karen stood facing one another, as if ready to swing.

"Let's see what Andrew thinks. He knows what a horrible kid you are." Karen's eyes looked violent, Jordan a rebellious teenager ready to prove a point.

I stood silent as they each yelled their case.

"Andrew, you see what I have to deal with?" Karen took her eyes off Jordan. Before I could answer, Jordan turned around, walking past the marble-lined bathtub and into Karen's walk-in closet. I peered around the corner, watching Jordan reach up to a shoe box, open it, and remove Karen's pistol.

"WHAT ARE YOU DOING?" Karen screamed.

Jordan walked towards us with the pistol. Karen roared louder than ever, "PUT THAT FUCKING THING DOWN!"

I curled into a ball, afraid to watch. The yelling continued. Jordan with the gun. Karen with her rage. Eventually, Jordan agreed to put the weapon away.

That year, 1999, wore on as I wore down. As teenage me fell into the depths of depression, the suicidal ideation intensified, going from occasional to daily. What a thing to mourn, that someone so young would have to talk themselves into living. I faked being sick to avoid school, developed chronic pain and an eye twitch, started binge eating, and stopped brushing my teeth. My teeth formed yellow stains that surrounded each bracket of my braces. My smile still bears those stains today.

Before my first therapy session, I received an email with intake paperwork. One of the documents was a trauma timeline. I was to write down in chronological order my life's hardest events. What I thought would be some simple back and forth about my dating issues turned into a full reprocessing of the past. My therapist and I went through many events, but one theme gained more attention than the rest. It was when I was twelve to fourteen years old, the two years I lived with my father and Karen. How could two years take over a decade to heal?

Aside from dabbling with the university counseling services in grad school, I had not been in therapy since 1999. That was when, after the gun incident, my father forced us all to see a family psychologist. It lasted a couple of months until Karen claimed the shrink tried to have sex with her.

My father didn't put up a fight when, at the age of 14, I sat with him at Starbucks and told him I was leaving. Even though I had not spoken to my real mom in over a year, she quickly welcomed me back and offered me a safe living space.

As an adult, I never told my father about the panic attacks. Nor did I tell him about my suicidal thoughts when I lived under his roof. The one time I admitted to beginning therapy, he replied, "They're good at teaching you who to blame."

Maybe that statement had some truth. My one-hour sessions were out of pocket, costing me nearly an entire day's salary. And how many times had I left, angrier at my father than when I arrived?

The digging was too much. I got up. My knees popped, ending the silence. I wandered over to Rudy and knelt down to look in the side-view mirror. My own face looked unfamiliar. After moving into Rudy, I went from looking in the mirror a dozen times a day, to only a couple of times a week. And here, in the Valley of the Gods, I caught a glimpse of myself for the first time that day.

I forced a smile. I didn't feel happy, far from it. I just wanted to see those teeth, those stains. To grieve for the kid who just wanted the yelling to stop, wanted some silence to breathe in. That boy who had hurt so much he stopped caring for himself, stopped brushing his own teeth. The boy who started thinking about how easier things would be if he were dead. And in the mirror's reflection, I didn't see that boy. I saw a man with a beard, some gray hairs, a layering of wrinkles, and those same tooth stains that I had been so self-conscious of. I also saw a man who was too uncomfortable to make it through a few minutes of silence.

I took a deep breath and marched back to the same rock, where I once again sat down and crossed my legs. Digging may look like I'm seeking nirvana or some euphoric existential state, but the truth is I'd be happy with some simple contentment. So, two decades after I left that dysfunctional house, I went back into stillness and tried to connect the dots. The trauma and daddy issues. The dating dilemmas and panic attacks. My addiction to escape. The willingness to get better. Without it, I wouldn't be here, in this divine desert, with its horrific silence. With Sarah, a woman who had her own share of turmoil; in a relationship only made possible because of hardships and repair. Without that, Sarah and I couldn't share this love, this home, this passion for the road.

I thought about how I fell in love with the road in the first place. It was that same awful year of 1999. Karen's father, Hank, took me in for a month in his RV. Away from my father. Away from Karen. To the two-lane backroads that opened my mind and freed my spirit. That year, all my happiest moments came in that RV passenger seat, studying a road atlas or looking out the windshield. Hank introduced me to all of this. He showed me that you don't have to escape something old, rather you can go towards something new. I don't know how that sweet man raised such a broken woman, but thinking about Hank's RV, I finally understood that even Karens have their purpose. That even she had played a role in making this all possible.

With that acknowledgment, the visceral stronghold of the memories loosened. The land felt more primordial and sacred than ever. I opened my eyes and stood up, craving the sun on my skin. Off with the shirt, then the shorts. I scanned the area. Aside from Sarah, no one was in sight. How badly I craved to feel it all. I kicked off my sandals and removed my underwear. My bare feet turned soil-red as I slowly walked towards nothing. Once confined to business casual, I was now naked in the desert. A car drove by. We exchanged an awkward glance. My hippie bush had finally gone public.

That night, the cold gust of winter's breath raised the red dust. The wind of the Arctic needed no Dugway as it flew down the cliff at magnificent speeds. Morning trickled a light snow, which stuck to the tops of mesas like icing on red velvet cupcakes.

Now Is the Time

Golden hours and silver linings, every day could be a new season, every moment a new lesson. Summer in the desert can leave scars that last months, but the right season amongst the cacti can bring revelations that last lifetimes. Once again, the desert's divinity did something to me, and I fell deeper in love with the arid and elevated lands of Utah.

Chapter 20
Somewhere in the
Middle

EMPTY HUTS DOTTED the gravel pullouts off UT-163. Drained beer cans sparkled along the land, the labels faded by sun and time. Navajo Nation had been hit hard by the pandemic. Visitors were permitted to drive through Monument Valley, but no businesses had reopened. Meanwhile, road-tripping millennials like myself parked along the shoulder of the road to snap photos of the iconic landscape of the American West. The scenery was astounding, but I carried the guilt of filtered exploitation, forcing smiles on camera while the locals stayed home. The only Navajo I saw sat in folding chairs in a parking lot in downtown Bluff, Utah. Next to their table, a sign: HONK IF YOU VOTED! FREE NAVAJO TACOS.

Rudy tooted. The polls closed in six days.

Goodbye San Juan County, Utah, a place where optimism came in the form of vacant nature that wowed the mind. In designated wilderness, Sarah and I answered the calling to bushwhack north. We climbed up and down the smooth sandstone walls of an empty wash, crunching over dried terrain until we reached a section that required a short scramble. Tucked under the overhang, a cliff dwelling made from stacked rocks had held firm for an unknown number of years. A single room, cramped and scarred with a charred ceiling. We analyzed a field of broken pottery painted with art from another time, when even the "trash" was made from the land. How amazing it felt to find this place on our own, leaving only footprints, taking only memories.

UT-162 led to CO-160. In the distance, a peculiar monolith rose from the land. Sarah took to Google to figure out how we had never heard of Shiprock Peak. The Navajo protect their sacred site by not allowing visitors to access the area via the dirt road, nor is climbing allowed.

Across the expanse, Rudy roared up an incline that wrapped around a mountain big enough to drop the temperature and encourage the wind. Unlike the main parks that struggled to adapt to the surge in visitors, Mesa Verde National Park was quiet—uninhibited by traffic and lines, no concessions, drones or live feeds. On the stereo played a podcast recorded by an Ancestral Puebloan, who gave us our tour as we drove from ruin to ruin. Wrapped in puffy jackets and beanies, we marveled from the bluff's edge at the intricate and expansive cliff dwellings.

The cold front lingered like a talkative neighbor. In the small city of Durango, Colorado, we inquired about a shower at a laundromat. COVID looked like the safest thing you could catch in the cesspool of rust, bacteria, and stains of God-knows-what. Our outdoor showers went from refreshing to cruel. We resorted to bathing inside the van, soaking a cloth in warm soapy water, standing next to one another, cleaning what we called the "pits n bits." Sarah and I weren't red-carpet clean, but we found laughter in how strange our new way of living was. After all, a couple's love should never be valued in how much money was spent on Valentine's Day, but in how lovers react to a wet wipe wash within arm's reach.

North for the day, up CO-550, best known as the Million Dollar Highway. I didn't know the nickname at the time and took in the majesty of the mountains without putting a price on it. Silverton was an endearing little town with a friendly general store surrounded by snowy peaks. Just down the road in Ouray, we scouted out a hot spring resort; but after seeing the crowd, I determined my quota of hippie bushes had been met long ago.

We drove on with greased hair, tinged with the irritability of a generation foreign to filth. Sarah read me the news about the Pentagon releasing videos of UFOs. This year was getting stranger each day.

Before we left San Diego, the ocean had turned blood red during the day and glowed electric blue from bioluminescence at night. Pandemic, fires, red tide, civil unrest, and now aliens. The Earth wanted to say something. I wanted a shower.

Given the times, making conclusions about a town in 2020 would be unfair. But hey, there's always next year to be less judgmental. Point in case: Montrose, Colorado, a town with so many Remingtons, Winchesters, and Colts (and that's just the names of the gas station attendants). I saw more open-carry pistols than people saying hi. Inside the grocery store, people went out of their way to give us an unwelcoming scowl.

If you have never been to the conservative outpost that is Montrose, Colorado, then allow me to sum it up. Montrose is like finding a strand of Ted Nugent's goatee hair in your freedom fries. It's like a militia founder and a doomsday prepper had a son, named him Ricky Bobby, and told that aspiring incel that if he stockpiled enough firearms and listened to enough InfoWars, they'd survive the Second Coming. I used to like a good conspiracy theory, but after my first visit to Montrose, I realized that most conspiracies lead to blaming the Jews for everything, and that's not why I had a Bar Mitzvah.

Inside Walmart was an eerie site. The shelves for ammunition and the displays for guns sat empty; not sold out, only hidden. The corporation had deemed the times too likely for civil unrest and pulled the weapons from potential looters' reach. (Walmart reversed the decision the following day, and the weapons returned.) Ten days before staying with friends came the vigilant protocol of people aversion. We stocked up on rations, resisted the temptation of truck stop showers, and kept to ourselves as a courtesy quarantine.

Oddly enough, a short distance from the fury of Montrose resides the best place in the world to yell out your frustrations. Black

Canyon of the Gunnison National Park contains Colorado's tallest cliffs, which are razorblade sharp, catapult close, dark and lined with regal stripes. If the Empire State Building stood on the Gunnison River at the canyon's bottom, the top of the tower would make it about halfway up the wall. Unlike most western canyons, Black Canyon was formed by tectonic activity, not river erosion, making the walls smooth and proximate.

Got anger? Repression makes depression. I screamed like I had never screamed before. My yell found its way across the magnificent trench. Two marathon-long seconds of silence until the howl bounced off the opposite wall. The echo carried the realization of how pitiful my "problems" sounded. The silence returned and I marveled at the view.

Colorado towns have more marijuana stores than banks and churches. We saw many, ranging from little huts to full-sized weed warehouses. Rudy followed the Gunnison River on CO-50, then turned left on CO-285, dodging the Denver city limits until arriving in Coal Creek, Colorado, a town tucked in the trees of the Rockies' eastern slope. My friends opened the doors of their mountain home. As ripened vagabonds, Sarah and I smelled the part. Our dirty clothes bag overflowed. We skipped the formalities and went straight for the shower. I should have picked up their water bill; the washer spun for hours and I took a long, hot shower every day for the next week.

November 4, 2020 arrived. It was a day of questions. I woke up the morning after the election and immediately went to the phone for updates. With the results in limbo, my mental defenses went down, my curiosities spiked. What was the world thinking? What were my "friends" posting? Mmm, the scroll. No. Yes. No, don't do it. Ah, fuck it. It felt like texting an ex-lover after dark. Within seconds I was in the app store. An anxious tremble moved through me as I waited for the Facebook and Instagram icons to finish downloading.

My thumb began scrolling with the ferocious curiosities of a man who had worked hard to rid drama from his life, only to welcome it back on a 3x5 inch screen. Radical posts flooded my feed, until Silicon

Valley went into censorship mode, flagging some and deleting many more. The tech titans had created a monster; now they sought to amputate its limbs. The Great Culture War stormed on; Facebook, Google, and Twitter were its arms dealers. I wish I could say I stopped there, but I'm an addict. Even when I know I've had too much, I keep going. Not for minutes or hours, but for months, addicted to speed reading others' thought vomit.

November 7, 2020 arrived. Biden had been declared the Commander in Disbelief. While Trump's supporters were on fire, the flames in Rocky Mountain National Park finally reached containment. The park reopened in time for Sarah and I to drive the long way to Boulder.

Ironically, the town's first two letters are B.O., because you immediately smell the harsh reality that all-natural deodorant isn't getting the job done. If you have never been to the progressive head-quarters of Boulder, Colorado, then allow me to sum it up. Boulder is like finding a piece of Janice Joplin's armpit hair in your granola. It's like a flower child and a vegan had a baby, named it Hope, and told Hope that if they annoyed enough people to sign their petition, there would be world peace. I used to consider myself progressive, but after my first visit to Boulder, I just went ahead and canceled myself.

Sarah and I met up with a friend and toured downtown to see the scene. A victory parade was underway. Horns honked, masks slipped below the noses of the cheerful. One could only wonder what was happening on the other side of the Rockies, in those armed and riled mountain towns. I'm not sure if Colorado's ability to have a Montrose and a Boulder is a thing of beauty or a bomb that ought to be disarmed.

When you keep pulling a rubber band, it's not the right or left that snaps, it's the center. The geriatric political orgy was in full swing, with no safe word to be found. Though America's problems weren't yet in the rearview, my literal foot was on the pedal. The future was down the road. I drove on, even if it felt like I was lost in the middle of Middle America.

Chapter 21
Bearded Jews

"I JUST GOT a text from my brother, the pastor," said Sarah. "They're excited to have us. We're welcome to stay in their house, but we would have to sleep in two separate rooms."

"Two separate rooms?"

"Yeah, because we're not married. It's easier if they don't have to explain it to the kids."

"But we're in our thirties. And it's supposed to be 17 degrees tonight with at least three inches of snow."

"Or we can stay in the van in front of their house?"

Rudy listened intently. Our home had a lot of love but no heater. Share Paul the pastor's house with his four young children or test Rudy's lower limits?

"What do you want to do?" I asked.

Sarah shrugged her shoulders. "We can think about it and tell him when we get there."

As a Jew from Texas, this wasn't the first time dating in a Christian culture had created some inconveniences. Words from prior dating experiences rang in my head:

"This can never work if you don't accept Jesus into your life."

"Don't tell my parents that you're Jewish."

"I can't date someone that's going to Hell because they're not Christian."

Here's some unsolicited feedback from the outside: believe what I believe or burn forever is a terrible sales pitch for anything, especially your loving savior. I have hidden in the kosher closet before. Sometimes to avoid conflict, other times to learn what people truly think. After all, how many meals have I shared with people who smiled and laughed at my jokes, only to pity my inevitable damnation after I was out of sight?

It's hard to find anyone without some religious baggage. Mine began at age eight when my single mother enrolled me in a church's after-school program so she could put in a full day's work. Whatever the bait—price, reputation, convenience—a shuttle van with a large cross decal picked me up from elementary school. The hours after school were spent playing with my new Christian buddies.

A week in, I let them in on my Jewish heritage. The next day a gang of peers cornered me near the playground's edge. The lead bully went on about how the Jews killed Jesus. East Texas pinecones grow to the size of softballs and come with thorny tips. The gang armed up, throwing dozens of pinecones at me. I turned around and fell. That's when the details get hazy. Stinging pain, shock, and confusion blackened my vision until the torment ended and whip-like scratches covered my body.

That evening, my father picked my siblings and me up from daycare. I told him the story.

"Don't listen to those little shitheads. You know my parents made me go to a private Jewish school in Brooklyn?"

"Yeah."

"Well, I used to have to walk home from school every day through an Irish Catholic neighborhood. And every week I'd get jumped by a group of them and have to fight off four or five at a time."

"Really?"

"Yeah. Their priest told them that the Jews killed Jesus."

"Did we kill Jesus, Dad?"

"No. The Romans killed him."

"Then why did they say that the Jews did?"

"I don't know, because they're idiots. Do you know how to fight?"

"Yeah," I lied.

"Good. Then fight."

End of talk.

A couple years after the divorce, my mother downsized and moved us a few miles away. We weren't in the new house long when I watched her paint over swastikas that had been sprayed onto the neighborhood entrance. She explained things a little better, but I still didn't understand why, "some people just don't like Jews." I was a little kid learning a big word: antisemitism.

Hundreds of times I've been told, "You don't look Jewish." It's a statement I often translated into: *How come you don't have a big nose? Where's your funny little hat? You don't sound smart enough to be one of those global elitists ruling the world.*

The answer to my appearance came later in life when my Jewish paternal grandparents revealed my father's origins: a black-market adoption. The couple that raised him didn't share any blood with me; in fact, they had purchased my father off-the-record in New York City. My father was in his late forties when he learned about the adoption. Can you imagine, learning your entire life was built on a giant lie? His adoptive parents died shortly after they disclosed the truth. Even my father's extended family had kept the secret for over four decades. My dad hired a private investigator, who failed to locate his biological parents. It wasn't until 2016 when a DNA test revealed that I had a good portion of Irish blood flowing through my veins, explaining why I "don't look Jewish."

In my high school class of nearly 900 students, I knew only one other Jew. And after a couple decades in The Lone Star State, I can say that I'm a lot of people's only Jewish friend. But you don't need to be raised in Texas to be a Jew with an identity crisis. The ethnic, cultural, and religious overlap can be confusing to sort through. Especially since I rarely practice the religious aspects of Judaism, or any religion for that matter.

Texan Jew, sober raver, overeducated drifter—they are clashing labels that I'm now proud of. I no longer envy those born knowing who they are. That would be too easy, like taking the interstate. My road to authenticity looked more like the Moki Dugway, challenging to navigate but beautiful and rewarding nonetheless.

Yoga, crystals, tarot cards—now Sarah was the woo-woo one in the family. She faced her own challenges since departing from her strict Christian upbringing. Heck, she even went to undergrad at a Christian university that didn't allow dancing. No wonder my twerking seduced her.

Sarah drove on, the question of our sleeping arrangement unresolved. GPS took us off I-25 and onto CO-86 towards Elizabeth, Colorado. In triangular proximity to the cities of Colorado Springs and Denver, Elizabeth felt like one of those places you would only go if you lived there or were visiting someone. Rudy rolled up and down the foothills, which rippled into the lower earth like the roots of an old tree. If Elizabeth has a downtown, I never saw it. By the time neighborhoods started to crop up, Sarah and I had made the decision to sleep in the van. Call it love, call it loyalty, or go ahead and label it the honeymoon phase. We might not be warm, but at least we'd be home.

Authenticity—when you find yourself and lose the desire to make others like you. Paul and his wife, Jillian, knew who they were. Unlike the Christians of my past, they opened their home and opened my mind. It seemed clear to me that I posed no threat to their faith, nor did I appear to have a stake in their savior's death. I was a guest, a traveler of the road, welcomed into a home of love, hospitality, and homemade tacos.

Tacos are a good start to any friendship. We sat across a big dining room table. Jillian spoke like a mom in quarantine, excited at the rare opportunity to converse with people her age. Paul caught us up on life as a small-town preacher in 2020. I tried hard not to use any profanity around the kids, and Sarah quickly threw an elbow each time I failed. After dinner came family time. No TV or Xbox, just good old-fashioned charades and the laughter that goes with it.

There is an art to temperature control in a furnace-free van. We parked Rudy with the windshield facing the sun. The sealed windows and fan created a Greenhouse Effect, which went a long way. By 8:30 p.m., we left the warm house for Rudy's cold vinyl floor. As we changed into a double layer of pajamas, a 12-volt electric blanket removed the chill from the sheets. Night fell little-town dark; under the stacks of blankets, Sarah and I cuddled warm.

My pinecone scratches had healed, but the wounds from persecution still haven't entirely gone away, because it took some time before I fell asleep, pondering religion and its role in my life. Like the man who sold us the van, Rudy's namesake, Paul and Jillian were more show than tell, and that's a sermon I can sit through.

There was no fire and brimstone, only ice and powder. In the morning, I took a broom to Rudy's carcass and swept off a thick coating of snow. After all the years of seeking, I'm not sure I've found God, but at least I found myself in the process.

On the go, we had seen a lot in a few days. From Great Sand Dunes National Park and fourteener vistas, through towns with tongue-friendly names: Walsenburg, Trinidad, and Raton. NM-64/TX-87 was where I said goodbye to what I thought would be the last hill for quite a while, only to see another one bless the view as we sank further away from the taken-for-granted topography of the West.

The drive went through an unindustrialized chunk of flatland. Spanish bonnets, roadrunners, sagebrush, grass, prairie dogs, and tumbleweeds. No wheat, corn, or cotton—the plains before we made them plain. Spotting trees became a way to pass the time, each one spaced out far enough to have listened to several songs until the next sighting. The plains are pleasant for the length of an album, and by the time U2's *Joshua Tree* ended, the West had flattened out to a forever view of despondency. The scent of natural gas blew in through the cracked windows. Oil derricks churned out of sync, welcoming us into Texas, the Long Road State.

A dilapidated boat rusted on top of dried grass to the left of the road. On the right was a yard littered with a dozen inoperable lawn mowers. Next door, three donkeys grazed in between piles of trash. Big ruts rocked Rudy and clattered the kitchenware. The road looked so rough even it appeared to be on meth. We drove through a dot on the map labeled Sanford (population 500).

We arrived at Sanford-Yake Campground in the North Texas Panhandle. Rudy purred in neutral, cooling down from a long drive. The campsite bordered a shallow, wide canyon filled with murky water. Lake Meredith was Middle America pretty, a place that broke the boredom of the high plains but would never hold up as an attraction west of Texas. Nevertheless, we managed more than our money's worth. The free site came with showers, and the sun of the lower latitudes made 54 degrees seem like a warm summer day.

Campground mornings started with birds chirping, until our neighbor played a podcast at concert-volume levels. The open, flat land brought strong cell signal. At night, as I lay in bed, I put down my book for the brain-numbing movement of the scroll. Even as a phantom behind the screen, intentionally not liking or commenting on anything, I felt bursts of judgment and frustration, comparison and envy. There were similarities to my addiction to alcohol. Highs, lows, and a lack of authenticity. The hope that I could fool others into thinking I had something better than I did. The illusion of control and the pitiful feeling that something had more power over me, than I had over it.

I closed down Instagram and went to Google Maps. I zoomed in and out of the nearby towns, mentally editing the grammar in reviews for restaurants I had no intention of eating at. I pinched the zoom on the nearby town of Borger, Texas, and began counting churches until I got to forty. Methodist, Mormon, Baptist, Episcopal, Pentecostal, Catholic, Lutheran, Presbyterian, Evangelical, and non-denominational. More preachers than cowboys these days. No synagogues, probably no minyan for a million miles.

If aliens ever drop you off on a road in far-north Texas, merely follow the FREE 72 oz. STEAK IF YOU FINISH billboards until you get to Amarillo. We averted the city and a triple bypass, heading southeast on a zigzag of Farm to Market (FM) roads. I grew up near FM1960, but the markets were Walmart and Target. These North Texas FM's actually transported things from the ground. Cotton covered the land and picking season must have been in full swing. Trucks zoomed by, filled with white balls, of which many escaped and littered the shoulder. For miles, the roadside looked like the aftermath of one epic pillow fight. Then there was wheat, corn, cows, some goats, and plenty of churches. Some chapels had funny signs: EAT THE BREAD OF LIFE OR YOU'LL BE TOAST. Too bad I'm gluten-free.

I examined the prairie off FM 2373. The empty road and vacant land made Amarillo feel days away, but the crow could fly there in a half hour. I love a good middle-of-nowhere mystery, and Texas has many. This one consisted of a massive, multistory white building surrounded by miles of pasture. The parking lot was filled with a hundred cars. No signs, no labels. Where did the vehicles come from? What did the people do? No cell signal to answer the riddle. I pictured classrooms for "enhanced interrogation" training. When cell signal returned, I found my conspiratorial guess not far-fetched. The building belonged to Pantex, and according to their website: "The Pantex Plant, located northeast of Amarillo, Texas, is the nation's primary facility for the final assembly, dismantlement, and maintenance of nuclear weapons." *Wow*. We had just driven by an apocalypse factory. Only in America?

A different hour, a different road, another large facility. This one was fenced in with barbed wire, razor wire, and barbed wire wrapped with razor wire. The road sign: HITCHHIKERS MAY BE ESCAPING INMATES.

What's more nostalgic than boredom? To combat it, Sarah and I unleashed the arsenal of the iPhone. Spotify played Horse Meat Disco's *Love and Dancing*, and somewhere near Childress, Texas, I declared it the best album of 2020. Audible provided a welcomed distraction with Bradley Garrett's *Bunker*, a book that investigates the world of doomsday preppers. Glitterbox Radio Show brought the grooves on Soundcloud. Brene Brown enlightened us on the Podcast app. ARE YOU NOT ENTERTAINED? Oh, look, a hill! Never mind, just a landfill. Keep driving, you're likely to find Jesus at some point.

When I was ten years old, Papa Herb joined us on a Texas road trip. When we passed one of the many billboards that said—JESUS IS THE ANSWER—he blurted out in his Brooklyn burr, "Well, what the fuck is the question?" I pictured him back in San Diego, dressed in business casual, watching the news from his recliner. I missed the ole clean-shaven charmer. But I was far from clean-shaven, with my beard growing thick and curling towards the steering wheel—long, but not as long as the rubber slog across Texas.

Let Texans know the bearded Jew had returned. Not the one with answers to unasked questions. Not the one whose face appears on billboards or candles. Not the one worthy of worship. No, the bearded Jew who had turned wine into puke. The one who died for no one's sins, not even his own. The bearded Jew who needed all the grace, simply to do life a little better.

Chapter 22
D.W.D.I.
(Driving with Daddy Issues)

MY BODY WAS exhausted, pushed to the brink. My eyelids slipped closed. I forced them back open for another mile. Cruise control was set at 75 mph. My right foot relaxed as I barreled on in the fast lane. A sprinkling of Sunday churchgoers replaced the usual midmorning rush hour. December made for a late sunrise that whitened the heavy clouds and brightened the sky. The light did nothing to penetrate the darkness of my soul. My eyelids surrendered; I fell asleep. The world went black and took me with it.

BOOM! A collision. The front driver-side tire bounced off the concrete median. I jolted awake, yanking the steering wheel like an angler fighting the catch of his life. I jerked right, then left, trying to reel the beast in. The friction of rubber and road sent a shrill screech into the air. The vehicle steadied, but my inner monster continued its roar.

I cruised northbound again. RPMs still churning. 75 mph still on the speedometer. My friend looked over from the passenger seat. He stared, hoping his face could say the words he couldn't speak as he began crying. Terror sank his eyeballs behind the bunkers of his cheeks. Bunkers are built for a beating, and his tear-covered cheeks looked like targets. With my left hand, I grabbed the steering wheel in the center. With my right, I reared back, then slapped him across the face. My open hand sent the tears flying away with whatever dignity I had left.

"Get it together!" I shouted at him, possessed by alcohol and haunted by no sleep. In the backseat, the ghoulish laughter of a different drunk friend echoed through the SUV. "*Ha-ha, ha-hahaha!*" Next to him, two beers floated in a cooler of melted ice. Thirty cans had filled the cooler when we started the drive, already drunk. Before I passed out again, I pulled over and crawled into the backseat. The bloodshot whites of my eyes became the white flag of surrender, retreating to the darkness of that day.

The year was 2007. I wasn't always a decent person, a recovered person. The antonyms of today's personality are the synonyms of my past: delusional, arrogant, sick, and lost. All of that is still in me, only tempered and restrained. I once resembled a cracked iPhone screen: performing but broken, like looking at something you know should get fixed. My actions were inexcusable, my graces undeserving.

Yet those graces kept me alive when I was apathetic about living. One of my saviors was the strong cage of that SUV, a used Chevy Tahoe that was champagne in color but malt liquor in use. That vehicle saved more lives than mine. The only damage rendered from that collision was a wheel misalignment so crooked that the steering wheel had to be forced twenty degrees counter-clockwise to make the vehicle go straight.

If the concrete barrier had a different curvature. If the road had been at a different angle. If someone had been in the lane next to me. If I had the decency to not drive drunk. It was the only time in my life I was awoken by a collision, but not the only time my alcoholism should have cost me my life.

I-45 is a freeway that should bear a memorial with my name. The same freeway Rudy cruised south on in November of 2020, heading to the same city. Back then, Houston was still home. Now, it's "where I'm from."

In the left lane, a familiar nervousness arose. After my near-death collision, the anxiousness returns anytime I have a concrete barrier near the driver's side. The same sweaty palms and curled knuckles belong to the same body, of the same name, but to a different man. I looked over at the small space between Rudy's tire and the concrete wall with the eyes of a sane person. *I'll stay in the right lane*, I thought. Rudy drifted to the slow lane, letting pickup trucks and SUVs zoom by on the left.

Sarah's bare feet pressed against the glovebox. The purple phoenix feather atop her foot was still and strong. She stared out the window with a thousand thoughts of her own. A hundred pine trees sprayed pollen into the winds of an approaching thunderstorm. "Angel On My Shoulder" by Kaskade played on the stereo, but the actual tune was nostalgia. Every part of the drive triggered a memory: pinecones, freeway barriers, and the songs I played during tougher times. Somewhere east of Decatur, the small rolling hills with rocky dry bushes had turned into the East Texas forests, and the climate of my childhood.

Surrounded by the flapjack flatlands of inescapable redundancy, the windshield brought up emotions that even a 35,000-foot-high vantage could not. I had not driven to Houston since I moved away in 2011. And for good reason. It takes three hours to fly home and three days to drive home. On a plane, with limited legroom and recycled air— man counts the time. In a vehicle, with the piney scents and humid, pollen-choking air of lost years—time counts the man. Flying brings you home, and driving brings home to you.

Texas extends the South and starts the West. We had crossed the climate threshold. The warm, southern air congealed like sitting grits, simmering memories I wished I didn't have.

The fast lane out of the past was to obsess about the future. In a few hours, my fears and hopes would be battling it out. Sarah was about to meet my immediate family for the first time. If judgment is a family gene, ours fit tight like Wranglers on a cowboy. Of course, Sarah would get a proper assessment, but it was our lifestyle that worried me most. I silently began crafting my responses to imaginary questions. *So, when are ya'll getting jobs? You're not gonna live in that thing forever, are you? Have you thought about marriage? Don't ya'll want kids?*

My family's love language is not quality time or acts of service—it's words of worry. Support usually comes in the form of suppressed opinions, and no comments would be the hope of tolerant times. Loaded questions and condescending statements would be the tests of my growth. My therapist was on standby.

My father pushed his walker down the sidewalk. Karen had been gone for over a decade. Now his fourth wife, Sheryl, walked beside him. To ensure my dad didn't have another fall, Sheryl wrapped her fingers around his arm to help steady him. My old man looked more fragile than ever, his walk more shuffling than stepping.

At this time, my relationship with my father was the kind of good you know could be better. Usually cordial, surface-level, and void of vulnerability. He was never absent, very supportive in some areas, hypercritical in others. And he loved me. He loved me so much—that I never doubted. I suppose it's the emotional duality we shared more than anything: the ability to judge one another hard, and love regardless.

A poor kid from Brooklyn to a guy who sought prenuptial agreements, my dad had worked for the same company for thirty years, retiring with a lofty title and a healthy pension. Yet he was a mysterious man whose mood swung like a metronome. Would Sarah see his charm or witness his rage?

It was lunchtime at a popular Cajun restaurant. Sarah and I sat across from my father and his wife.

"It's so nice to finally meet you, Dave and Sheryl," said Sarah.

My father smiled. "It's nice to meet you, too. How do you like Houston?"

"Um, well, I'm looking forward to seeing where Andrew's fr—"

"It's hot as hell," my dad interjected.

"Ha, yes. I can't believe it's November."

"It muss get hot in the van," said Sheryl.

"Yeah, it can," Sarah admitted, "but honestly, it was so cold before we got to Texas."

"Well that doesn't sound fun," said Sheryl, her southern drawl extended certain syllables and cut others off.

"Yeah, I don't like the cold, but it's been worth it," Sarah replied. "Has Andrew shown you pictures of the van?"

"No," replied my dad, disinterested.

I pulled out my phone.

"Oh, it's a lot bigger than I thought," he said. "You guys did a good job."

"Do you like to travel?" Sarah asked.

"I used to travel for work a lot," replied my dad.

"Uh-huh, and did you like it?"

"It was work. The firm sent me to Brazil, Mexico, and Europe. Paris was my favorite."

"And how about you, Sheryl?" Sarah angled towards her.

"Well, we use-ta go to Vegas. Dave loves the Bellagio. And we travel to see my son's competitions—"

"Ugh, don't get me started on that," interrupted my dad.

Sheryl shot a look at him. "Oh, come on. You had fun the lass time we went. But to be honest, it's hard with Dave's balance. When we were in the Caribbean lass, Dave just had the wurss fall."

My father shot her a more intense look. An awkward silence fell as we all began eating.

My dad finished chewing and glared at me. "You been thinking about teaching?"

I looked at my food. "Uh, yeah I think about it. I miss my students. But I can't say I miss the job. At least not right now."

"Are you going back to teaching after the trip?"

"I don't know."

He looked at Sarah, "I keep telling him that I hope teaching will get him back to a *real* career."

My molars ground into one another.

Sarah reacted quickly, "So, what was Andrew like as a kid?"

My dad went into his favorite story, which involves me throwing an empty bottle from my crib and nailing my mom in the face with it.

"And how long have you two been married?" Sarah asked.

"Umm," my father looked over at his wife.

"Well, it was in the summer," she said. "I guess it would've been six years or—"

"No, it's been longer than that," he said.

I chimed in, "Well, it would have been 2013."

"Right. Seven years," said my dad.

"Yeah, that's right," agreed Sheryl.

"So, what's been the highlight of your marriage?" asked Sarah.

I grabbed my iced tea and took a nervous pull, bracing myself for impact. Sarah had no idea, but I had asked the same exact question three years before, on their anniversary.

My dad's face went flat. He looked at his wife, then back to Sarah. He paused. "After all my health issues ... I'm just lucky to be alive."

His wife winced, waiting for more, then spoke, "Ummm ... I ain't thought about that. Hmm. It's been hard with his health, and his balance is jus gettin wurrse. Well, he did jus buy me this ring." She extended her diamond-studded fingers and looked down. "And I was fixin-ta get the Bentley—"

My dad interrupted her, "It's not *fixin-ta*, it's pronounced *fixing to*. You have to learn how to speak *English*."

"That's enough, Dave," she snapped.

My stomach churned. Their answers hadn't changed.

Dad looked over at Sarah, "They don't speak English in *Al-uh-bam-uh*."

I cringed. A waiter stopped at our table. "Can I get ya'll anything?"

"More Diet Coke," grunted my dad.

"I need more tea. Unsweet with three Sweet-n-Lows," demanded Sheryl.

"We're good, thanks," I said.

"Oh, and I need a new fork for this carrot cake," commanded my father.

"Two forks," his wife declared, "Do you want any, Sarah? Better bring a few forks."

"You don't need any carrot cake," my father said, looking at his wife.

Sheryl looked down, the color exiting her face. "Dave thinks I need-ta lose weight," she mumbled.

"I'm gonna go to the bathroom," said my father.

"I'll help you," I said, pushing away from the table and grabbing his walker.

Afterwards, my father dug into his cake.

"You gotta try this, Sarah," he said.

Sarah took a bite. Sheryl went in for another.

"That's enough," my father scolded her.

I anxiously tapped my foot until we were done. The meal was the only thing that left a good taste in my mouth.

Sarah let out a sigh when we were alone and back in Rudy. "Ugh. I'm so glad that's over," she said.

"I know."

"They didn't ask me a single question about myself! They made zero effort to get to know me."

"I know, I noticed that too," I said. Seeing Sarah so upset was surprising, but oddly validating.

"And when you went to take your dad to the bathroom, Sheryl said, 'You know Andrew's father doesn't approve of ya'lls van trip.'"

"What? Are you serious?"

"Yeah. No lead into it or anything. Like she had been waiting to say that the whole time."

"You gotta be kidding me ..."

Yeah, goodbye serenity. The spiral began its spin. My rising anger morphed into an obsession. I spent the afternoon fuming, embarrassed, disappointed. It wasn't my first time, but something about having Sarah there pulled the trigger that family squeezes best. My panic symptoms began to flare up. The chest pains. The lightheadedness. The deteriorating thoughts.

Sarah interrupted my pity party, bringing up my therapist, suggesting, "Maybe you should see if Mary has an opening."

Who was I kidding, thinking I could sort through it on my own? By the end of the day, I had a session booked.

2020, a boom year for the therapist. And my therapist, Mary, had a full caseload. Mary offered more than her ears; she knew how to peel a big onion. And God bless her, she always made time for me when I needed it most.

I had been to enough sessions and should have seen it coming. The things we don't want to hear rarely sound predictable. Mary spoke the question with equal parts neutrality and curiosity, ever timely and poignant.

"Have you thought about telling your father what you just told me?"

The question terrified me, shook me. I took a dry swallow. "No, not really. I'd be too scared to."

"Have you tried before?"

"Once. About four years ago."

"How'd that go?"

"Umm, terrible."

"What happened?"

"Well, we went to our favorite restaurant. He was in a good mood. It seemed like a perfect time. My mentor helped me craft what to say, in a way that wouldn't be blamey. My dad saw right through it. In the middle of the restaurant, he started yelling, 'That was Karen's fault! What do you want me to do about it, huh? I won't make amends for things I didn't do!' I forget what else he said. I shut down and didn't push it any further."

"Are you willing to try again?"

"Ugh." Hourly rate earned. I paused, looking away from the phone screen. Then the thought came: *If I permit myself the right to change, then I'm obligated to give others the same opportunity.* "Damn it. I guess so. Yeah, I'm willing."

The annoying pain in my sternum felt like it would never go away as Mary coached me through the action. I took notes, and we did some role-play. (I'm sure if you googled "therapist role play," you'd get something completely different.)

Per her advice, I met my father alone, at his home. No Sheryl, no Sarah. Just my old man, who leaned against his walker. The same jawline I see in the mirror stared back at me, only I could see the consequence of age and stress. More than the balding scalp and graying hair, the lack of a smile struck me the most. Here stood a man who had worked hard to provide his kids with a giant step forward but never found the balance to give himself more. How do I know? He had retired three separate times, returning to corporations not for the money but for whatever challenge and sense of importance he found there.

Now he withered away his senior years, handicapped with bad balance. Western medicine had kept him alive through prostate cancer, heart stints, kidney infections, E. coli, and now Parkinson's Disease (though this diagnosis wouldn't come for another six months). He was as intelligent as anyone I knew, but since his final retirement, he lived without much purpose. The only times I saw him genuinely smile were when he was around his grandchildren. While my father and I shared features inside and out, our perspectives on life seemed to be growing further and further apart. My dad did want me to succeed, but we were two men who measured success by different metrics—one by money, the other by emotions.

"You been watching football?" asked my dad.

"No," I replied.

My father went on, groveling about the Houston Texans' defense. My mind drifted. I lifted my gaze. A chandelier dangled above the breakfast table. Then another one above the dining room table. Two more chandeliers hung in the entryway. He had almost as many chandeliers as I had T-shirts. The midday sun danced in each dangling crystal. The realization sparkled back at me: I was just another kid doing the opposite of the parent they resented the most.

How naive I was, driving around with a self-righteous chip on my shoulder, thinking that my minimalism was inspired by my love of nature and my willingness to live differently; all in the hope that it would make me happier. Could it be that simple? That I was just a textbook rebel kid, acting out his daddy issues? That I was willing to take more drastic measures to be happy, not because of human nature, but because my father was so miserable? I thought about all the anger I suppressed so I didn't rage like him. Why I left corporate America so I wouldn't come home mad at the world like he did. Why I put so much intention into my relationship with Sarah, just so she never felt like one of my father's wives. It was like each bulb on the chandelier lit up, one rebellious realization at a time.

My father ended his rant about the NFL. "So, did Sarah say anything about meeting us?"

The body kept the score. My sinuses grew hot, my shoulders became bastions of stress. Those pestilent chest pains intensified. The panic was doing what it does: telling me to quit, to avoid, to keep things safe and distant. But I kept my word. Lord knows, I'm too cheap to spend another $130 to tell my therapist I wimped out. A deep breath, a prayer, and a step into the discomfort.

"Yes, she did. But, Dad, can we get serious for a second?"

"Yeah ... "

"I want you to know how grateful I am for everything you've done for me. Even though I don't have a traditional job, I still use the education you provided me every day. But I'm thirty-four now. I know I'm wired differently. The same things don't energize me that energize you. I have to ask, why do you hate that I'm a teacher?"

He sat still. Silent. Calm. "I don't hate that you're a teacher."

"Then why do you still pressure me to live like you did?"

"You know, I was a teacher once. The firm paid me to teach night classes at NYU."

"Isn't that how you met Mom? Wasn't she your student?"

"Yeah."

"Dad, I literally wouldn't be here if you didn't teach."

"True. But I hated it. So, I … I was hoping it was a stepping stone to get you back into something more lucrative. I worry about how little money you make, especially because you refuse to let me help you."

"Dad, I'm not saying I'm going back to teaching. But you need to know that I didn't hate it. I loved it. But the point is … the point is that I may never have a traditional career. Or get married. Or have kids. Or make the kind of money you did. And I don't … I don't want it to keep getting in the way of our relationship—"

"Andrew—"

"Dad, you don't have to agree with it. Just don't voice it all the time."

Stillness. A straight face. Is this what healing looks like? Father and son having a conversation we'd both rather avoid. Me judging him for his crystal chandeliers, him resenting me for taking all of the sacrifices he made in his own life, all the advantages he provided me, to go live in a van and travel around.

"Okay," he said.

I almost didn't know how to respond. Had he found the acceptance to be okay with my lifestyle?

"Thanks," I replied.

"It's just, having kids was the best thing in my life. I'd hate for you to miss that experience."

"I get it. I'm not saying never. Just not now."

"Okay," he took his eyes off mine, "and I … I want to spend more time together. I miss you."

I fidgeted in my seat. My armpits burning, my brow ready to burst with sweat. The scariest panic symptom, the lightheadedness, came on. But it wasn't the panic's voice that I wanted to listen to. It was

Mary's: *Go towards the panic, it won't kill you. It can't. And after it intensifies, it will lose strength. You'll feel it dissolve.*

My eyes drifted to the chandelier, to those damn crystals. I looked back at my father. His skinny legs, his frail and failing body. I had never seen him cry, never even seen him come close to it. If I had gone sixteen years, he could have easily gone sixty without shedding a tear. I wondered how all that suppressed pain affected his health. Yes, he was physically weak, but what about his presence? Was the same man I feared still in there, or had his anger fizzled away with his strength?

I ended the silence, "Okay. But, there's something we need to discuss if that's going to happen."

"Okay…"

"Dad, when we're alone, we have a nice time. But there's something different when you're with your wife. You act different and boss her around. I don't want to be around ya'll if that's how you're gonna treat her. And I definitely don't want to bring Sarah around it."

"What do you mean?"

"Dad, I shouldn't have to spell it out for you. Her accent … her weight."

"Oh, yeah? What are you saying?" his tone stiff, daring me to challenge him.

"Jesus, Dad. I'm not telling you what to do with your marriage. You want to use money and control her, tell her how to speak and look, that's between ya'll. But why would I want to spend time with you if that's what it looks like? And why would I want to bring my girlfriend around that? I mean, c'mon. Ya'll didn't ask Sarah a single question, and you had never even met her. You were too busy belittling Sheryl."

I felt as if I was staring into a gurgling volcano. A darkness consumed his eyes. The silence stretched. I felt dizzy.

Then, his demeanor shifted. He spoke, "You're right. I could be nicer."

I was aghast, almost too shocked to feel the relief, the hope, the panic dissolve away.

"Thanks," I said, "I love you."

"I love you too," he replied.

Maybe I was naive to think he would be a different man after that day. But I knew one thing for certain: something big changed within me. My mental health struggles had created the desire to take action, to not live with the turmoil of suppressed emotions and the regret of tight lips. Perhaps aging had brought my father a tenderness that I didn't know survived. I left that conversation with an unfamiliar sentiment—a desire to spend more time with my old man.

It wasn't about a chandelier or a van, it wasn't even about money. It was about life, our most precious resource. And time, the ultimate commodity. It was about change, the real cash crop. My therapist's question altered more than my trip, it enhanced my life. It undoubtedly transformed the dynamic with my father, which seemed more crucial given the uncertain amount of days he had left.

I praised Mary's work and honored the road. This time there would be no plane ride, toting a backpack full of clothes and a duffle bag full of resentments. This time the road had brought new pace, and with it, opportunity.

Cruise control had nearly killed me before. I would not let it again.

Chapter 23
Home, Part II

MY LIFE, MUCH like anyone's, has been filled with highs and lows. I have shat my pants in the Andes Mountains and have been rescued from the bottom of the Grand Canyon. I have danced all night until the Ibiza sunrise, and surfed waves so long they started in one zip code and ended in another. I have let an agonizing ten days of silent meditation break and rebuild me, and more than once, I have lost hope until it had to be borrowed. Choices and consequences, depression to bliss. Among all the peaks of happiness or plateaus of joy, there upholds a consistent trend: my happiest moments are when I feel free.

In 2011, at the age of twenty-five, I got my first hit of freedom and have chased that high ever since. West was the way. Eddie Vedder's "Setting Forth" blared on the stereo. In the rearview mirror, the skyline of downtown Houston reflected the afternoon sun off the thousands of skyscraper windows. I had spent the last few years behind some of those windows. Not next to any of them—no, I had not earned the privilege of having my desk next to a window. So, I would walk the width of a cubicle to get from my workstation to the glass, where I looked out across land that was tortilla flat and concrete gray.

There, I dreamt of a different way to spend my time. I contemplated various schemes to make money that didn't involve me working indoors for nine hours a day. I thought of the places I might go, all the other locations I could live. "Houston is a great place to make money and save money," my father would say. He was right, but every day I tried this rationale, *free* felt less like an emotion and more like a concept.

That must have been why leaving Houston in 2011 was one of the more pivotal moments of my life. I would be moving to Florida to go back to school, where routines and obligations would be commonplace again. But until then, for three glorious summer months, *I was free*—from cubicles and copy machines, surface-level conversations and conference room meetings. Free from clothes that needed dry cleaning, and free from playing the CSI detective in the case of which asshole coworker microwaved fish for lunch. Above all, I was free from that pestering question—*what if?*

I said goodbye to a loving community of people in Houston, and I said goodbye to the obligations of adulthood: no rent, bills, or meal prep. No more lease, and no more commute. Moreover, I was experiencing a new liberation from my own demons. Sober for one year, I was free from the vicious cycle of alcoholism. Free from hangovers, and gut-emptying trips to the toilet. Free from the guilt that looked back in the mirror, and free from the ball and chain of self-centered delusion. Getting sober was the hardest thing I had ever done. I knew life's shackles would always be there if I wanted them back. I chose to drive instead.

Everything I needed for several weeks of living was tucked into my small SUV. Minimalism was not a word I knew, but it was an experience I was about to have. And how it changed me. By the end of the trip, I recognized that in choosing little, I was in fact opening myself up to so much more.

Houston had not been home for many years. More like an old friend I never talk to on the phone and only see in person once a year. No hard feelings, just lots to catch up on. H-Town and its people had always been good to me, even when I wasn't good to them. That's why Houston is more than where I'm from, it's where I burned bridges and began building better ones. After all, a place doesn't raise you, but it does leave its mark—scars of regrets or stretch marks of growth.

Nine years later, with more scars and stretch marks than I could count, Sarah and I returned to the city where I nearly lost my life. Once again, we watched the forest turn to suburb, then to city sprawl. Past fajita restaurants, BBQ joints, and Whataburger. Past strip clubs, furniture stores, and mega-churches that seated more people than the population of towns I had grown accustomed to driving through. The skyscrapers appeared as the interstate continued its slither. Familiar, yes. But home? Nay.

Texas and California have their prejudices and I have worn both. How many times had I been in California and heard them say, "I wish Texas would go ahead and secede already." Or been in Texas and heard them say, "I wish California would have its earthquake and just fall into the ocean." I had shot guns with Republicans in Lufkin, and danced with elephant-pant-wearing hippies in Encinitas. I had drunk beer floating the Guadalupe in the Texas heat, and attended parties with "clothing optional" yurts in the underbelly of California weirdness. Experience the yin-yang of a nation but fear the echo chamber, where bad ideas get worse support.

In Houston I claimed both identities by drinking green juice in the morning and consuming a pound of smoked brisket before nightfall. Sarah cringed a little when I ate homemade goat curry with my hands for one meal and a slab of BBQ ribs for another. We both agreed that Houston isn't the ideal foodie destination for a vegetarian. Her open mind was rewarded with Connie's Frozen Custard and tubs of Blue Bell Ice Cream.

Those most impressed with van life still attended elementary school. My nephew and niece, eight and five, thought Rudy was the coolest thing they had ever seen. They were amazed by every feature, jumping up and down, wanting more. I showed my niece all of our photos. "I didn't know places like this really existed!" she exclaimed when she saw the snow-capped peaks and strange deserts. They both got souvenirs of polished crystals that had traveled the long way from Yachats, Oregon.

Home has many connotations: where you live, where you sleep, where you were raised. Home is where you hang your hat. Home is where the heart is. There's no place like home. It's an easy word if you go from the house of your parents to a house of your own. But Rudy had no address. My answers to *where are you from?* were feeling too lengthy or inauthentic.

Sarah and I spent two weeks in Houston, and while we slept at a relative's house, Rudy sat idle along the curb, bored but never neglected. In Houston, everything can change in a day. I never regret visiting, and I never regretted leaving.

Cruising around the suburb I once called home, Sarah appeared amused with the tour: "That's where I lived. That's the Walmart I worked at. Oh, and over there is the middle school my friends and I nearly exploded with fireworks."

En route to one of those friends' houses, we drove past Cypress Creek High School, my alma mater. The exterior had been renovated, but the appearance was still similar enough to transport me down the wormhole of memories, specifically a day engraved in the mural of my life.

It was my Junior year there, everything familiar, as it should be. Baggy jeans, tight T-shirt, Motorola cell phone in the left pocket, Honda Civic keys and a note from my girlfriend in the right. Entering the classroom, my favorite teacher, Mr. Aricio, greeted me. He taught history, always wearing a suit but removing his loafers while he lectured, pacing in silk socks. The bell rang for class to start. My teacher's demeanor shifted, his drastic words and serious tone capturing everyone's attention.

"You might not realize it, but today your lives changed and they will *never* be the same," he stated, then paused for an uncomfortable length of silence before explaining.

That day, the United States had invaded Iraq. Mr. Aricio was a Vietnam veteran. Before his tour ended, he had watched his best friend get shot right in front of him. In the middle of the night, the glow of my teacher's lit cigarette had given up their location. He never smoked again.

Like most my age, I comprehended the severity of 9-11. Yet, I couldn't help but think my teacher was being overly dramatic. Consumed by youthful naiveness, my friends and I stayed busy, reveling in the glorious years of pre-adulthood. My clique was half-wholesome, half-hooligan. A tight-knit clan of males that personified American diversity: Mexican, Vietnamese, Black, Italian, Honduran, Pakistani, German, and myself, "Tha Jew," as my friends called me. We were of the *Jackass* and *Chappelle's Show* era, and our cultural banter forced me to get witty or get ridiculed. As teenagers, we used to wander into the woods outside our neighborhood, toting pellet guns to hunt squirrels and doves. We looked like the Model UN meets *Lord of the Flies*. Oh, the things you could get away with back then.

However, by the end of high school, Mr. Aricio's prophecy started to come true. A US Marine Corp recruiter made his rounds at the cafeteria. One by one, my friends enlisted until half of them deployed to Iraq and Afghanistan.

Then, one by one, I watched them come home, returning to a Texas that had changed little. Though they'd be called heroes and get applauded at sporting events, there wasn't a military discount or a VA appointment that could undo the things that had been done. Gone were the pranksters and boys brimming with hubris. Home were the men scarred and transformed. My friends, once teenagers who laughed and pranked, were now men who screamed in their sleep. How I came to hate war, even though I'd never been. This disdain wasn't born from romantic ideology or Oliver Stone films, rather from those screams—the PTSD of soldiers, the darkened dreams of my once-innocent peers.

Now, my friends grow bellies, bank accounts, and babies. Cop, electrician, mechanic, teacher, computer programmer, graphic designer, insurance sales, and career-less me. To the Texans, I'm the California hippie: strange but not a stranger. As the only one who no longer lived in the county, I feared the time when we'd retell twenty-year-old stories too many times, and I'd resemble too outside of an outsider. Whether it be politics or life experiences, jobs or living situation, every return left me feeling more like a foreigner—a chameleon on a good day, awkwardly out of place on a bad.

One statistic that describes the cast of characters I call my friends—three of eight men were diagnosed with gout before the age of thirty. Sarah and I arrived at a gout-survivor's house. A single-story home with a big yard, tucked in a neighborhood near the high school. The smell of red meat above charcoal filled the air outside. Inside, a pot of slow-cooked ranchero beans simmered next to Mexican rice. Our group never needed incentives to relive the past, but the boxing ring provided it nonetheless: Mike Tyson (age fifty-four) vs Roy Jones Jr. (age fifty-one). Nothing says *old* like paying pay-per-view to watch the favorite fighters of your childhood try to give each other a concussion a few years before their social security kicks in.

My desires and doubts had a boxing match of their own. Despite the longevity of my friendships, my friends in recovery knew much more about me, and I knew more about them. Being in an environment where sober men opened up made it harder to watch the other men I love suffer in suppression. How badly I wanted to talk with my oldest friends about everything—about war and struggles, alcoholism and nightmares. But my friends had not been trained to talk about their hardships, they had been trained to kill, to be tough, to destroy their enemy. In reality, we had set them up to destroy themselves.

One by one, my friends climbed in Rudy and got a tour of my new home. There was the one who had come home to discover that no amount of prescriptions or alcoholic beverages could relieve the unrelievable. The one who had put a gun to his own head, frantically crying for help. And the ones who, like me, would never know the experience of war, only the toll it takes on the ones you love.

I thought a lot about Mr. Aricio's prophecy that night, and about the war within. Two decades prior, my friends had pulled me out of the suicidal depths of my early-teen depression without knowing it—just by being there, a distraction, a return to innocence. If only I could return that to them now.

Though years had passed, those horrific seconds when war showed its true colors still haunted us all, filling the gathering with an inadequate nostalgia. Surely, I wasn't the only one asking that pestering question: *what if?*

I had to remember, it wasn't just about me coming home, and that others had returned to this neighborhood with baggage I could never truly comprehend. Whether returning from war or coming back from vacation, the return to home isn't so much about inventorying what has changed, but identifying what needs to.

Mr. Aricio was right ... life was never the same for all of us after that day.

In Texas, van life was about as popular as communism. Heck, we saw more van conversions in the town of Moab than in the entire state. Around Houston, Rudy got his catwalk. Some were amazed; others curled their upper lip when they saw the size of our closets, the way we shower, and of course ... the toilet. "Bigger is better in Texas," they say; and the smaller the sweeter in van life. Houstonians love to make money and spend money. Sarah and I were unemployed and showering with a weed sprayer, living off an average of $750 per person each month, including: gas, car insurance, food, supplies, activities, entertainment, and laundry (2020 figure, not adjusted for inflation). Most people I knew spent that in a couple of days. Sarah and I left each suburban house saying, "I'm so glad we don't live that way, I couldn't do it." And I assume that most whispered the same to their spouse after they toured Rudy.

Once again, Houston shrunk in the rearview mirror. I might have left the familiar lands and lifestyles of my childhood without a morsel of envy; however, I didn't leave without baggage. For in my self-centered head was still that made-up conversation. In between my ears, I continued rambling off justifications for why I live the way I live. Between the van's windows and inside my mind lingered that pest of assumption. Where I internalized the judgments of friends and family. Where I wasted energy defending a lifestyle to people who didn't want it. Why couldn't I let other people live their lives, free from my judgment? Why couldn't I live my own, free from my pestilent overthinking?

Extended time on the road can spotlight the most limiting parts of ourselves. I said goodbye to friends and family but realized one more farewell needed sendoff if I were to truly be free. If I were to finally have an answer to the question: *Am I finally ready to live for myself?* Thus, I cast aside that fear of what others thought of me, for it bound me to places I wished to leave.

Our nation claims to be founded on freedom. In reality, it's founded on the fence … or the wall … or the mortgage, title, lease, or gate code. Warehouse floors to towering offices. Cubicles to corner suites. Apartments to gated mansions. The first Europeans that went west were trappers; now almost everyone is trapped.

We are fortified by walls of debt, gated by the boundaries of social pressure, and imprisoned by the concept of career. A house is only a dream if your finances are not a nightmare, and freedom is only realized when you don't feel trapped. Those that are the freest—that play by their own rules—often receive the most ridicule. They're threats, not heroes or pioneers. Most Americans don't want less, they want more. Even if it means more debt, more obligations, more worrying, and more stuck. The earn-it, take-it, compete-for-it, *Home of the Conformed.* The Land of the Free, *where?* The great reality is most Americans fear true freedom or so many wouldn't have a long list of reasons for why they avoid it.

What makes a home is not its size or decor, its approval or valuation—it's whether the owners know joy and the guests feel welcomed. If you have to ask, "How do you know if you're in love?", then you're probably not in love. And feeling *at home* is no different. The sensation is so desirable that many convince themselves that they know it, that they have it. Only when home truly takes form does this awareness sink in.

Of course, I am speaking from experience. Because for thirty-four years I had convinced myself I had a home until Rudy became my forever standard. I can't fully explain it, but things felt different for me inside that van. What can I say? Rudy was the one. So if *home* is a noble title, then Rudy deserved to be knighted. The road was now my stallion, my moving address of opportunity.

I won't rule out houses forever, but I'm done forcing myself to go to sleep in someone else's American Dream. Trying to keep up with others could have cost me an interesting life. While I encourage everyone to think critically about their own choices, freedom means not crucifying or converting those that pursue the opposite. As my mom always says, "It takes a lot of people to make a world."

Chapter 24
Deep in the Heart of Texas

IN THE WEST, Sarah and I were a couple of nobodies, another set of millennials living in a photogenic van. However, in Texas, we were gas station famous.

"Are ya'll the Willets?" said a man with a heavy twang. His belly ballooned out, ready to pop and unleash the entire Whataburger menu. Two suspenders strained with the stress of a barge's bowline, struggling to keep his denim pants afloat.

"The what?" I said.

"The Willets."

"Um, no Sir." I gave him a quizzical yet amicable look.

"Oh, well I hurd thair was a famuhlee nearby witha big white van named the Willets. I ain't met 'em yet. Thought ya'll might be'um."

"No, Sir."

"I hear they gotta buncha kids so they gotta use-uh big van like this to drive 'em all around."

I smiled. "Nope. We live in this thing. Just the two of us."

He gave the van one more look, a head tilt, a smile, and craned himself back into his dually truck.

Even the most fuel-efficient vehicles have to hit up a Texas gas station (or twenty) to cross from the South to the West, or from the Plains to the Swamps. And none says *welcome ya'll* more than Buc-ee's—technically a gas station, but more a beacon of Good-Ole-Boy excess. Everything is bigger in Texas and everything certainly is inside of a Buc-ee's. Sarah let Rudy hum under the big beaver face logo while I went to decide which of the eighteen urinals to decorate. As soon as I exited the restroom, a short woman crept up behind me and got my attention. Even if there was no pandemic, she stood uncomfortably close, bringing her face towards me as if coming in for a kiss. I arched back like it was my turn in the limbo line.

"Sorry to bother you but are ya'll that couple from *People* magazine?" she asked.

"Huh?"

"I saw your big white van outside and just had to check. There's some bloggers featured in *People* magazine and I thought ya'll might be them. Your van looks just like theirs."

"Nope, not us."

"Oh." She walked away, disappointed.

I came out to escort Sarah inside. I wanted to see her face as soon as she stepped in.

"What the ..." Sarah gawked, astounded at the monstrosity of the place. "How is this a gas station?"

She tried to take it all in. The smell of kolaches filled the air. I took her over to the bakery to explain the local delicacy, a sweet bread stuffed with meat and cheese, or with a fruit filling. The next counter over featured more types of beef jerky than breeds of cattle. Gift sets, every soda imaginable, a candy station, and a dozen touch screens to order BBQ. Racks of clothes displayed Lone Star State slogans (GOD BLESS TEXAS; EVERYTHING'S BIGGER IN TEXAS; DON'T MESS WITH TEXAS).

Rudy let down the gas station locals, but the Texas prices didn't let us down—$1.72/gallon, the cheapest we paid for diesel the entire trip. ($3.89/gallon back in California was the highest.)

We couldn't avoid I-10, the nation's femoral vein connecting Jacksonville, Florida, to Los Angeles, California. Westward, Rudy spun his slippers on the long straight interstate. I leaned back, guiding with three fingers from the bottom of the wheel. The speed limit hit 80, but we cruised at a sedated 68 mph. Rudy dragged heavier after putting on some holiday weight. Sarah and I had full bellies and a fridge stocked with leftovers from the Thanksgiving feast. We had done what you do in Houston: gain weight. As the humidity gave way to the desert, Sarah glowed brighter than the headlights, shining her way West, taking me along.

Meriwether Lewis and John Muir, Alexander Supertramp and Fievel. They all went West. A body needs many parts and the East functions as America's brains, the Middle its belly, the South its heart, and the West its pretty-eyed, smooth-skinned, muscular frame. The don't-need-it-but-like-to-look-at-it sexy physique of America. Sure, the West wins the eyes, but the land is more than some stereotypical description of beauty. The West is America's soul, where anyone can find God, and come up with the questions to ask Him.

So, giddy-up Rudy. To the terrains so diverse they can't be gentrified. To the places where freedom is a feeling. With jagged mountains and shimmering lakes. With the can't-cross'em canyons and mystical badlands. To the places pretty enough they need processing. To the West.

Yes, Rudy, take me *to the West*.

Wide and tall but thin on public land, Texas joined the union but gave over little. Instead of Forest Service or BLM banners, we saw posts with PRIVATE PROPERTY and NO TRESPASSING. Goodbye shared land, hello fences. Sure, you got your rest stops and Walmarts with long-haulers blaring through the night. We tried to avoid them, but often they were the only legal option for free overnight parking.

Westward, in Junction, we found southern hospitality in the form of free spots on the Llano River, tucked under oak and mesquite trees that had been decorated with Christmas lights. The only curious neighbor was a long-tailed weasel scavenging through the evening. We slept for twelve hours that night. So long to city sounds and WiFi frequencies.

Now Is the Time

A counterclockwise turn to TX-385. The Sierra Madera Astro-
bleme sign made an ordinary drive extraterrestrial. Rudy coasted
down the remains of the eight-mile-wide impact crater, then churned
up and on, to Big Bend National Park.

Reservation-less and surrounded by ranches of fenced-in nothing,
we opted to do things in the spirit of America's early road-trippers by
pulling over and utilizing the space of gravel between the road and
the fence. While Rudy rested, the horror of noiseless land lunged for
my thoughts. Silence. Stillness. Insanity. I yelled as loud as I could.
The scream disappeared. I did it again. It was a sound vacuum,
consuming every decibel. *Where did the noise go?* It didn't matter. I had
reacclimated by shouting my way back into the culture-less chasms of
West Texas.

Sarah and I took a walk, listening to fighting javelina squealing in
the thickets of juniper and cacti. It was West Texas wild, with more
roadrunners than cars, *beep beep.* One roadrunner walked right up to
our feet and looked up. Its eye swirled, resembling a divine portal, a
cosmic gate. I found the ethereal lens of this trotting bird as
transcendent as anything on Earth. The city of Houston was now a
constellation: shining lights connected by man's imagination, light
years away.

It's no secret that Texans hate handouts, and we paid the price.
Our first paid campsite of the trip was Cottonwood Campground,
under the watchful eye of a great horned owl. The hooter reminded
me of old Papa Herb: looks to be asleep but is actually in deep
thought.

Up the Chisos Mountains we hiked, finding a quiet overlook to
snack and enjoy the view. Then, the sound of incessant buzzing. I
looked up to see a drone, something the park prohibited.

"NO DRONES ALLOWED!" I yelled. The three males piloting
the thing looked over at me, shrugged their shoulders, then went back
to the remote control. The blades continued to chop away at the view,
destroying the silence I sought to savor.

Armed with park permits, Sarah and I set up camp in eyesight of Mexico. Strange sounds of deep and hungry voices broke the silence. Then the sound of crunching vegetation. The grass stood two-humans tall. I scanned the perimeter. Cartels? Immigration coyotes? Nope, it was just cows. Sarah and I followed the *moos* through the game trails, chasing the scent of water. Mexican cattle had come over for some American grazing, ate their share, and left their diplomacy in the form of cow patties. Then they returned home, no visa required. I watched them cross the Rio Grande and there was nothing grand about it. A murky flow of gray water that tempted one to jump across, instead of wade through.

Santa Elena Canyon was a ranger's recommendation that didn't disappoint. We marched along the water's edge, between the sheer canyon walls. Finally, here I saw the grand: an exquisite, nature-crafted channel. It wasn't the river's borders that were of interest, rather, its transformation. One could appreciate the Rio Grande's journey, for it had traveled a long way, through obstacles and detours, to create something so beautiful. It was a journey I could relate to.

Study Butte, Texas (population 188), took up the sides of the tarmac. The town didn't even make a dot in my 2012 Rand McNally Atlas, yet an assortment of structures lined the road. Abandoned buildings, a dusty store selling cash-only crystals, and a gas station with a sign above the urinal that said: ONLY FLUSH WHEN NECESSARY. I deemed my urine unnecessary (still not sure what that says about me).

As I saw with Moab, a national park designation can simultaneously protect the wilderness and transform a town. Down TX-170, Rudy rolled by river rafting outfitters and an assortment of rental properties. Teepees, yurts, adobe houses, condos, RV parks, and glamping sites hung onto the sides of the road.

Rudy, short for Rodolfo, is Mexican by blood—mostly manufactured south of the border and initially purchased by a Mexican American. In a past life, our van had ruled the roads of Baja and sheltered a Mexican family. Rudy loved churning so close to his cultural origins, smiling with bug-stained teeth as we wrapped around the Rio Grande. Up and down canyons and desert mountains, Mexico in sight when we curved to the left, Texas forever to the right. The Chihuahuan Desert never lost intrigue with its exotic birds and expansive views. The most popular vehicle—the big SUVs painted white and decaled with US Border Patrol logos—hid around every other bend. At every checkpoint we crossed, the agents took a glance at our faces and waved us by.

We entered the town of Presidio, where I stopped for an all-important question.

"Hi, do you know anywhere that sells *chilaquiles*?" I asked.

She was large, Latina, and undeniably confused. "Sells what?"

"Chill-uh-kill-ez." I said again.

"Chill-uh-what?" She looked at this gringo as if I had driven in from Omaha or Anchorage.

"You know, the breakfast food, with the chips." *Pinche gringo.*

"AHHH! You mean chill-AH-keel-lez."

I gushed. "Yes, chill-AHHH-keeel-eggs," I tried. She laughed.

"No, I don't. Sorry." She gave me a recommendation for a Mexican restaurant anyhow.

A mile down the road I pulled in. The place croaked, just how I like it—a sign with no neon left, ring the bell, order at the counter, eat outside, don't ask to use the restroom if you know what's good for you. This should be good.

A sweet Mexican gal answered the bell, sliding open a glass window. Behind her, I saw her old *abuela* stirring a pot.

"Hi," I smiled, "do you have any *chilaquiles*?"

"What?"

Damn it. "Chill-ahh-kill-ez?"

She looked like I asked to see a gynecologist. I tried one more time.

"AHHH! You mean chill-AH-keel-lez." She laughed harder than the first *señorita*. Somewhere, my Mexican ex-girlfriends danced *banda* around my disgrace.

I butchered the word one more time. She laughed, "No, we don't."

Tacos, guacamole, and gringo shame it was. With Mexico in sight, the meal delivered. Sarah and I had eaten at Mexican restaurants in every state thus far. The torture done to tortillas north of the border states was as tormenting as my pronunciation of *chilaquiles*. These tacos in Presidio made my tastebuds sing, *"Cucurrucucu!"* Sarah had the best chile relleno of her life, then the stomach ache to go with it. She grumbled harder than Rudy as we drove up TX-67, heading towards Texas's most peculiar town.

I love a good anomaly, and Marfa, Texas (population 1,831), has the reputation as such. Weird, artsy, out-of-place, I had been told. Though I approached this contemporary art hub with low expectations, it still felt as if they might be too high. Oh expectations, the travelers' trap. After all, contemporary art failed to enlighten me on the plague of narcissism on a good day, and this day, the 2020 vibes wore on drearily in West Texas. Closed signs hung on glass doors. Art galleries posted phone numbers for appointment-only visitations. A bulletin board read: WEAR A MASK, STOP THE SPREAD. WE HAVE NO HOSPITAL HERE AND NEED YOUR HELP.

We stepped into one of the few businesses that was open, a thrift store. Fifty-year-old flannels retailed for seventy dollars. Marfa branded T-shirts sold for thirty-five dollars. A case displayed bronzed jewelry built by hipster hands. A town that relies on tourism was mainly void of visitors. I questioned the proprietor, a gay man from Austin who relocated to Marfa in 2018, about life here.

"It's got that small-town wonder and friendliness, with a cloud of sadness hanging over it."

"Poetic," I replied.

Overnight, the cloud of sadness dumped another anomaly. West Texas was the last place I expected to awake to a whiteout. I stepped out of Rudy, onto the high plateau covered with inches of snow. Across the park, an Australian Shepard jumped up and down, smiling, rolling, and barking. The snow fell harder than anywhere I had ever been. I marveled how so much precipitation could be so silent.

One of the greatest feelings of the human experience is being far away and witnessing those rare moments when timing and travel put on their best performance. In 2013, I pulled onto a dirt road in the Blue Ridge Mountains near Asheville, North Carolina. Two hours later, the fireflies surprised me with one of nature's hard-to-find phenomena. The insects lit the woods up like a great rave. I had never felt so blessed and aware of how every turn took me to a new future. It's still a memory I hold tight. And that same blissful feeling returned, on December 5, 2020, in that snow powder pileup. Sarah and I used Rudy as a wall while running around having a snowball fight. Until I gave out, huffing and laughing on the white grounds of a forgotten park in Presidio County, Texas.

Rudy needed a good snow sweeping while we waited to find the answer to the mystery: do roads in West Texas get plowed?

The answer is yes. For thirty-five minutes, we drove northwest on TX-90, past some abandoned buildings that interrupted the nothingness of it all. We arrived at the infamous Prada Marfa, an art installation that is a replica of the luxury store, situated in the vast humdrum of West Texas. The snow slowed to a trickle. Beyond the white flakes, four twenty-something women posed for their photo shoot in front of the faux-store turned Instagram obsession. The photo shoot lasted several minutes as they jumped, did yoga poses, pursed their lips, sat in the middle of the road, looked left, right, up, down, turned around, and grabbed each other's butts. Then I saw it, the art coming to life—the plague of narcissism on full display. I tip my hat to you after all, Marfa.

We drove north with Marfa waving goodbye. The cloud of sadness stopped its crying, and sunny skies dried the wet roads of TX-54. The views widened to another middle-of-nowhere puzzle. Behind secured gates, a new facility rose above the squandered desert with enormous holding tanks of combustible fuel and massive cement platforms. We guessed before we googled—*perhaps the richest man in the world's hidden facility, where he prepares his plot to take over the universe?*

This time I was right. We drove past Blue Origin Launch Site One, where Amazon founder Jeff Bezos's space company launches its trials and rockets. (A year and a half later, the billionaire would strap himself into a penis-shaped aircraft and depart for space from this exact spot. Glad all our Amazon orders paid off.)

A trip without firsts is no trip at all. The driveway to the Guadalupe Mountain trailhead wired the nerves from the brain to the heart. In 2011, I had so many firsts here: my first big road trip, my first experience camping as an adult, and my first go at SUV-dwelling. The trunk of my Nissan Murano became my bedroom, where I'd lie awake with my headlamp illuminating the pages of my road atlas. With camping's idle time, I opened up a notebook to journal the emotions—my first travelogue. I've kept one for every trip since. With more foresight I could have vlogged about it and become a digital pioneer. But alas, I am not your influencer.

Nine years later, I led the way up the first mountain I ever summited, Guadalupe Peak, the highest point in Texas. Sarah and I were celebrating our four-month *van-iversary*. Over a quarter of our relationship had been spent living in Rudy. We sauntered up the mountain with ease. The summit took about two hours this time. In 2011 it took me twice as long. I had the thighs of a Westerner now, not the flexible straws of a city-slicking flatlander. How good it felt to be back, not because of speed or strength, but for a joyful adaptation to this way of life.

The weather was delightful, cloudless with a slight haze fading the horizon. A 360-degree view presented lower mountains rising from an ocean of arid and dreary land. Last time, the summit had three other people. This time, I didn't bother to count the flapping lips of fellow national park-baggers. Every conversation I heard was about trips to national parks. Each roadie claimed their chariot: vans, Subarus, run-down RVs, and a school bus. No one lived within a twelve-hour drive of Guadalupe Mountains National Park. No one except a vagabond named Patty.

Wearing a gray uniform with an NPS Volunteer patch, Patty tucked three shades of thick gray hair under her hat and smiled as she gave me her story. A retired EMT from Vermont, she was seventy-five and lived at various national parks. Instead of answering the same questions all day long in visitor centers, Patty took only backcountry patrol posts. Her current home was the park's dormitory.

"It's great," she said with the speed of someone high on life. "It's got four beds, but I'm the only one in there. Got my own shower and even a furnace."

"How long will you stay?" I asked.

"Oh, a few months. When the seasons change I'll try and get one of the coveted spots at Zion or Glacier," she interrupted herself whenever someone left the summit, "Bye! Keep enjoying your-selves!"

"Have you ever seen a mountain lion?" I asked.

She put the brights on her headlight eyes. "Oh yeah!! Twice. Once in the backcountry, I saw two deer run by and thought, *Betcha there's a mountain lion.* So, I waited. Sure enough, ten minutes later, a cougar comes walking through the meadow. Maaaan, was she be-U-tiful!"

"Wow."

"But that's nothing. Another time I was backpacking off the same trail. Hadn't seen a soul. So, I stepped off the trail. You know, to dehydrate. [Her cute way of saying urinate.] All of the sudden, I hear a scream. Then a deer ran down the trail, right where I was walking. Never heard a deer scream before! And it had a big wound on its side and I thought, *Oh boy!* Five seconds later here comes this young cougar, running after it. Good thing my bladder was empty or I prolly woulda wet myself!"

Sarah and I packed up and got ready for the descent. I thanked Patty for her story and her service. Before she could say goodbye, I beat her to her own punchline, "Keep enjoying yourself!" I said, and had no doubt that this adventurous grandmother would.

Back in the parking lot, the travelers of the road filled jugs of water and dried their sweaty socks. Our acquaintances from the summit became friends for happy minutes before we all rolled away in different directions. A father-daughter combo came by Rudy, asking for a tour before they started the long drive back to Boston. Brea, the twenty-year-young gal, had the eyes of a future wayfarer. She lit up when she looked inside Rudy.

"Oh my God! This is my dream!" she exclaimed.

"Well, if we can do it, you definitely can," I replied.

Back in Houston, our contrarian lifestyle had served as a measly conversation piece. But, in this parking lot, Rudy was now the example for the next generation of the restless that you *can* go your own way. I watched as Brea glowed from behind the steering wheel of her old Subaru. I imagined her dreams flashing as quickly as her waving hand.

We all need to meet those people that live life more fully than we do. Thank you for my reminder, Patty. And thank you, Brea, for making me realize that we all have this potential. After all, what is a life if it inspires no one?

I didn't know what the future had in store for Patty or Brea. I didn't even know what the future had in store for myself. But if the present moment had anything to say, it was this:

Now is the time. The time to wander and drive. To listen and learn. To smile and accept every slow-down and U-turn. *Now is the time to live*. To turn an in-between chapter in life into its own book. To look around, take it in, and digest it all. To feel aligned and be content. *Now is the time* to be back on the road. To be myself and no one else.

Chapter 25
Riddles of the Southwest

A FEW MILES into New Mexico, I realized that the state loves its historical markers. On NM-285, we drove by an abandoned strip club, then an abandoned adult video store. When would they get their historical marker? *2007—Here lie the relics of life before free internet porn.*

Back on the highway, a shirtless man with prison tattoos and a cigarette hanging from his lip scurried across the road. I had seen many like him throughout the day. Onward for an errand day and New Mexico's alien towns. We drove to Roswell, down Main Street, past UFO everything. The McDonald's had aliens, the Dunkin' Donuts had aliens, even the UFO museum had aliens!

We pulled into a laundromat. Across the street, the Adventure Bible Church had an electric guitar logo and a banner that read: JESUS SAVES. Rock on, Roswell. With clean clothes, we drove across town to the recycling center. I handed over my tin and plastic to a thin Latino in a T-shirt and trucker hat.

"Can I recycle this here?" I showed him a dozen empty glass bottles.

"No, we don't take glass. But I got a trash can right there."

He pointed to a waste bin behind me. We had been carrying the bottles since Marfa, 250 miles away. Like most people, I pretended my hypocrisies would save the planet, hoarding my recyclables while driving a diesel-burning vehicle across the country. *Where was my Nobel Peace Prize?* My hypocrisies brought me hope—the decadent candy of delusional hope. Small-town recycling shed light on things we city folk take for granted, like the ability to feel good about yourself without any serious effort. Some towns' recycling centers were impressive; others missed the mark (looking at you mister-throw-it-in-the-trash).

"You know anywhere else in town I can recycle this?" I asked him.

"There's some bins by Target."

Great, add *make sure Sarah doesn't spend too much money at Target* to the errands list. Done. To the gas station: $1.89, close enough to Texas for the last under-$2-per-gallon giveaway.

"Good God! Look at the line!" I said as we pulled up to Walmart, next on the errands list. People eyeballed six-foot gaps from one another at *both* entrances, covering nearly the entire width of the massive building. Lines bring out the worst in me, but I shoved my hands in my pockets and got in the queue, infrequently inching forward. An hour later, we entered. The Walmart felt apocalyptic and eerily empty, not even the music played. It reminded me of those late-night shifts when only the desperate shopped. When I inquired why this Walmart was so strict, I was told the New Mexico governor had declared 25 percent to be the magic number for store occupancy during the pandemic.

Like a kid who eats all his veggies, I earned a reward. We parked in an empty lot across from a Mexican eatery. *Pop quiz, gringo-boy.*

"Do you have any chill-AH-kill-egs?" I asked.

She grinned. No laugh. No confusion. She shouted back into the kitchen, "Hey mom! Will you make *chilaquiles*?"

Some Spanish went back and forth.

"Do you want red or green sauce?"

I'd give my pronunciation a C-. I'd give the *chilaquiles* an A+.

Only the best towns make me want to stay. Roswell failed the test, so we rolled on, to those two-lane marvels of America. So many scenic roads to set the scene. NM-380 served as the byway, emancipating us from the horrid scents of factory-farmed cattle and natural gas wells. Down the windows and up we went, past historical markers unread and trees underappreciated. Away from the dust devils and political division of the lowlands, to the calming road and the altitudes closer to the clouds. We followed our favorite license plate—the New

Mexican turquoise and yellow—until no car remained on the road but our own. Rudy relished the attention like a spoiled only child.

"Ah, dang," Sarah spoke, "we forgot to empty the toilet."

She had forgotten; I had not. The repulsive chore was written on my list. A list I had read. It should also be noted that it was *my* turn to empty it.

"Oh, yeah. It's all good. We haven't used it that much. Plus, I think we'll be camping near a privy."

"Okay," she conceded.

At least I was right about the privy. When we arrived in Lincoln National Forest, I walked into what must have been my thousandth outhouse of the trip. I had added to the inventory of privies across our nation, from the far northwest corner of the lower forty-eight to this doo-doo hut in middle-of-nowhere New Mexico.

All national forest privies are creepy, no matter how isolated or well-maintained. The sixteen-square-foot shit shack. The welcome committee of flies. The don't-look-up ceiling of spider webs. And don't forget the nasal uppercut of a hundred decomposing turds.

I lifted the lid of the too-tall throne. *How many poor little-leg people must be dangling their feet across our public lands at this very moment?* Inside, the usual scene. No matter how recently cleaned, they all have that rank spray of feces lining the back wall of the bowl. I never understood the physics.

I took the riddle to Sarah. "How does all that dookie splatter end up in the privies?"

She took her gaze off the mountains and gave it some proper thought. "You know, bubs ... I don't know."

And *maybe* we never will.

A park less packed; a ticket for a drone,
where color leaves the dirt alone.
A detour I doubted, yet proved me wrong,
curve after curve, where ancients belong;
to learn of the past and soak in the heat,
winter's fresh breath blew me to the driver's seat.
Over the divide to find the sun's rays,
oh how I longed for some zero days.

Every trip deserves a detour—the unplanned unraveling of the road's riddle.

After our detour, Rudy flung the loose gravel off Old Ajo Road, just outside Tucson, Arizona. Empty beer and energy drink cans sparkled in the Arizona sun. Used toilet paper stuck to thorny bushes. Even the BLM land seemed gentrified. Multiple RVs covered one plot of soil, some with missing tires, parked next to tarp-covered cars, Breaking Bad and breaking rules. On to the next lot. We pulled into a plot of land occupied by vans and trailers, middle-class and diverse. Urban boondocking brought more shine from the headlights of cars than from the stars above.

Nearby, Saguaro National Park decorated the desert. As lush as a desert can get, it felt like the Southwest's equivalent of a jungle. Giant saguaros towered over sprawling fields of cholla. Barrel, prickly pear, hedgehog—there was one thorn for every star in the sky. This desert had a billion ways to get stabbed (hopefully from the cacti and not from the neighbors). Strangers camped ten yards in every direction. I assumed some commuted to work in Tucson, a few had fallen on hard times, and others, like us, overnighted after exploring the national park.

Never boondock bashful, I walked out of the van in the tight black underwear I had worn on our hike. I hung a dromedary bag from the rear door hinge, grabbed the little bottle of Dr. Bronner's soap, and pulled the spout. A stream of water the width of a piece of fettuccine sprang out. The bag had been sitting on our dash all day, taking in the sun. I appreciated the warm water as I began the hobo shower dance—moving my head, my back, bending the knees to get my armpits wet, stepping back to get my legs, and pulling the elastic band on my underwear to spray where the sun don't shine. I closed the spout, soaped up, then danced again. Inside the van, a kettle sat on the stove. When the right temperature hit, Sarah poured it into our weed sprayer, and did her own dance. The average American uses approximately seventeen gallons of water per shower. Sarah and I used one gallon each. Strap on a dress and take us to the ball, we were clean.

Tucson was our last city stop. The next ten days would serve as our self-imposed quarantine while we crossed the desert to California to spend Christmas with Sarah's grandma. The trip would finally end back "home" in San Diego, in time to celebrate the New Year with Papa Herb.

Leaving Tucson behind, Rudy revved down I-10 until exit 251. Mountain ranges fortified the horizon in every direction. A field of old commercial airplanes dried out in the desert like retirees in Palm Springs. A dirt road took us closer to Ironwood Forest National Monument, deeper into BLM land, until the freeway lights flickered on the horizon. There, we settled on our next backyard.

Each desert has its own personality and I have dated them all. This one was flirtatious and playful during the day, with small birds chirping from the arms of goofy-shaped cacti. At night, things got serious—look me in the eye and tell me your secrets. Alas, how I wanted what I could not have! How I longed for my lake swims and surfboard! But why focus on a long-distance relationship? I let the beautiful landlocked goddess lure me in.

By 7 p.m., the night sky glittered, seducing my mind. A shooting star. What to wish for? Another flew by before I had my answer. Then another, bright green, and trailing far enough across the sky that my eyes followed, then my neck, until the streak was out of sight.

"Sarah! Get out here and see this!"

We lay down on Mama Earth, two lovers of the stars wedged between the sand and infinity. The Geminids meteor shower lasted much longer than my one-gallon hobo shower. We crawled into bed with more wishes than one person needs. I closed my eyes, savoring that delectable sensation again—time and place's prized performance. Then, the sound of gunfire echoed through the air. BANG! BANG! BANG-BANG! Welcome to BLM land.

A clanking on the roof rousted me from my slumber. The bird hopped off Rudy and found a perch on an ironwood tree. She sang to me. A sweet, bouncing beat of a new day. I stepped out of the van to applaud. It was 7:30 a.m., just in time for a dawn fashion show. A lone cloud shifted shapes, twirling a variety of colors on the catwalk of the sky. The crescent moon beat the sun to rise, climbing above the distant brown peaks. Winter days might be short, but a desert day resembles a worthy book, knowing a good beginning and ending.

I glistened, so grateful for it all. The late morning sunrises and evening meteor showers. The tiny home and giant backyard. The bird's song and the desert's blissful silence. Then, I heard more gunfire.

My college roommate, from Brownsboro, Texas (population 1,185), once told me, "If you start an ice cream cone on one side of a town and finish it before you drive to the other side … then that town is too big." Phoenix drove ten scoops too big. Ice cream would have been helpful to liven the mood inside Rudy, where a Marfa-like cloud of sadness rained a heavy melancholy. Each mile nearer to the end. Each hour closer to the proverbial fork in the road.

Sarah and I rotated shifts until we exited for AZ-95 in the town of Quartzsite, Arizona. I discovered the area on a boondocking app and determined it a logical stop to break up the westward flight. The town was short on services but long on RV Parks. One after another, RV after RV. (While the book *Nomadland* was released in 2017,

Quartzsite would gain pop culture notoriety when the Oscar-winning film of the same title debuted in 2021.)

Rudy trotted out to public land. Airport-sized clearings of flat desert were occupied by campers, some in clusters, others distant and reclusive. Ranch-sized spacing separated each party. I reckoned tens of thousands of RVers could consume the miles of clearings. The seasonal migration of nomads to the low desert during winter brings with it every kind of snowbird. The happy, vivacious, and free, and the lonely, destitute, and beaten. I discovered you could be both sides of the coin on the same day.

Rudy guzzled lunch at a Quartzsite truck stop. I took to the iPhone, searching for a spot to fill up on water. Some RV blogger mentioned filling up at truck stop spigots. *Brilliant!* I was at a truck stop. I saw a spigot. No need to deal with the usual search through city parks and public campgrounds. I drove Rudy over to the hose bib. A rank smell of dried diesel socked my nostrils. Puddles of fuel gleamed around the spigot. I began this journey with a statement that deserves repeating: *I have a reputation for making mistakes.* I filled up our six-gallon jugs and took off.

Evening fell. An animal groaned an angry moan, "ARRGHHH!"

A hungry coyote? A dying deer? A constipated jackrabbit? The answer: *me*, curled in the fetal position, my stomach churning. I called the truck stop.

"Is the water spigot by the pump drinkable?"

"Nope, that water is not potable."

Slap my tits and call me Tanya, I'm screwed. What foulness comes out of a truck stop's dark tank? Rudy had a high-grade water filter designed for bacteria and parasites, not mercury and lead. Sarah had drunk only a little. Within days her skin began to itch, and a rash developed; my toes swelled up and burned. I should have stuck to mining uranium and Nairing my nipples. My poor body, *oh how it must hate me!* Eight years of alcoholism, half of which I spent hugging the toilet roughly ten times a week. Now, *this.* I lay awake taking bets on which orifice would be the geyser—a 3:1 spread I would be peeing out of my ass before sunrise.

Emptying Vladimir Poopin remained the worst part of van life. Our chemical toilet neared capacity as our desert days dragged on. AZ-95 took us north to the tiny, desperate town of Parker, Arizona. The dust-covered, hapless land seemed as good as any to drain our throne. We did the usual city park scout, looking for a secure bathroom with commercial flush toilets. Western Park passed the test. Sarah detached the seat from the case. I nearly strained my back lifting the plastic box of waste. *How long had it been?* Procrastination is a deadly sin after all. My sloth was about to be measured in slop.

I waddled like a kid carrying a year's worth of textbooks. Sarah had to hold the bathroom door open so I could enter. I shuffled over the dark gray floor, stained so many times I couldn't tell what the original shade was. Graffiti inked the brick walls and covered the mirror. The familiar foulness of public restrooms fought the fibers of my mask. *Now was the time,* alright. Time to man up. Time for dookie duty.

I turned Vladimir Poopin's spout. My forearm veins protruded as I fought the awkward dimensions for the best grip. A tilt. The green stew shot from the spout, into the toilet, splashing the surrounding basin. But I was dry, *thank God*. I flushed and repeated this twice more. Vladimir Poopin remained fat and heavy. The thicker matter struggled to exit. I began shaking the container until some contents shot out. Another flush. I tilted the case back and forth. Nothing. A shake. Nothing. It was a jam. A dookie jam!

I increased the angle of my tilt, up and down. A little shake. A big shake. A fast tilt. Then a ferocious roar bellowed from the spout. I went to retreat, but the beast cannoned too fast. My hand slipped. The case fell. A bomb of feces fired out at great speed, overshooting the toilet bowl and splattering the floor and lower wall.

Perhaps this is how all the privies get stained? No time to answer riddles. I stared at the vile mess I made—a poo-poo platter of waste layered over hobos' urine stains. It was the greatest moral dilemma of my life:

leave it or clean it? I couldn't fabricate a more disgusting case study in social ethics.

My dear readers, you have traveled with me far. I have opened up my life for your judgment. You have followed me across America, covering sensitive topics such as race and religion. You have endured my ramblings of the road, my daddy issues, and my drunk-a-logs. I have mocked your towns and ridiculed your Gods. Hate me if you must, but please—*I beg of you, please!*—should mercy reside in your hearts, then let it soar! Assess me not by my written words and dark thoughts, not by my degenerate past or my privileged future, but by my humble actions in that dreadful stall. For what would you do if you were in a rundown town like Parker, Arizona ... in a city park restroom ... a sickening soup of you and your partner's fecal matter covering a floor already stained with tramps' piss ... *and* only one-ply toilet paper available to clean the mess?

I stared, contemplating my options. What a horrible yet hilarious situation. I couldn't help but laugh. It was a panting, wicked, ghoulish laugh. A cackle that was part jovial, part evil. I looked over at the thin toilet paper, then pulled a long line of the fragile stuff. I balled it up and got down on my knees. I had to find out the answer to the question: *Who really is Andrew Singer?*

And I got the answer, one saturated ball of toilet paper at a time. That's right, I did it. I mopped that dookie jam right up. My mask did little to lessen the stench, and I gagged frequently. Occasionally, when I went back for more toilet paper, I found myself smiling. I don't know why I was smiling, in what was the grossest situation of my life. All I know is that ten minutes later, that bathroom looked better than it did when I walked in, with that God-awful, heavy suitcase of shit.

Never have I felt more like a good human being.

Chapter 26
Home, Part III

YOU KNOW YOU had a good trip when you're sad to see California. For miles, I stared at her from across the Colorado River as we continued north on AZ-95. Like a seaman spotting the shore after a great voyage, I was unsure how life had gone on or how my old house would feel. We topped off Rudy's fuel tank before the harsh return to California economics, got on I-40, and made the crossing.

Music played but I can't say what song. For the travel blues—that deep bass of sadness, that heartache of return—wailed in my head. People drive to the Pacific to live out their daydreams; I was driving back with mine complete. We still had a couple of stops left, but I wondered if I should let our trip play out like a dream I had the option not to wake from. To keep driving, to let Rudy ride like a winning streak.

Sarah and I had feared the transition for the last week. Though we still had a few more days on the road, within California's borders, the end felt in sight. Not many people schedule time to feel, but that's what we did. Two nights and one intention. Avoidance would be an invitation for emotional catastrophe. So, we pulled off the interstate for the familiar terrain of Mojave National Preserve.

2020 brought first dates with the high deserts of Utah, the plateaus of West Texas, and the lowlands of Arizona. Now I called up my ex—the Mojave—that familiar lover to return to after seeing what else was out there. She looked as beautiful as ever, with her stony mountains and sandy roads, her geological mysteries and sensual night sky. Beauty is ever the distraction, never the antidote. My travel blues went on tour with me everywhere. Bushwhacking up no-name mountains. Sitting silently in the sand. Laying down in Rudy, staring at the pine ceiling, thinking about it all.

Zero miles but a million thoughts. Sarah and I honored the five months on the road by journaling, then scheduling a date. After dinner, we lay in bed and pulled out our phones, beginning the multi-hour scroll through twenty-nine weeks of photos. From an empty tin shell to the home that changed everything. We dreamt our build, then built our dream. From the Muir-made mountains of the Eastern Sierras to the volcanoes ready to blow—America, hot damn you're beautiful! The alps of the North Cascades, the wild walls of the Black Canyon, the waterfalls and river bends, hot springs and badlands. Our trip was the American equivalent of hopping from the Louvre to the Sistine Chapel, the Notre Dame to the Coliseum. How fortunate can one man be, to wake up for the first time in a country so vast and diverse, with a culture so hungry to drive it all?

Between the photos of natural wonders were memories in towns and cities, littered with the harsh veracity of the times. The scenes in Salt Lake replayed in my mind daily. The horrid smoke that chased us across the West. The absence of community and the struggling faces that went along with it. I marveled at our photos but also mourned the great rift in America. The one giant canyon that would never be a national park but should be designated its national demise.

Thank heavens for those moments in nature when we all remembered we could do more than tolerate. Once, Rudy camped between parties of either political extreme: the eco-camper from Oregon and the alt-right truck-n-trailer from Idaho. There, on that gravel plot of public land, I witnessed the contrarian people laugh and converse with one another, carrying the camaraderie of opposites not seen on a phone scroll or a news program. They loved the land they shared and shared the land they loved. What a year to live on the road. To let the conversations and windshield views serve as the news. To listen to actual birds' tweets and not read the limited characters of culture clashes.

Sarah and I put down the phone and stepped outside. The desert sky wrapped me up, reminding me again that everything would be alright. The only difference between everything having meaning and nothing mattering is the vitality of the stars. To the west, Jupiter and Saturn courted one another for a dance humans had not seen for 397 years: the Great Conjunction, last recorded by Galileo himself. Tonight, they twirled oh-so-close. Tomorrow, the big finale.

To the east, an even stranger phenomenon. Between the ridgelines, a long trail of lights connected the horizon to some unknown height. At first, I thought it was Christmas lights hung by another camper. Sarah was hopeful it was aliens. We walked closer, noticing the lights had no wires.

"I think it's the freeway," said Sarah.

"No way."

"Look at the map."

She was right. One after another: long haulers making sure your automatic replenishment of dog food arrives on time, the land yachts and the drifters getting by, the Vegas victims and the national park-baggers. They all drove. I watched late into the night. When would the traffic die down? It never did. A sleepless night; I was in the desert but the sandman held an empty bag. I checked the lights again at 4 a.m. Still there. The interstate never slept. America's obsession with the road had become a dependence. The road was an addiction, no one more a junkie than I.

CA-58 served as my next fix, freeing me from the interstate's boredom. Over the mountain pass and down into the unkept taint of California. The Central Valley was as polluted as ever. A thick, putrid steam rose from the land that grows much of our food. To the left, the gray air curdled like spoiled milk. To the right, it appeared that chemical warfare had been unleashed. The air quality made it look like the world was ending, and no one cared. Sarah googled for fire reports. None. Just another day in Bakersfield. America's breadbasket had turned into its fart. But, similar to your own stench, I speculated that the residents didn't even notice.

No other state boasts beauty and diversity like California. Some-where in Encinitas, a woman sips a matcha latte with oat milk, enjoying the ocean as blue as the sky, while some immigrant farmer in a straw hat plucks table grapes in the Central Valley, unable to see the sun on a clear day. Somewhere a person stands under a redwood and has a revelation, another person drives the tarmac of Highway 1, wondering how life will play out. Skid Row's population grows, as does the scroll-makers' mansions in the Bay Area. It sure does take a lot of people to make a California.

The green slopes of CA-166 clawed above the smog until the sky became blue again. Over the Sierra Madre and up the 101, to Shell Beach. *Ahoy! There she blows!* The Pacific. Bluer and bigger than I remembered. The greatest of all the healers. The lover of all lovers. My favorite think-tank. I was many miles from San Diego but within view of home, whatever that word now meant.

After Christmas, Rudy looked south, squinting through the husky smog. Buildings with corporate logos came and went. The offices were vacant, but the people clearly not at home either. Los Angeles traffic inched back and forth, up and down, side to side, worrying and honking. The city changed lanes but not directions. San Diegans excel at two things: talking about the weather and how much they hate Los Angeles.

Homeless encampments occupied nearly every exit. Around each corner, lines of immobile RVs, vehicles, and tents sheltered the growing ranks of the unhoused. The state associated with so much of America's wealth reminded me of the class discrepancies I had seen in faraway countries, lavish high-rises and roadsides filled with trash and human feces.

A drive that should take five hours went beyond eight. The stream of cars plodded on at a painful pace. Driving through Southern California, it's easy to let traffic exhaust all the things you love. I drove by the city without stars, thinking about how many people abide, changing who they are, stressing to be what others want them to be. How many people exist, fighting their way to the top or skidding their way to the rows of defeat?

Road-tripping is not Hollywood. There are no perfectly timed climaxes or scripted comebacks. No sex scenes to spice it up, no savior to save us all. Sometimes the heroes have no names, sometimes they're not even people. Life on the road fails to maintain that constant Hollywood excitement. The road is long, with miles of nothing. Maybe your car breaks down, maybe you do. Sometimes the ending drags on, usually it comes too soon. God forbid it all goes as planned.

So, I don't have a Hollywood response to the question Sarah and I got the most: *How do you get along as a couple living in such a small space?* Sure, I could lie and give you something suited for a screenplay. Something about a fight, a separation, and a magical reunion. Or, I could be curt, and tell you we went those five months without a fight, give a smile, and be done with it. Maybe lean on one of those clichés: "*I just found the one*," and "*I'm a lucky guy*," or the gag-worthy, "*Happy wife, happy life*."

However, these statements would miss the power the whole truth carries. Whenever I get asked how Sarah and I manage to get along living in such a small space, I think about Sarah's backstory and her early marriage. A woman who endured things no person should. My gratitude extends each day that I met a woman who prioritizes her own recovery. I think about my own story. The unfortunate others who suffered the brunt of my alcoholism and commitment phobia. All the stupid arguments. All the heartbreak. All the panic attacks.

The truth is that most humans prefer characters who need therapy, not ones that have already been. So, this is my big letdown to the drama-fiends out there: not only did Sarah and I not fight living in the van, but our relationship actually flourished. Rudy left no room to hide—no weird quirk or pet peeve, no manscaping or waxing of the upper lip. You can't hide a candy bar, let alone your own emotions. Sarah and I bonded not only as wanderlusts, but as travelers seeking to stitch the wounds within. Let me be clear, van life is definitely not for everyone, but I would be amiss if I attributed our success to clichés or luck, rather than our commitment to doing better.

How much I appreciated the evolution of our love story. How great it felt to return without settling. Not on my relationships or on my mental health, not on my home or on my life.

I didn't discover the definition of home until I traded a white picket fence for a white plumber's van. Inside that steel shell, I felt more like myself than any other place I had been. The longest journey yet—the one to honor what was right for me, not what others said, and certainly not what the nasty pressure I had put on myself negotiated.

So, goodbye to the careers to get others off my back. Farewell to the safety of conformity. So long to the toxic people-pleasing and the obnoxious people-impressing. And a big rejection letter to the scripts I let others sell. Hello to individuality. Hello to living a life that needs no justification. And hello, San Diego. I did miss you.

San Diego, I told you I would return one day and reflect on how much I had grown. I'm afraid I come without a story of growth. Instead, I return to show you how much I have shrunk. Six feet, 185 pounds, and 72 square feet of me. How I moved into a small space, left behind material luxuries, and dropped along America's unrelenting roads many of the unnecessary stories I carried in my head.

Grown ... no. I have minimized. A smaller, simpler life. A life void of monotony and excess. A life measured in emotion and experience. For I have never felt bigger on the inside, in a home so small, with a land so vast.

The road has brought me to a place in my soul I never want to leave.

Welcome home.

Epilogue

AT THE END of 2020 we could have sold Rudy for a nice profit, somewhere close to double our investment. However, by the end of the trip, my attachment to Rudy was so strong I would have been more likely to sell a kidney. The big conversation about our future lasted under a minute. Sarah and I agreed to sell, donate, and trash all those unnecessary things. My uncle and aunt would move in to care for Papa Herb, and our anchor chain to lives with stationary comforts would be cut.

We looked at what upgrades Rudy needed to thrive for full-time living. We paid a professional to mount a propane tank, and he hooked up the oven and a furnace. We upgraded our outdoor shower and purchased some leveling blocks. Needless to say, our final stimulus checks went into the economy rather quickly.

By the time our departure arrived, our lives had narrowed down to what we brought in the van and the few things we left behind in ole Herbie's garage. I sold my car and all my furniture, in essence my salary for the coming year on the road. This next departure wasn't going to be about driving all over the continent, checking off national parks. Instead, we intended to find beautiful places to camp while we wrote our books. A few things would stay the same: the less money we spent, the longer we could go; the less stuff we had, the freer we would be.

On April 20, 2021, I removed the house key from its ring. Only Rudy's sword remained. I was finally going all in. A minimalist. A nomad. A full-time van-lifer. These labels I gladly slapped onto the box that has become my life.

Papa Herb insisted on waving us off from the driveway. His age had brought about a sentimentality that didn't define his earlier years.

Each time our departure had come up in conversation, he spoke words of encouragement behind the broken voice and fallen tears of a man torn between saying goodbye, thank you, and *what if*.

"I'm not sure I'll be around if you guys end up having a family," he said with emotion in his eyes, "But if you do, I'll give you the most important lesson: raise them to know the difference between right and wrong."

I squeezed his frame until his belly poked hard into mine. I cried. Openly, willingly, gratefully. Sarah climbed in the passenger door, her face glistening. Rudy roared back to life. From the side mirror, I watched Papa Herb wave his arm until his figure vanished out of sight.

I looked across the cab at Sarah. "Do you wanna scream with me?" I asked.

She counted us down, "Three ... two ... one ..."

We screamed. Then I cried some more.

Though it was a year with many hardships, 2020 proved to be one of the most pivotal years of my life. And 2021 took that momentum even further. Rudy's upgrades made for a deeper level of comfort, and a stronger identity as our home. Out the slider door, we watched spring turn to summer. From New Mexico to the Canadian Rockies, we worked our way north. Rivers, lakes, and hot springs. Always a few mountains, always more stars. Sarah and I wrote and wrote, often going several hours each day not speaking to one another. Something beautiful was under creation, like living in a lucid dream. Life can be a fairytale, at least without the ever after.

Things took a turn in the summer of 2021, with my father's Parkinson's diagnosis. I took several lengthy breaks from van life to care for him as his body gave out. It was an arduous time, filled with drama, growth, mistakes, and immense grief. In April 2022, I got the call and arrived to see him in bed, taking slow, rattling gasps for air. I held my father's hand and said the things a son should say as he took his final breath. Nothing ensures the triviality of resentment more than mortality. When I reflect on the words in this book, I see how much I still had to learn, not only as a van-lifer, but also as a human. So, if the first half of my thirties was spent sorting out the shortcomings of my parents, I'd like to think the second half has been spent truly appreciating just how much they've given me. Thankfully, I can report that Papa Herb is still alive (ninety-six years old at the time of writing).

Three years into our relationship, Sarah and I had our first fight. It was literally over spilled water. I guess we're human after all. Though I have no window into the future, my panic attacks have been mostly nonexistent since 2022.

Sarah and I have returned to the Valley of the Gods many times since our initial visit. It's become a ritual to park Rudy amidst those vermillion mesas and reflect on how things have changed. There, in October 2023, I got on one knee and proposed. She said yes. Sarah and I wed a couple of weeks later.

Rudy is still our primary home and the best we've ever had. We have no children or pets, but the van now has eight plants. We get asked often how long we intend to live this way. Frequently, I miss community, in the stationary sense, but for now, the pros of van life still outweigh the cons. The day may come when home changes, but one thing that will never leave is my enduring love of the road.

While I am not your influencer, I do hope that you find your own inspiration to take to the tarmac. To meet new people and take in some silence. To see what comes up when you expand the border of your comfort zone and challenge what others call *normal* or *traditional*. To find what feels right within you.

After all, *now is the time to do it.* To go when others give you the green light, and by God, to go when others say you shouldn't. Go it alone or go it together. Go when you're young. Go when you're old. Go when you're neither. Go for the weekend or go for a lifetime. Never forget: the road only welcomes those willing to leave.

So, go.
Go count your firsts and avoid your lasts,
Grab an atlas and leave the GPS in the past.
Go down a highway you have never known,
Towards the horizon and away from home.
Go unravel the riddles of the sacred road,
Grow or shrink, ***just go.***

Gratitude

I HOPE IT doesn't come across as cliché or insincere when I say my deepest gratitude goes to you, my dear reader. Thank you for your time and purchase. I would love to hear from you directly; please feel free to send me an email: AuthorAndrewSinger@gmail.com. As an independent writer I need all the help I can get, so if you enjoyed this book, please consider leaving a review or recommending it to someone else.

To my family, who has gifted me many privileges in this life, I love and appreciate you all. A special shoutout to my mom, who sacrificed her own creative pursuits to ensure I had a stable upbringing. And Dad, I miss you, thank you for proofreading my earliest essays and insisting on the importance of writing and education.

Gerald Burke, our two-man writing group has been pivotal to this journey. Your edits delivered massive leaps forward, your encouragement was always timely, and your friendship remains forever valuable. (Check out his novel, *Just Vic*).

Andy and Jim, thank you for always reading my work and providing feedback. Your mentorship has been a tremendous asset to my life. And Henry, I'm not sure I'd be here without you, thanks for saving my life. To all my sober supporters, thanks for teaching me the language of the heart.

Much gratitude to the professionals, Tatiana Wilde and Jennifer Duardo, your edits were critical to this book's improvement. A huge shoutout to Eric McKinney at Wonderland Studios for the production of the audiobook. Gülsah Keles for the incredible cover art. Ijaz Saleem for the formatting. My appreciation to the beta readers for earlier versions of this manuscript: Dallas, Alex, Brent, Lindsey,

Emma, Michael, Jana, Dwight, and Andrea. And of course a round of applause to the people in this book that let me interview them.

If something in this book made you laugh, you can thank The BDC, my band of brothers who have been inspiring my wit for twenty-five years. Several jokes were gifted by Denis F. Arce and one joke by Chris Mills (OnlyVans).

Our mechanic and friend Justin, the ProMaster Forum, Diesel ProMaster Facebook Group, and all those that post how-to content online, Rudy wouldn't be so awesome without you.

To our tremendous public lands and all the people who work to protect and preserve them, you have gifted us the most beautiful backyards one could dream up. Much of this book was written in, and inspired by, these incredible places.

Mandy, you've contributed so much to my story, thank you. And to Josiah Johnson, get out there and live life!

Lastly, to end where we began: To Sarah May, my wife, partner, best friend, and an incredible writer and editor. Thank you for all of your contributions, readings, edits, and suggestions to this book. There is no one else on this planet whose poo I would dump. I love you.

www.ingramcontent.com/pod-product-compliance
Lightning Source LLC
Chambersburg PA
CBHW021225130626
46554CB00004B/1378